Porn on the Couch

This book considers pornography as a bridge between screen cultures and screen memories. The screen as a conceptual apparatus, in both pornographic production/viewership and psychoanalysis, becomes important to unpack as such—what does the screen hold in with respect to desire and pleasure? What does it keep out? Are sex and memory interconnected? And if so, what is the status of memory as it informs sexual choices, practices, and fantasies and, thereby, informs the use of porn? Following Eve Kosofsky Sedgwick, might there be the possibility for a reparative or redemptive reading of pornography that is informed by a psychoanalytic emphasis on the study of desire? Who or what are the subjects and objects of desire in the visual field of pornography? What sorts of psychoanalytic readings are possible of pornographic texts (in any media) and to what end might we undertake such an interpretative approach? How do well-worn psychoanalytic categories, such as loss, lack, mourning, melancholia, attachment, trauma, and the fetish, inform pornographic interpellation in both the producer and viewer? What are the ethical and methodological implications connected to thinking psychoanalytically about pornography? These are but some of the questions that this collection of essays explores. It will be of interest to researchers and advanced students of media and cultural studies, sociology, psychology, and mental health. This book was originally published as a special issue of the journal, *Porn Studies*.

Ricky Varghese is a psychoanalyst and psychotherapist based in Toronto and Senior Research Associate at the Toronto Metropolitan University (formerly known as Ryerson University) and Toronto Psychoanalytic Society and Institute, Toronto, Canada.

Porn on the Couch
Sex, Psychoanalysis, and Screen Cultures/Memories

Edited by
Ricky Varghese

LONDON AND NEW YORK

First published 2023
by Routledge
4 Park Square, Milton Park, Abingdon, Oxon OX14 4RN

and by Routledge
605 Third Avenue, New York, NY 10158

Routledge is an imprint of the Taylor & Francis Group, an informa business

Foreword, Chapters 1–10 © 2023 Taylor & Francis

All rights reserved. No part of this book may be reprinted or reproduced or utilised in any form or by any electronic, mechanical, or other means, now known or hereafter invented, including photocopying and recording, or in any information storage or retrieval system, without permission in writing from the publishers.

Trademark notice: Product or corporate names may be trademarks or registered trademarks, and are used only for identification and explanation without intent to infringe.

British Library Cataloguing in Publication Data
A catalogue record for this book is available from the British Library

ISBN13: 978-1-032-43427-8 (hbk)
ISBN13: 978-1-032-43428-5 (pbk)
ISBN13: 978-1-003-36725-3 (ebk)

DOI: 10.4324/9781003367253

Typeset in Myriad Pro
by Newgen Publishing UK

Publisher's Note
The publisher accepts responsibility for any inconsistencies that may have arisen during the conversion of this book from journal articles to book chapters, namely the inclusion of journal terminology.

Disclaimer
Every effort has been made to contact copyright holders for their permission to reprint material in this book. The publishers would be grateful to hear from any copyright holder who is not here acknowledged and will undertake to rectify any errors or omissions in future editions of this book.

Contents

Citation Information	vii
Notes on Contributors	ix
Foreword	x
Feona Attwood, Clarissa Smith and John Mercer	

1 Introduction: an orgasm by any other name   1
Ricky Varghese

2 Form for the blind (porn and description without guarantee)   7
Eugenie Brinkema

3 Paranoid pleasure: surveillance, online pornography, and scopophilia   20
Chris Vanderwees

4 A porn voyeur's discourse   35
Fan Wu

5 Looking for Pei Lim's penis: melancholia, mimicry, pedagogy   45
David K. Seitz

6 Pornography, psychoanalysis and the sinthome: ignorance and ethics   56
Katie Goss

7 'Bodies that splutter': theorizing jouissance in bareback and chemsex porn   71
Gareth Longstaff

8 A psychoanalytic ethics of the pornographic aesthetic   84
Alison Horbury

9 The social/political potential of illusions: enthusiasm and feminist porn   97
Maggie Ann Labinski

10 More than vanilla sex: reading gay post-pornography with affect theory and psychoanalysis 111
Peter Rehberg

Index 126

Citation Information

The chapters in this book were originally published in the journal *Porn Studies*, volume 6, issue 1 (2019). When citing this material, please use the original page numbering for each article, as follows:

Foreword
Editorial
Feona Attwood, Clarissa Smith and John Mercer
Porn Studies, volume 6, issue 1 (2019), pp. 1–3

Chapter 1
Introduction: an orgasm by any other name
Ricky Varghese
Porn Studies, volume 6, issue 1 (2019), pp. 4–9

Chapter 2
Form for the blind (porn and description without guarantee)
Eugenie Brinkema
Porn Studies, volume 6, issue 1 (2019), pp. 10–22

Chapter 3
Paranoid pleasure: surveillance, online pornography, and scopophilia
Chris Vanderwees
Porn Studies, volume 6, issue 1 (2019), pp. 23–37

Chapter 4
A porn voyeur's discourse
Fan Wu
Porn Studies, volume 6, issue 1 (2019), pp. 38–47

Chapter 5
Looking for Pei Lim's penis: melancholia, mimicry, pedagogy
David K. Seitz
Porn Studies, volume 6, issue 1 (2019), pp. 48–58

Chapter 6

Pornography, psychoanalysis and the sinthome: ignorance and ethics
Katie Goss
Porn Studies, volume 6, issue 1 (2019), pp. 59–73

Chapter 7

'Bodies that splutter' – theorizing jouissance in bareback and chemsex porn
Gareth Longstaff
Porn Studies, volume 6, issue 1 (2019), pp. 74–86

Chapter 8

A psychoanalytic ethics of the pornographic aesthetic
Alison Horbury
Porn Studies, volume 6, issue 1 (2019), pp. 87–99

Chapter 9

The social/political potential of illusions: enthusiasm and feminist porn
Maggie Ann Labinski
Porn Studies, volume 6, issue 1 (2019), pp. 100–113

Chapter 10

More than vanilla sex: reading gay post-pornography with affect theory and psychoanalysis
Peter Rehberg
Porn Studies, volume 6, issue 1 (2019), pp. 114–128

For any permission-related enquiries please visit:
www.tandfonline.com/page/help/permissions

Notes on Contributors

Feona Attwood, Cultural Studies, Communication and Media, Middlesex University, London, UK.

Eugenie Brinkema, Massachusetts Institute of Technology, Cambridge, USA.

Katie Goss, School of English and Drama, Queen Mary University of London, London, UK.

Alison Horbury, Collarts (Australian College of the Arts), Melbourne, Australia.

Maggie Ann Labinski, Department of Philosophy, Fairfield University, Fairfield, USA.

Gareth Longstaff, Media, Culture, Heritage, Newcastle University, Newcastle upon Tyne, UK.

John Mercer, Birmingham Centre for Media and Cultural Research, Birmingham City University, UK.

Peter Rehberg, Institute for Cultural Inquiry, Berlin, Germany and Schwules Museum, Berlin, Germany.

David K. Seitz, Department of Humanities, Social Sciences and Arts, Harvey Mudd College, Claremont, USA.

Clarissa Smith, Department of Arts, Northumbria University, Newcastle upon Tyne, UK.

Chris Vanderwees, Toronto Psychoanalytic Society and Institute, Toronto, Canada, and The Lacanian School of Psychoanalysis, Berkeley, USA.

Ricky Varghese, School of Disability Studies, Toronto Metropolitan University (formerly known as Ryerson University) and Toronto Psychoanalytic Society and Institute, Toronto, Canada.

Fan Wu, Screen Cultures and Curatorial Studies, Queen's University, Kingston, Canada.

Foreword

In this special issue of *Porn Studies*, Ricky Varghese has pulled together a great selection of articles which explore the complex and layered relationships between pornography and psychoanalysis across films, internet videos, pornographic literature, and pulp fiction.

Theories of sexuality have preoccupied psychoanalytic scholars but there has perhaps been a dearth of rigorous application to pornography – the exploration of how categories such as desire and pleasure are so entangled in pornographic production, consumption, and practices is the focus of the articles presented here, beginning with Varghese's account of why psychoanalysis might have value for contemporary research into sexually explicit representation.

Pornography is usually understood as a visual medium; indeed, this understanding is sedimented in the various ways that pornography is publicly discussed – from the subtitle of Linda Williams' foundational text *Hardcore* to the calls for censorship of pornographic imagery, pornography's 'frenzy of the visible' all too constantly renders the sounds of pornography redundant. Eugenie Brinkema's article 'Form for the Blind' takes a different approach, exploring the unwieldy, difficult to categorize, and ignored category of audio porn. Taking examples from Pornhub's growing archive of professional vocal transcriptions of conventional visual pornographic texts, Brinkema works through the difficulties of describing description alongside its relations to forms of interpretation and the ways that description overwrites the action onscreen. Cinematically specific visual language is only one aspect of the 'unmoved viewer' who retells the action producing two registers of performed desire. Brinkema finds that 'Description thus indexes the *interpretability* of pornography as such, making clear in its unfolding performance that pornographic labour is inextricable from its formal activity.'

For Chris Vanderwees, new media technologies not only interpellate desiring subjects as Peeping Toms – watching, stalking, looking at each other – but he also contends that contemporary viewers must also live with the anxiety of being 'peeped' at themselves – cultures of surveillance extend even into our most private spaces, collecting data on our screen-time, use of social media and online pornography. In 'Paranoid Pleasure: Surveillance, Online Pornography, and Scopophilia', Vanderwees uses Sartre's conception of the man looking through the keyhole to explore the complexities of scopophilic pleasures and desire, and their relationships with anxieties around voyeurism, shame, narcissism, and the self. His article strives to understand the possible connections between 'fantasies of looking and being looked at through the keyholes of technology' that characterize consumption of contemporary online pornographies.

Voyeurism is also the subject of Fan Wu's 'A Porn Voyeur's Discourse'. Inspired by Roland Barthes' *A Lover's Discourse* and his idiosyncratic, particularly literary, understanding of psychoanalysis, Wu offers a lyrical exposition of the different pleasures offered by amateur and studio gay pornography. Moving away from depersonalized enumerations of the cultural significances (too often negative) of pornographic texts, Wu offers a more personal exploration of his reactions to the texts in a set of moves which seem to echo Barthes' assertion that signs 'are only important to me if they seduce or irritate me. Signs in themselves are never enough for me, I must have the desire to read them.' Barthes famously rejected pornography (in his *Camera Lucida*), separating 'the "heavy" desire of pornography from the "light" (good) desire of eroticism', but Wu diverges from Barthes on this. Exploring edging, authenticity effect, and the pleasures of personal porn archives, Wu argues for a renewed appraisal of porn's pedagogies for our desire(s).

Psychoanalysis is, of course, an interpretative science and particularly of the complexities of desire(s). David K. Seitz employs the interpretative lens of melancholia in 'Looking for Pei Lim's Penis: Melancholia, Mimicry, Pedagogy'. Freud's account of melancholia and its constitutive role of loss in subject formation is the foundation for Seitz's exploration of the racialization of queer sexuality and its mediation in pornography, particularly through the staging of 'repudiated desire'. Seitz focuses on the artistic, activist, and porn careers of Lim Pei-Hsien, an important, if rarely acknowledged, figure in Canadian LGBTQ, AIDS, and anti-racist circles. Focusing on Lim's work read through a psychoanalytic lens enables Seitz to argue that Lim is a profoundly and perhaps instructively melancholic figure with significant resonance for apprehending the interconnections of race, queerness, and pornography.

Katie Goss' contribution to this special issue, 'Pornography, Psychoanalysis, and the Sinthome: Ignorance and Ethics', takes us on a journey through the knots and entanglements of knowing and ignorance, art and porn, repression and liberation, and the Imaginary and the Real. Moving across a range of films and texts, from Bette Gordon's 1983 *Variety*, through Dennis Cooper's transgressive novel *Frisk*, and on to Conor Habib's 2015 essay 'The Name of Your First Pet and the Street You Grew Up On', Goss conjoins pornography and the radical ethics of psychoanalysis to 'demonstrate how the "savoir-faire" (Lacan [1975–76] 2016, 47) pornography supports and can engender – an absolute unknowability that exposes our essential ignorance – holds unique possibilities for creative appropriation of the Real in modes of artistic and ethical sexual practice'.

The Lacanian concept of 'jouissance', or the enjoyment that goes beyond the pleasure principle, makes its appearance in many of the articles in this special issue. For Gareth Longstaff the interpretation of jouissance makes possible the exploration and repositioning of a queer and psychoanalytic politics of bareback and chemsex as porn. In '"Bodies that Splutter" – Theorizing Jouissance in Bareback and Chemsex Porn', Longstaff examines the output of UK director Liam Cole and US website RawFuckClub.com alongside a transposition of Judith Butler's concept of performative bodies that matter and Tim Dean's unconscious bodies that mutter in order to frame gay male desires for bareback and chemsex as instances of phallic jouissance.

Lacanian ethics are the subject of Alison Horbury's 'A Psychoanalytic Ethics of the Pornographic Aesthetic'. As Horbury explains, Lacan positions a psychoanalytic ethics in opposition to traditional ethics, enabling 'the cleaning up of desire', through 'modesty', and 'temperateness'. Utilizing this psychoanalytic ethics, Horbury attempts its application to a pornographic aesthetic. Once again Roland Barthes is useful to our author – the theoretical concept of the punctum enabling her examination of the pornographic 'artefact of the libido' and its aesthetic, which she argues, despite Barthes' protestations to the contrary, 'may "prick" our symbolic identifications and political ideals to generate a more honest engagement with the (libidinal) truth of our desire'.

While pornography has traditionally been derided as fake and speaking to our basest desires, one form of pornographic production has more recently been claimed to embody honesty, truth, and authenticity. Feminist porn has become the story *du jour*, although its substance and impact have divided opinion. Madison Young has argued that 'Feminist porn takes a cultural form that has historically been seen as the purview of men. It reworks sexual images and conventions to explore new and more diverse kinds of desires' (in Martincic 2017); while anti-porn activists deride feminist porn as an oxymoron. In 'The Social/Political Potential of Illusions: Enthusiasm and Feminist Porn', Maggie Ann Labinski argues that the Freudian strategy of leading with 'enthusiasm' might offer a way through the impasse of 'ambivalence' towards more developed understandings of the impact of feminist porn within the social/political sphere.

The exploration of significances and impacts forms the basis of the final article in this special issue authored by Peter Rehberg, an academic and archivist at the ICI Berlin and Schwules Museum. Rehberg takes the realcore of Porn 2.0 and its new post-pornographic cultures to explore the limitations of psychoanalytic accounts of subjectivity and desire, to consider the possibility that psychoanalysis might be obsolete, or that we now live in a post-psychoanalytic pornographic universe. Rehberg's article 'More than Vanilla Sex: Reading Gay Post-Pornography' develops its thesis through the juxtaposition of Eve Sedgwick's theories of affect with Freudian theories of the drives. Rehberg's contribution moves beyond the purely theoretical through exploration of the culture of affective sexualities as presented in the Dutch gay fanzine *Butt*.

In each of these articles our authors explore the multiple ways in which desire manifests in relation to pornographic authorship and viewership/consumption, drawing out the experiences and meanings of pleasure and moving beyond the negative connotations of perversion and pathology which have dogged pornographic consumption. Taken together, these articles reinvigorate some of the well-worn psychoanalytic categories, of jouissance, loss, lack, mourning, melancholia, attachment, trauma, and the fetish, to argue for the importance of taking a fresh look at thinking psychoanalytically about pornography.

Feona Attwood
Clarissa Smith
John Mercer

Reference

Martincic, Julia. 2017. 'Girls on Top: The Rise of Feminist Porn'. *The Daily Telegraph*. April 20. https://www.telegraph.co.uk/women/sex/girls-top-rise-feminist-porn/

Introduction: an orgasm by any other name

Ricky Varghese

Memory is dangerous, and so is remembering. Or so the response to Shailaja Padindala's (2016a) *Memories of a Machine* would have us believe. The short Malayalam film, 9 minutes and 47 seconds in length, has polarized viewer responses since it was released in late 2016. To be sure, *Memories of a Machine* is not pornographic, at least not in the strictest sense. Part *mise en scène*, part retelling, a recalling (or even a conjuring – is not 'all' representation, cinematic or otherwise, a sort of conjuring of desire?) as such, and, to recall Freud himself here for a moment, part a remembrance, a repetition, and a working through, *Memories of a Machine*, as the name suggests, is precisely just about that: a memory, now of a long departed past, and what it might mean – accounting for 'its' many meanings and implications, of course – to remember it in the present conjecture. Here, put simply, the memory is that of a sexual awakening, of one's first orgasm, or the memory of the first orgasm one might remember having, the remembrance of an inaugural experience of one's own sexuality and of one's coming-to-awareness of one's own body as a technology – an affective apparatus, a thinking, feeling machine, even – of sex.

The premise – if the film can be considered to have one – appears to be simple enough. Set in what appears to be a bedroom, a young woman, unnamed for the duration of the film, is roused from playfully pretending to sleep – pretending, itself, as a kind of erotic play, or a play of Eros – by an unknown man behind a camera, also unnamed for the duration of the film. The man, here, is always a disembodied voice. Non-existent, never seen, invisible, seemingly privileged, as the case may be, to be invisible. Much can be, and has been, said about such a heteronormative and heteropatriarchal dyad. Laura Mulvey in 'Visual Pleasure and Narrative Cinema', for instance, immediately comes to mind:

> In a world ordered by sexual imbalance, pleasure in looking has been split between active/ male and passive/female. The determining male gaze projects its phantasy on to the female figure which is styled accordingly. In their traditional exhibitionist role women are simultaneously looked at and displayed ... Woman displayed as sexual object is the leit-motif of erotic spectacle ... ([1975] 2012, 584)

Still further, speaking from an art historical register regarding such a dyad, John Berger has suggested:

> One might simplify this by saying: men act and women appear. Men look at women. Women watch themselves being looked at. This determines not only most relations between men and women but also the relation of women to themselves. The surveyor of woman in herself is male: the surveyed female. Thus, she turns herself into an object – and most particularly an object of vision: a sight. (1972, 47)

Figure 1 Film still from *Memories of a Machine* (2016), directed by Shailaja Padindala. https://www.youtube.com/watch?v=ZnZwPY7uJuI, 26 February 2016.

Approaching such a coupling still – the appearing woman, the non-appearing man – from a literary angle, one might hear in the scene described echoes of the poetic Anne Michaels: 'How much of a woman's body belongs to her, how much the clay of man's gaze' (2009, 115). All of these discursively critical approaches may be quite effortlessly applied, even adequately and necessarily so, in reading the scene. However, the woman in front of the camera is not 'merely' a passive sight (Figure 1).

The audience is not made sure of the nature of the relationship between the woman and the man until much later; that they are a young married couple is only disclosed to us through their dialogue towards the end of the narrative. Up until this point, we may very well assume, or may be led by Padindala to believe, that they may be a pair of unmarried lovers. Even in the context of the otherwise progressive, leftist landscape of Kerala, pre-marital sex, as is the case elsewhere in the subcontinent, is a taboo matter; so to believe that they may be lovers is enticing, even perhaps scandalously exciting for the audience. This, however, is not the 'scandal' at the heart of the film; its traumatic kernel, so to speak, that has had audience members up in arms. As the film begins, after the woman is roused from pretending to sleep, she is asked by the man beyond the frame to confess to something. It is alluded to that, earlier, before the camera started rolling, the woman had subjected the man to a playful interrogation; a series of 'quirky questions' to which, he states, he willingly provided answers. Now, it is her turn to be subjected to a similar line of questioning. He wants to know about the same thing he claims she asked him prior to the start of the film's narrative; he asks her: 'Tell me about the first time you felt sexual and wondered … ' – indicating a desire to know of her earliest memory of experiencing being sexually aroused, her earliest memory of an orgasm.

The figure of the woman – skilfully executed as coy, unassuming, yet brilliantly in charge of her own narrative by the gifted actress Kani Kusruti – goes on to describe a scene she remembers from her childhood. It is this childhood memory, the act of remembering this scene from her childhood, that has led to the deeply polemical response to the film and its presumed intentions. According to how she remembers it, she was eight years of age when the incident took place. She describes how there was a 'peon' – the word used in certain contexts in India to refer to custodial and janitorial staff – at school, a young man she describes as 'tall and handsome', and who she claims was her 'first crush'. After the end of the final examinations on the last day of the school year, after all her friends had left, she found herself alone in the school grounds waiting for her father, who was running late from work, to pick her up. After the peon had checked all of the classrooms and shuttered all of the classroom doors, he arrived at the steps to the school, saw her waiting, and sat down on the steps. He 'called [out to her] and gestured [her] to sit on his lap'. She remembers acceding to his request. She then recalls:

> When I sat, I felt something hard under my thighs. I did not know what it was. I was curious and scared, so I touched him. I wondered if it was flesh or bone. I was confused, did not know what it was … I was extremely curious! And then he softly tried touching the place I pee from. He was very gentle … very gently, like he knew how I would like it or rather knew how to do it. I felt wet and confused as to why I was feeling wet without urinating. It scared me. He figured out that and asked me if I was scared. I didn't say anything. He stopped, put me down, and went away.

After recounting this incident, she becomes shy and playful again, and admits that this is the first time she has ever told anyone what happened to her that day in the grounds of her school. Her off-screen male counterpart and interrogator, clearly alarmed by what he has just learned, then asks her questions reverberating with nothing short of seemingly genuine concern: 'Did he threaten you to keep it a secret?' She responds with a resounding 'No! He asked me if I got scared. He did not threaten me … Perhaps, I wanted it to happen again hence I kept it as a secret.' He pushes further: 'So do you feel anger toward him now?' 'No', she says in a demeanour that is so matter of fact, to which he responds, almost in a sense of being defeated by the casualness of her response and her repose: 'Fuck.' He continues to insist with his line of inquiry: 'Do you think whatever happened was wrong?' She continues with an air suggestive of confidence:

> I don't know if it was right or wrong. At the time, it was just a moment of sexual exploration for me. I liked the way he touched me and he stopped when I did not want it. I'm not concluding that it's right or wrong for that matter. I didn't think it was wrong then or now. That's all.

He responds cheekily: 'Don't tell this to a paedophile.' The mood of the exchange shifts for a very brief, perhaps all too brief, moment. All along, she was lying on the bed, peeling a fruit and eating it, as she responded to his questions. When he made the aforementioned indignant remark, she was inserting a piece of fruit into her mouth; she stopped mid bite and looked squarely at the camera, which is also to say at him, and in a look that almost predicts the negative responses to this film, she also looks in order to break the fourth wall, she looks at us the audience. This brief moment is heavy; Kusruti masterfully holds her look and holds the silence between her and the man behind the camera that envelops this look. These – the look, the silence, the moment – clearly make her male counterpart uncomfortable and so as to rupture all of these, he asks: 'And then, what happened?'

She goes on to recount that, that very summer, her father got transferred to a new job, and, as a result, she had to move away and to a new school. She never saw the peon after that day. To his query about whether she ever wished to see the peon ever again, she says 'No. But that day after going back home from school. I went to pee in the toilet and began

Figure 2 Film still from *Memories of a Machine* (2016), directed by Shailaja Padindala. https://www.youtube.com/watch?v=ZnZwPY7uJul, 26 February 2016.

touching myself the way he touched me. I went on in a rhythm and then something happened!' (Figure 2). He asks '… what happened?' She responds almost in a knowing manner: 'Orgasm! … by the way, what is orgasm called in Malayalam?' She recounts how she did not know, at the time, what had happened to her was an orgasm; that '[she] thought [she had] invented this thing nobody else knew about in the world'. The man laughs and responds: 'I thought the same the first time I did it too … !!' She says 'You too?! … after that day, I started doing it every day … ' When asked whether she had any boyfriends growing up, she recounts that she had one for a brief period of four months when she was in Grade 10. The first time they kissed, she describes getting wet, and when she asked him whether he would touch her 'down there' (as she is describing all this she is lying in bed, she unclips her bra and removes it from underneath the top she is wearing; she sighs, 'Ahh!! What a relief!'), he 'got shocked and acted weird, called [her] shameless and slapped [her]. [She] pelted a stone at him and left … the asshole!' She says that 'he was the last. [She] did not feel the need for a boyfriend after [her] "invention"'.

The dialogue goes on for a few more moments, at which point she asks whether he will now answer a question for her, and grabs his phone from his hands. She uses it to search for something online. When asked as to what she is searching for, she states: 'I'm googling the Malayalam word for orgasm.' She discovers that there are two words: '*rathimoorcha*' (രതിമൂർച്ഛ) and what she reads as '*rathimoorCHA*' (രതിമൂർച്ഛ) – she jokingly infers that 'cha' possibly indicates just one orgasm whilst 'CHA' means multiple orgasms. Laughter ensues between the two and the film ends.

Charged with accusations of supporting paedophilia, childhood sexual assault, and abuse, the film has been read through a regressive lens by some quarters of the viewing public. Both Kusruti and Padindala have come out and countered these readings of the film. In a video statement released by Padindala on YouTube on 7 February 2017, a few months after the release of the film, she states:

> As a teenager, when I discussed sexuality with my peers, almost every girl was touched as a child by an adult … almost every girl was guilty, she felt miserable about that, but there was one girl who was open about it and she thought that it was a pleasurable act. I started understanding how she looked at sexuality, and as a collective, how we look at sexuality and how the basic for everything in this world is the way we address sexuality. So that was the inception for making this film. (Padindala 2016b)

In a similar vein, in an interview she did with *The News Minute*, Kusruti (2016) observes:

> I feel very certain that the film doesn't normalize or defend abuse of any kind, whatsoever. So I don't think it's a fair assessment at all. The fallacy arises from conflating the domain of child sexual experiences with the rubric of child sexual abuse. This makes it very challenging to speak about various encounters that many people may have had which don't fall within a victim/trauma narrative, and as the film shows, can be accounted from the domain of curiosity and desire. The actions of the peon would constitute an offence under the law, but the scene is not a legal or moral deconstruction of his actions – the scene is about the girl, her sexuality, her power dynamics, and her memories, which are neither juridical nor prescriptive.

Yet a memory feels dangerous here. Also remembering, too. I decided to introduce this issue of *Porn Studies* on the potential furtive ground that exists for research into the interplay between pornography and psychoanalysis through a description of this film, a film that has stirred up some bit of controversy, precisely because I wanted to underscore how psychoanalysis, understood as the study of the relationship between memory and the unconscious – both in its applied academic and in its clinical registers – can be, in itself, a dangerous but necessary endeavour. I use the word 'danger' here not as an alarm to signal something nefarious, but to highlight the structure of risk upon which it is founded. Memory work is risky business – it has the potential to unfurl how the subject experiences and determines desire for themselves. It is still particularly risky because it has the potential to take us to difficult-to-fathom terrains such as the nuanced landscape of childhood sexuality and sexual experience. To think desire, alongside childhood sexuality, is a difficult conversation to have, still more difficult might be to incorporate the pornographic into these debates. How might we develop an understanding of how desire determines what we choose to consume and how we go about the work of choosing the object(s) of our consumption? How do judgement, taste, form, and desire relate to the pornographic and subsequently to how we come to underscore and understand our sexualities? What kinds of personal historical and subjective memorial contexts are evoked in how and what we consume as far as the pornographic is concerned? What kind of legal, juridical, moral, and philosophical registers – all of which may be ideologically and politically charged valences – are energized when we think of the interplay between sex, desire, pornography, and the screens, both in culture and memory, that we use to either occlude or release forms of pleasure that may be important to us? These are but some of the very few concerns that I was hoping would be interrogated in this issue, which, in the final analysis, might be a gesture towards conjoining sex and a longing for the image, or images in the plural; images, either as represented vis-à-vis the pornographic or in the form of a memory culled from childhood experience, that allow us to make sense of our desires and of ourselves as desiring subjects.

This longing, for instance, might already be found in a linguistic deconstruction of the word that the unnamed woman in *Memories of a Machine* goes searching for, the Malayalam word for orgasm. An example of how a history of colonization may have impacted and determined what words remain or become forgotten or left out of colloquial discourse, the Malayalam word for orgasm – a classical Malayalam word, at that – is clunky in a way, feels heavy-handed in another register, and is perhaps too beautiful-sounding and even operatic to mean the 'mere' expenditure of sexual energy. Most Keralites or Malayalees may not even know the word because it has long gone out of fashion and usage and has been replaced by the English 'orgasm', and yet something about '*rathimoorcha*' captures the essential meaning of what our character's recounting of her memory meant to her and for her understanding a part, a fragment to be sure, of the history of her desire and her sexuality. *Rathimoorcha* is a portmanteau of two other words: '*rathi*' which stands for the Hindu goddess Rathi (or 'Rati' depending on how you transliterate the word from Malayalam to English), the goddess of sex, lust, and desire, the consort of the god Kama (the same 'Kama' as in the *Kama Sutra*, the ancient Hindu text dealing with matters concerning human sexual behaviour) who is the god of love, and the word '*moorcha*' which can refer to the 'unconscious' or a fall (to be sure, not the lapsarian fall of man in the Abrahamic traditions) or slip into unconsciousness. That sex and love are uncannily gendered in the names of the divine in most Indian languages is in and of itself deserving of a full linguistic exploration. However, I want to return to the second word that makes the portmanteau complete – '*moorcha*' in Malayalam also means 'to cut', 'to gash', or 'to wound'. One might hear in this word a tremolo of Freud's description of melancholia as an 'open wound', what philosopher Rebecca Comay, in her turn, has succinctly described as 'the unappeasable attachment to an ungrievable loss' (2005, 88). Perhaps, the orgasm, or the memory of that first orgasm and the psychical implications of this memory (whether it happened in 'exactly' the manner by which it is recalled or not) for our young character, and, perhaps, for all of us to an extent, is always already melancholic, an open wound that cannot be sutured up too easily or that cannot heal quickly enough. My wager is that the story of the memory of this, which is at its core a memory of loss, can tell us so much about ourselves.

Disclosure statement

No potential conflict of interest was reported by the author.

References

Berger, John. 1972. *Ways of Seeing*. London: Penguin Books.
Comay, Rebecca. 2005. "The Sickness of Tradition: Between Melancholia and Fetishism." In *Walter Benjamin and History*, edited by Andrew Benjamin, 88–101. London: Continuum.
Kusruti, Kani. 2016. "Memories of a Machine is about Sexuality, Not Abuse: Actor Kani on Controversial Film." *The News Minute*, November 29. Accessed October 25, 2018. https://www.thenewsminute.com/article/memories-machine-about-sexuality-not-abuse-actor-kani-controversial-film-53596
Michaels, Anne. 2009. *The Winter Vault*. Toronto: Mclelland & Stewart.
Mulvey, Laura. [1975] 2012. "Visual Pleasure and Narrative Cinema." In *The Bloomsbury Anthology of Aesthetics*, edited by Joseph Tanke and Colin McQuillan, 581–590. London: Bloomsbury Academic.
Padindala, Shailaja, dir. 2016a. *Memories of a Machine*. India.
Padindala, Shailaja. 2016b. "Why the Title 'Memories of a Machine'." *YouTube*, February 7. Accessed October 25, 2018. https://www.youtube.com/watch?v=QhLZ9sH4iA0

Form for the blind (porn and description without guarantee)

Eugenie Brinkema

ABSTRACT

This article reads the paradoxical, curious, and seemingly self-negating pornographic category known as 'Described Video' – focusing on PornHub's growing archive of professional vocal transcriptions of conventional visual pornographic texts, which are described in great detail, in real time alongside the source video, ostensibly for the benefit of the visually impaired. Through a close reading of the way in which the formal language of each text is described alongside narration of sexual practices, the article argues that described video reveals the tension at the heart of pornographic form: the inadequate mediation that all pornography attempts to contravene and disavow, a confusion of description with action. While pornography might seem the Antivalue of description – *Don't tell me, show me!* – I argue that the pornographic commodity is itself a positive claim about the nature of description, one that is complicated in the case of described video. Ultimately, description comes to name an interpretation of pornography, making clear that pornographic labour is inextricable from its formal activity, and that desire is not a result of fantasies or flesh, but that *form* is what gets viewers off.

Ultimately – or at the limit – in order to see a photograph well, it is best to look away or close your eyes. (Roland Barthes, *Camera Lucida*)
Decidedly this eye is hard of hearing. (Samuel Beckett, *The Unnamable*)

Fermer les yeux

So maybe it is a *fap* or a *schlick* track, the onomatopoetically named sub-genre of audio recordings of men (the former) or women (the latter) masturbating, that male neologism, per one archaeology, derived from written sound effects in several works of 1990s manga, the female taking longer to consolidate into a single term – metonymizing everything that has ever been said about the unwieldy polysemy of feminine sexuality – having been offered in the early 2000s as *paf* or *squish* before settling into its current dominant form (Dean 2016). Or maybe it is a 1970s erotic radio play written and performed for that medium, composed of moans showcasing the grains of professionally trained voices. Then again, if we follow McLuhan and radio is merely the realized joining of records and tapes, perhaps it is just another version of that cassette they found, and – luckily –

were still able to play, of people they did not know fucking in some way or other, recording it they cannot imagine why or when or where. Late at night, listening for the same from the apartments across the way when back-room windows are open due to the heat. Or one prefers the soundtracks of their porn, the images exhausted or distressing or boring or distracting; She likes literotica posted on blogs, he loves Tumblr screamer tracks; and tonight you call a phone line with recorded tones at the press on the keypad or your usual troll for chat sex finds, this time – for once – a stranger you really like the sound of so you can – finally – banter and barter a shared fantasy in your 'fiber-optical' back room as in Nicholson Baker's *Vox*; or it is the face-fucking domination posts on Gone Wild Audio, the sonic outgrowth of Reddit's Gone Wild, or, just a link away, the sentimental drowse of the narrated second-person tenderness of [M4F] Good Morning [Australian Accent] [Morning Sex] [Sweet], posted for anyone but it feels with absolute certainty like that voice is speaking just to you, breathing right on your skin – and who, on finding themselves thus listening, is not reminded of the philosophical tradition that insists on the radical openness of the ear, gaping organ, running from Rousseau's '*Essai sur l'origine des langues*', where he describes musical accents

> to which one cannot close one's ear and which by way of it penetrate to the very depths of the heart, in spite of ourselves convey to it the emotions that wring them, and cause us to feel what we hear, (1997, 250–251)

to Lacan's insistence that because the ears are not burdened with lids, they will not, cannot, bar shut the world ('the invocatory drive has the privilege of not being able to close' [1998, 200]). Or maybe it has been a rough few months and now you can only get off listening to autonomous sensory meridian response (ASMR) whispering, that crackle at the corner of the lips, that mouth-to-cochlea clicking that calms. But it could also, I suppose, just be my lover leaving a short dirty voice mail. What we will do later.

There is nothing simple or direct in any effort at classifying sub-genres and formations of any mode or kind of pornography, and it follows that defining, taxonomizing, and specifying a category of 'audio porn' immediately runs out of control, unwieldy in the scale, density, and heterogeneity of its membership, and thereby rapidly useless as a term of nomination for a subject of thinking. Nor is there anything new in this complaint about pornography and definition, nor is it in fact a complaint because the question of definition itself, the setting of boundaries in a statement of what something means, is, we might say, the essential project of pornography, which is why it constantly eludes definition in its own drive to proliferate beyond (all, every, any) set limits, and why it devastates thresholds of definition, most famously in *Jacobellis v. Ohio*, the 1964 juridical opinion which, right before uttering 'I know it when I see it', negatively affirms 'I shall not today attempt further to define the kinds of material I understand to be embraced within that shorthand description.' But I would argue that this is because pornography is, if it can be said to *be* anything at all, a speculative problem of and for the relation of definition to description. While pornography might seem the Antivalue of description – *Don't tell me, show me!* – my current work explores how the pornographic commodity is itself a positive claim about the nature of description.[1] The present article focuses on a sub-membership of that expansive, impossibly-defined mode of 'audio porn' – what is called 'Described Video' – a still-sizable tent that includes the amateur, donated descriptions of the non-profit Porn for the Blind and PornHub's growing archive of transcriptions of their most popular videos – in which conventional visual pornographic texts are elaborately described in real concurrent time by a human voice ('volunteer audiodescribers' in the case of the former, professional voice actors in the latter), ostensibly for the benefit of the visually impaired.[2] My argument is that this is the textual field that most radically unconceals a paradox central to (all) pornographic labour.[3] At the heart of this article is the straightforward yet perhaps aggressively unintuitive insistence that in pornography it is neither the wet nor the moan, but in fact *form* that is what gets viewers off.

Eyes are not the easiest way to see this.

Cut to a close-up of a cock

> To listen is to be straining toward a possible meaning, and consequently one that is not immediately accessible. (Jean-Luc Nancy, *Listening*)
> Words create silence. (Gilles Deleuze, 'He Stuttered')

Shall I then here proceed to describe a description? Or shall I engage the tradition of transcription, writing across, which is to say to insert some distance between *this* description and *that* one? Var.: in describing (only) the description, am I overtly failing to describe the textual object that ought to be my subject, the hybrid composed object of description-described source video? In speaking about the images, of course, the described video fails to hew to the specificity of *describere* – a writing down – so, once more, if I write to describe a description, have I in fact fulfilled its etymological end, brought it to some sort of realization?

I will transcribe, then. I will refuse to describe. Description is clearly a trap.

> [Female voice] *This is PornHub's Descriptive Audio of the video Teen Mom Farrah Abraham Sex Video by Vivid Celebs. The video opens with a shot of Farrah on a beige sofa with a blue and black gym bag beside her. She's wearing a bodycon minidress that's neon orange with black and is leaning forward to take off her shoes. The man she talks to, presumably James Deen, is off-screen.*

But I lied just now. For when I include, bracketed but present, the assertion that it is a female voice who speaks, a voice ageless and with a clipped rhythm to her consonants, I am of course already caught in description, and not a description of the description but a description of the describer, which transcription can never name itself within itself. (This is an ancient problem in pornographic thought, which is to say it dates back to Sade: as Klossowski phrases it,

> The description Sade gives of his own experience in the characters he created covers a twofold experimentation: (1) that of the representation of the sensuous in an aberrant act; (2) that of the described representation. There will then be a relationship between the actualization of the sensuous in an act through writing and the performing of the act independently of its description. With Sade, this writing is not purely descriptive (objective) but interpretive. [1991, 17]

Descriptive porn, however, inverts this logic of description, promising a priority of that 'purely descriptive (objective)' encounter, which is to say one that evades mediation, is not interpretive, but stands in *for* action.)

How to proceed, then?

> [Female voice] *This is PornHub's Descriptive Audio of the video Teen Mom Farrah Abraham Sex Video by Vivid Celebs. The video opens with a shot of Farrah on a beige sofa with a blue and black*

gym bag* beside her. She's wearing a bodycon minidress that's neon orange** with black and is leaning forward to take off her shoes. The man she talks to, presumably James Deen, is off-screen. It cuts to her walking from her tote bag from which she's removed some blue and pink lingerie to a bed covered in white bed linens with a gold bed frame. Deen, who is still off-screen, gets her to turn around, but she won't let him look up her skirt. She lies back on the bed with her legs crossed and closed while she untangles the bra she's preparing to put on. Then she stands back up and again demands help removing her dress. It looks like he's the one filming because he reaches out with only one hand and doesn't actually seem to be able to undo the top of her dress.*** It cuts to her in the blue and purple bra with matching panties. She's standing, but is bent over her bag again searching for better lingerie. She complains about her friend's lingerie selection.**** Then her***** and Deen start teasing each other and she hurls a pillow towards him, then she walks over to the bed and throws herself down on it laughing. Although you still can't see him, he starts hitting****** her with a pillow. She invites him to come over and we see a bit of his jeans and t-shirt as he walks over to stand beside her. They start talking about his cock and she compares the jeans he's wearing to armour.******* It cuts and now we have a close-up view from above of her blowing him. She sucks his cock but he's not hard yet.******** Then, when she decides that they should do anal, she springs up off the bed and walks away to get lube. She walks over to a metal staircase going downstairs but then they keep teasing each other for a few moments so she stands there by the railing for a few seconds in her pink and blue lingerie. After a moment of jostling, the camera settles on a side view of her giving him a blow job. He's still not really hard although he's getting there.********* She licks and sucks and rubs his shaft.********** Then the scene cuts and reopens on them doing anal on the bed. He's kneeling and is mostly off-screen and she is lying on the bed also partially cropped out, although you can see her tits and her face is turned toward us. *********** Got his right hand out and rubbing her pussy, his left hand is gripping her hip. It cuts to an extreme close-up below him pounding her pussy, and she has her left leg, the one nearer to us, raised completely so we can fully see her ass and her pussy as his cock moves in and out of her.************ She looks back over her right shoulder and gives the camera a sexy playful smile. He reaches out and brushes her hair away from her face over her left shoulder so now we can see her even better. She's beautiful. Her little************* brown tits point down towards the bed and look like little pyramids. He smacks her ass as he thrusts. He's very hard now and is moving all the way in and out of her ass really fast.**************

* It's just black (cf. proliferating network of associations from unwarranted evocation of the chromatic schema of a bruise).

** It's pink.

*** This figure of Deen's inadequacy will become a dominant topos in the narration.

**** NB: What is being described is a description of a complaint, one that describes negatively a series of available sartorial objects. We can generalize this as – what is here being narrated on a second-order recording is none other than another scene of recorded dialogue. These verbal negotiations, flirtations, demands, and complaints could, of course, be heard in the original audio track – and thus of course could have been conveyed in their original (which is to say initially recorded) form – but that original recorded audio is minimized and nearly inaudible, just tones not words, so that the description stands in redoubled place of all the recorded speech of the performers which, because the dress could not be unzipped, which, because the lingerie has been dubbed inadequate, has been the entirety of what has been taking place – talking, demanding, complaining – on the level of action.

***** Sic. (Also: for whom might this grammar sour an erotic mood instantly, absolutely?)

****** *Hurler*, thirteenth century, to come into collision, throw forcibly; OE *hittan*, come upon, to strike, forcible contact. Had the word been *throw*, we might have sensed a twisting, turning projection; had it been *toss*, a rhythmic lifting with sudden movement; or *lob*, the gentle elegance of sending up in a slow high arc; and so forth (– but of course it was not). The ineluctable specificity of specific signifiers had to be chosen: description demands that within its own workings. An arbitrary but determinate *choosing* cannot be outstripped from description. And so, here, now, unremittably, Deen, with all the force thereby imported, only ever hits.[+]

[+] It will thus become impossible, viewing at a historical remove, not to re-read this 2013 video through the lens of Abraham's repeated claims, beginning in 2015, of abuse against then boyfriend Deen.

******* NB: the voice is again describing dialogue, rendering direct speech reported speech. The narration thereby introduces, which is to say creates, adds newly to the text, a rhetoric of indirection.+

+ This reported speech hews fairly closely to the directly issued dialogue of the original text. However, several of the narrators of others of PornHub's described videos prefer employing *discours indirect libre*, blending into one commentary third-person narration with first-person consciousness: e.g., the mix of speech and thought in the opening minutes of PornHub's Described Audio of 'Schoolgirls Squirting', in which the female British-accented speaker with the uneven scansion of a digital transcription tool declares (which is to say interprets, or rather imagines, invents[++]) – 'Jillian and Christian look at each other longingly, knowing that what they are doing is bad, but loving it.'

[++] This narrator's flexibility with the adequacy of description introduces overt error, which in turn introduces paradox and contradiction, even in the case of trivial details. Narrator intones: 'Her legs are smooth and bare; her midsection firm and slim. She turns towards the man and moves towards the side of the sofa. Jillian reaches for his zipper.' However, a moment later it is further declared that the man's jeans are now being unbuttoned (as they in fact are; the zipper was always a mirage, imagined). The attentive listener will perhaps wonder whether this is some sort of unusual type of pant, but what it demonstrates is the descriptive law of inertia: that description is not passive but predictive, that its energetic line is apt to fill out formulas, always running ahead in an attempt to imagine and produce its object – which of course means it can – in minor, irrelevant, but profound ways – be totally at odds[+++] with that which it describes. Description is thus transformational; at a minimum, at the level of spoken description, it posits the signified of that which it describes – whether it has a visible referent in the accompanying video or not.

[+++] The other at-oddsness of the description of 'Schoolgirls Squirting' is that the listener is constantly reminded of their absent presence through a perverse negation: when the describing voice declares that 'Jillian's hand extends to touch the leg of the man who we see in part for the first time' – as the image on the screen indeed shows a close-up of a leg with a hand resting on a thigh – that spoken invocation of a 'we' who 'sees'[++++] unconceals the intentionality of the framing of the original video (*there* for some 'we' who 'sees'), despite the fact that the someone for whom the description is provided under the presumption (aegis? pretext? alibi?) of ocular impairment would definitionally be excluded from that 'we' who 'sees' that man 'for the first time'.

[++++] Throughout these narrations one encounters the impossible excising of the language of visibility, even in the midst of description motivated by an overt politics of accessibility. This indestructible opticentrism comes to a fascinating crisis in one of the more formally rigorous descriptive tracks, that for 'Puremature HD Lisa Ann gets fucked hard in the gym', in which the narration demonstrates both a jarring commitment to inventive synonyms – resulting in phrases like 'strokes his cockflesh down to the base' – and hews to the language of close analysis one associates with cinema scholars: 'Dissolve to later'; 'and now we cut to a side-front angle'; 'close-up on her tits'; and so forth. One consequence of this rabid formal specificity is a constant reference to the textual constructedness of the image. Narration that declares 'Back to a wide shot where he holds her wrists behind her back. Then an extreme close-up of her pussy and asshole from behind as his dick goes deep into that snatch and she holds her butt cheek apart *for the camera*' (emphasis added) makes clear that sexual practice, here spreading the buttocks, is not a move made for pleasure – ordered by a dominant partner, or spontaneously exposing the body to new sensations – but a gesture described overtly as *being for* the camera, a mediation that, if it deprives the text of the ideology of spontaneity or realism,[+++++] makes descriptively clear that the video's form is affirmatively staged for an idealism of maximum visibility[++++++] – thus simultaneously depriving the described text of any pretence of a description that could ever be adequate to stand in for that Vide-o. Transcribed here as: *I am telling you in precise detail that you do* not *see something that is there with a given visual form precisely so that the someone the film imagines you to be can* see everything that is there. This description is not a prosthetic eye but rather an account of the precise nature of the blindness.[+++++++]

[+++++] It is interesting to note cases where an exegetical commitment to descriptive fidelity, following from an ideology of accuracy, comes into competition with another pornographic valuation°: that of the virtuosic ease of particularly intense sexual practice. The descriptive audio for 'Kimmy Granger Likes it Rough', which is careful to include details about the stubble on a male performer's face, or the 'strand of spit' trailing from a mouth, also makes certain to note, in the midst of energetic fucking, 'his cock falls out briefly', an assertion that wagers that this avowal of realism, the unstaged spontaneous slippages of enacted practices, will provide a compensatory pleasure for any loss of signs of idealisms of ease, unstained fantasy, and the perfectibility of the pornographic act.

° Multiple competing valuations are in play; consider that descriptive audio polemically refrains from clinical naming for anatomy and sexual practices – not vulva, but *pussy*; not intercourse, *fucking*; not frottage, *titty-fucking*, and so forth – and yet simultaneously insists on technical rigour and precision in the formal language of time-based moving image media (*dissolve, fade, jump cut, medium shot, high-angle*, etc.). It poses the question of whether one ought to read *pussy, titty-fucking, sucking cock* as equivalent to the technical language of film analysis – or, more excitingly, whether the language of close textual analysis is less coolly dispassionate and clinical than imagined by opponents of formalism.

[++++++] The more profound question is how blindness can teach us new things about form, new ways of imagining form, new vocabularies for and questions to ask of form.

[+++++++] Likewise, when PornHub's descriptive audio for Kim Kardashian's sex tape with Vivid insists that it 'opens on a medium distance view', then proceeds to state that 'it cuts and now we get a shot from above of Ray's cock in Kim's face', and finally makes point to mention that 'the camera is blurry' – the reference to a view, an overhead framing, and the quality of the sharpness of the image all put description to work to name the irreducibly visual mediation of actions; under the alibi of the accessibility of (this, any) pornographic object, description proceeds to reinstate the ontological *inaccessibility* of that which is being described. What the description positively[++++++++] describes is an ever-narrower diagnosis of that inaccessibility.

[++++++++] Of course, there are also moments of unexpected, exquisite beauty. The male voice describing 'Hairy Dad Fucking Step Son', while carefully notating the editing syntax – 'The camera keeps moving back and forth between a side view of their bodies and the son's face and a close-up rear view of the dad's ass and balls as he thrusts his cock in and out of his son's asshole' – concludes his descriptive paragraph with an Anne Carson-esque 16-word list: 'There's a jump cut and now the camera is a bit further back. We see more of the room, the wooden headboard of the bed, the dark wood shelf, a green plant on the shelf.'

[********] There is a long period of silence here, from 2.22 to 2.48. During those 26 seconds what voicelessness unconceals is the negative knowledge that *some* event presently *not* being described is taking place – the duration of attempting to undo that 'isn't hard yet' qualifier. What the description textually introduces, then, is the possibility of a silence that names foreclosure (on the level of description) and simultaneously a continuity of action, the narration only resuming once a new practice is introduced. ([********] cont.: Of interest are further questions neither described nor answered: Why isn't Deen already hard? Isn't he the professional here [against which the rawness of Farrah's amateur performance is measured]? Will he ever get hard?[+] At what point does he get hard – and what, in the end, did it take? How does his lack of tumescence affect the rhythm and geometry of fellatio? And so forth.)

[+] This, as some know, is the pure form of an anxiogenic question.

[*********] That 'although' is delightful: a description of budding phallic adequacy would suffice without qualification. But that the absence of tumescence phrasally precedes the absence of this absence renders description more akin to encouragement, the narrative voice functioning like an in-game adjusting coach who senses a momentum shift from the sidelines and promises, ever the believer, that still yet their plucky team may rally in time.

[**********] What a description of action misses entirely is the rhythm of Farrah's performance: that everything she starts she stops seconds later. Some of the gaps are her stopping. Some are an index of that rhythm's insufficiency for producing new state changes. In its stead is the rhythm of the narrator's vocality – frenetic in its effort to describe in real time the movements of editing and shifting framing positions, languid in its relative uninvolvement in the movements of sexual practice: even if the fucking itself is rather busy, if formal arrangement does not locally change, the verbal pace is slow, even silent. What new there is to say relies on a newness in the textual construction; otherwise description falls to redundancy.

[***********] Of the infinite set of textual details the description does not describe, consider at least these three: that at this moment, Deen, who has been invoked in his various inabilities from the start of the video, is doubled in a thin, bent-postured, shadow homunculus in the reflecting television screen; that the most arresting, because most mobile, aspect of the *mise en scene* is the flashing digital time code that pulses around the grid of that same television screen, showing a real time second-by-second counting of the brief thrusting; and that the pillow that keeps obscuring Farrah's face creates a white blotch at the right side of the frame that resembles the ripped edge of a photograph

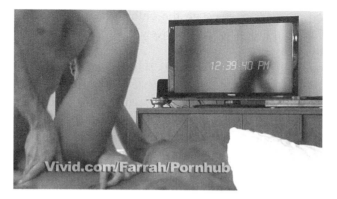

Figure 1. Screenshot from Teen Mom Farrah Abraham Sex Video by Vivid Celebs.

with a face excised – out of shame, revenge, for anonymity, or just the pure drive of iconoclasm: to wreck the image (Figure 1). (*********** cont.: evocations of that John Deakin photograph of Lucian Freud crumpled, half-destroyed and found on the floor of Francis Bacon's studio.)

************ Another 20-second silence, from 4.16 to 4.36, over a barely audible overheard whisper of 'Fuck that pussy', at such a sonic remove it is momentarily unclear which party issues the phrase, and whether it is a pleading imperative or, itself, a description of present action.

************ They are actually rather large. (************ cont.: Is this *little* declaration a *little* trace of the erotic preference of the narrating voice? And if so: is that preference for relative mammary scale, or, rather – and equally erotic, it should be said – a preference of the tip of the articulating tongue for forming the assonance that gets to pair *little* with *tits*? Who is to say that Voice should not have its own compensations, should not get some small aesthetic pleasure out of this whole describing thing? *Describe it to me* – what an imperious order! Always an obligation, a duty; always a gift to be done *for* some *you*. The good describer remains unmoved, careful; without desire. But maybe all this time, description was a little formal game I just felt like playing ...)

************ It ends here, abruptly; without closure, *in medias res*.

The wooden headboard of the bed, the dark wood shelf, a green plant on the shelf

> However detailed and complete it may be, and even if it says more, much more, than the film ever appeared to say, the written text can never capture anything but a kind of elementary skeleton, stripped of flesh from the beginning. (Raymond Bellour, *The Analysis of Film*)
> The lung, a stupid organ [...] swells but gets no erection. (Roland Barthes, 'The Grain of the Voice')

To the letter, what pornography sells are descriptions: *Pornographos*, the writings of whores, writing by whores about their whorish practices. But really, what the pornographic commodity sells is a particular *theory* of description. As Frances Ferguson frames it in her account of the co-constitution of pornography and utilitarianism in the late eighteenth century, 'pornography was not routing its claims through beliefs – however affectively intense – but rather through descriptions of actions' (2004, xiii). Specifically, the commodity put up for sale in pornography is a promise of a description so adequate to the activities of whores that there is a transferential contagion (of both pleasure and obscenity), a description that edges participation. What pornography assures is a description that can evade the distancing of forms of mediation, an assurance only amplified in pornographic inscription in indexical media ontologies.

Many questions present themselves in relation to descriptive porn videos, including: how would someone congenitally blind, an optic nerve damaged, say, during birth, interpret the spoken narration that opens 'Kimmy Granger Likes it Rough', which includes the information that 'the scene begins with the New Sensations logo', continues 'we fade to a windowed door', and promises that 'You can see the bittersweet struggle on her face' – all claims that make reference to cinematically specific visual language to which our hypothesized listener would have no literal point of reference, and a self-negating instruction in the second person at precisely the moment it is contraindicated by the logic of the described narration in the first place: 'You can see ... ' Are these descriptions accurate? What does it matter if they are not? And what kind of corrective could be made, let alone would be makeable?

While those are fine questions, they miss the most salient one: what precisely is being described in descriptive porn? For if description in relation to pornography is not equivalent to the question of description in relation to any other textual field – for a theory of description is what the pornographic commodity *is* – then a description of that description requires speculative care. For what is being described is not transcendent or general sexual practices, but situated, specific, particular ones. Above all, even in an indexical image, what are described are mediated actions, framed and edited and describable solely in reference to the concrete formal language of textual givenness. What is catalogued in PornHub's descriptive audio are formal differences: that shot as opposed to this one; *this* text – with its bodies, their shapes and tones, framed one way, with specific rhythms, under certain lighting conditions, framed by some, and not other, angles, cutting now as opposed to then – as distinct from *that* one. Description is not presented as equivalent to obviousness or unmediated accessibility (to bodies, pleasures, or practices). Rather, that that which is being described is formal language produces a negative claim about the general possibility of paraphrase, one that gives body, as it were, to Cleanth Brooks' famous 'heresy of paraphrase' in his 1947 *The Well-Wrought Urn*, that the 'paraphrase is not the real core of meaning which constitutes the essence of the poem. For the imagery and the rhythm are not merely the instruments by which this fancied core-of-meaning-which-can-be-expressed-in-a-paraphrase is directly rendered' (1947, 197). And in doing so, descriptive audio performs the essential logic of any formalist project – for as Ellen Rooney words it, all that is required to take form seriously is 'refusing to reduce reading entirely to the elucidation, essentially the paraphrase of themes' (2000, 29). To thematize pornography is to generalize transcendental bodies and practices; to formalize pornography is to describe the ineluctable specificity of textual details. What porn makes visible is that it is, in fact, impossible to paraphrase formal language: to describe form is to describe a failure of a description that would constitute a direct rendering.

Each describing voice thus functions as an ideal formalist/structuralist reader – possessed with knowledge of the various codes that comprise the text (equally the *pussy–cock–cum* system and the *fade–dissolve–close-up* system), able to decipher the assumptions and assertions of the work with an indifferent, unrestricted ease of observation, providing forms of knowledge and naming gender and race where observed, while remaining nameless, ungendered, unraced, and above all *unmoved* by the work. The describing voice, analogue to the transcendental critical reader, materializes the capacity to exhaustively describe textual rules and navigations without getting caught up in the messy affects that compromise, which is to say particularize and instrumentalize, an understanding of sexual action. This voice neither moans nor responds – this voice never comes. This voice thus indexes its own stance as an unmoved viewer in the service of an intention to move a listener. The transcribing voice, by describing formal systems without itself vocally attesting to those systems having the effect of arousal, assures above all that it has no body; that it is competent to name and describe textual form precisely *by virtue* of having no body.

With described porn, then, one is listening to two registers of performed desire simultaneously – the one a cause and consequence of corporeoerotic negotiation (the *body–practice–pleasure–pressure* level – the drive to come), and the other a cause and consequence of a linguistic negotiation aiming at a supplementary form of related but autonomous communication (the *accurate–specific–detailed–contingent* level – the drive to knowledge). But they are not equivalent; they are not sutured together, nor dialogically engaged. The descriptive drive overwhelms the erotic one; it sonically dominates. Thus, at the heart of described video is an affective paradox: if a goal of pornographic commodification is arousal, the described voice describes simultaneously an account of what an idealized, abstracted viewer is ostensibly seeing, while simultaneously affectively performing affective disinterest, non-arousal in the face of that which is being described. What described video thus attests to is the possibility of erotic neutrality towards pornographic descriptions – neutral because it tarries only with description without responding as if description was a proxy for action. If it also fails to provide any sense of a fully exhaustive account – exposing the limitation of description that would purport to be adequate, full, complete – the description that it does provide makes clear the dehiscence between pornographic inscription and telic erotic payoff.

Described porn thus demonstrates the three major risks of all description: that in attending to a single minute detail it overwhelms understanding through decontextualization; that in compiling an exhaustive catalogue of specificities it amasses a thicket of raw dangerous data, performing Naomi Schor's warning that 'There is always the danger that to write *on* the detail is to become lost *in* it' (2007, xlv; original emphases); and that description, an ostensible site of objectivity, neutrality and accuracy, itself is constitutively mired in the deferral of linguistic games, revealing its own reliance on formal strategies of metaphor, trope, and so forth, which themselves require infinite recursive description to come to terms with – becoming nothing but description all the way down. For imagine the case of the ideal described pornographic video, one that followed Borges' thought experiment from 'On Exactitude in Science' in which eventually cartographic art was able to create a 'Map of the Empire whose size was that of the Empire, which coincided point for point with it' (1999, 325). Perfect descriptive audio, in which description coincided so exquisitely and perfectly on every nuance and detail of the pornographic activity of the text, a one-to-one realization in description of practice so faithful as to transform description into an invisible analogue for that practice itself – would render the secondary description pornography proper. But that which would transform description into action is the ideology porn sells, but cannot be – and has a market in which to sell that precisely because some difference remains. In commodifying descriptions of actions, pornography names the irreducible non-coincidence of the two; turning on a promise of an asymptotic approach of description to a realization in action, the pornographic promise of a map the size of the Empire itself at once names the anxiety that description does not and never will approach action without mediation, which is to say: loss, noise, some lack of guarantee.

Description is precarious. We have known this at least since 1899, when an entire branch of philosophical thought – psychoanalysis – was founded on a theory of description as that which requires infinite (interminable) interpretation (analysis). The dehiscence, then, between the description of described video and the video as such performs *en abime* the fundamental rupture at the heart of pornographic form: the awkward inadequate mediation that all pornography attempts to contravene and disavow. It refuses to rally description for claims of a transparency of pleasure or practice, insisting in its imposed register of formal devices that there is no neutral accounting but only specific, infinitely different, formally given textual movements already and fundamentally in place intervening between viewer and practice, necessitating interpretation, with no final signified. The more detailed the description, the less description approaches some real or referent of action. Rather, the thicker the description of the formal mediation that is itself the rupture between *pornographos* and action, the stronger the *negation* of a fantasy of description adequate to action, the more description antagonizes a determination that description *could* ever be adequate to action. Instead of description offering an accumulation of meaning from the storehouse of the pornographic text, ready to give up a plenitude of stable, possessed knowledge (what Lacan criticizes as the Hegelian savoir-totalité), the more full the provision of description the more it ruptures the fantasy that the pornographic text is the sublimation of description into a proxy for action, each description a further deferral of a participation in the action that is the target and cause of desire. Description thus indexes the *interpretability* of pornography *as such*, making clear in its unfolding performance that pornographic labour is inextricable from its formal activity.

In the midst of this negative move, what descriptive pornography attests to is a positive speculative stance: description without guarantee. It unconceals the fragility of the pornographic project by making manifest description's debt to formal specificity that is only giveable through close, exhausting, and still yet never exhaustive, further description. *Form is the metalanguage of pornography*. Not a metalanguage in the sense of stabilizing pornographic discourse, but in its function as positioning formal description as unavoidably central to pornographic specificity, and form as unavoidably central to adjacent questions of pornographic discourse, including fantasy, identification, desire, all of which, psychoanalysis teaches us, are fundamentally formal enterprises. In many ways, the claim that form is the metalanguage of pornography articulates a version of the central insistence made by Laplanche and Pontalis, that in fantasy:

> the subject does not pursue the object or its sign; he appears caught up himself in the sequence of images. […] [T]he subject, though always present in the fantasy, may be so in a desubjectivized form, that is to say, in the very syntax of the sequence in question. (1986, 26–27)

What is internal to the pornographic project's effort to adequate description to action is what unavoidably cannot be outstripped from pornography: that its form will always require description; that form names what cannot be paraphrased about a pornographic text. This form, what gives the difference of different texts – the colour, light, cut, dissolve, space, angle, wood, plant, each of which demands while also producing more description – shows how form is the marker of difference that names the space in which desire comes down to *thisnesses*. As a result, an ideology or fantasy of description so adequate to action that it stands in its place is constructed through the negative index of a formal language which itself is only apprehensible through description. That form is the metalanguage of pornography means that there is no way for pornographic description to declare that its description is adequate to action without that description itself being given through formal means that are impossible to account for except through supplementary description. What is nakedly unconcealed in described pornography is not the lesson already taught by psychoanalysis – that desire proceeds without guarantee – but this far more abyssal claim: description itself is without guarantee. And pornography is merely form all the way down.

Notes

1. I engage in a longer, most robust discussion of pornography in relation to description in Brinkema (2017). This question of the nature, value, limitations, etc. of description – especially as a rejoinder to the hermeneutics of suspicion – has been hotly debated in the humanities in multiple fields in the last decade. See Best and Marcus (2009), Love (2010), and Marcus, Love and Best (2016).
2. The unwieldy size of even this subset archive makes strange a claim such as Dominic Pettman's:

   Given the erotic power and potential of the voice, then, what should we make of the dearth of sonic erotica, or 'audio porn,' on the Internet? Why are so many images sexualized but so few sound files […]? Why does the erotic voice lack 'stickiness' when it comes to the World Wide Web, given the power of the voice to summon seductive ghosts, quicken the heart, and whisper promises of bliss? (2017, 18–19)

   Although Pettman notes as an exception Porn for the Blind, because his focus on 'sonic intimacy' privileges the figure of seduction (of the ear), his searched-for vocality is reduced to performances of ecstasy and is unable to speak to the unseduced voice that describes.
3. Porn for the Blind is defunct as of this writing, but the interested can consult https://www.reddit.com/r/gonewildaudio/ and http://www.pornhub.com/described-video. See also Aronowitz (2015) and Henry (2016). The texts read in this article are from PornHub's Descriptive category, launched in 2016 and ongoing.

Disclosure statement

No potential conflict of interest was reported by the author.

References

Aronowitz, Nona Willis. 2015. 'Talk Dirty to Me: Deep Inside the Intimately Sexy World of Audio Porn,' *Playboy* February, 9.

Baker, Nicholson. 1992. *Vox*. New York: Random House.

Best, Stephen, and Sharon Marcus. 2009. 'Surface Reading: An Introduction.' In 'The Way We Read Now', edited by Stephen Best and Sharon Marcus, with Emily Apter and Elaine Freedgood. *Representations* 108: 1–21.

Borges, Jorge Luis. 1999. 'On Exactitude in Science.' In *Collected Fictions*, translated by Andrew Hurley, 325. New York: Penguin Books.

Brinkema, Eugenie. 2017. 'Irrumation, the Interrogative: Extreme Porn and the Crisis of Reading.' *Polygraph* 26: 130–164.

Brooks, Cleanth. 1947. *The Well Wrought Urn*. New York: Harcourt Brace.

Dean, Sam. 2016. 'Where Did "Fap" Come From?' *Mel Magazine*. October 31.

Ferguson, Frances. 2004. *Pornography, the Theory: What Utilitarianism Did to Action*. Chicago: University of Chicago Press.

Henry, Casey Michael. 2016. 'The Vibrating Wire: Nicholson Baker's *Vox* and the Art of Analog.' *Journal of Modern Literature* 39 (2): 20–38.

Klossowski, Pierre. 1991. *Sade my Neighbor*, translated by Alphonso Lingis. Evanston: Northwestern University Press.

Lacan, Jacques. 1998. *The Seminar of Jacques Lacan XI: The Four Fundamental Concepts of Psychoanalysis*, translated by Alan Sheridan, edited by Jacques-Alain Miller. London: Vintage.

Laplanche, Jean, and Jean-Bertrand Pontalis. 1986. 'Fantasy and the Origins of Sexuality.' In *Formations of Fantasy*, edited by Victor Burgin, James Donald and Cora Kaplan, 5–34. London: Methuen.

Love, Heather. 2010. 'Close but not Deep: Literary Ethics and the Descriptive Turn.' *New Literary History* 41 (2): 371–391.

Marcus, Sharon, Heather Love and Stephen Best, eds. 2016. 'Special Issue: Description Across Disciplines,' *Representations* 135.

Pettman, Dominic. 2017. *Sonic Intimacy: Voice, Species, Technics (or, How to Listen to the World)*. Stanford: Stanford University Press.

Rooney, Ellen. 2000. 'Form and Contentment.' *Modern Language Quarterly* 61 (1): 17–40.

Rousseau, Jean-Jacques. 1997. 'Essay on the Origin of Languages.' In *Rousseau: the Discourses and Other Political Writings*, edited and translated by Victor Gourevitch, 247–299. Cambridge: Cambridge University Press.

Schor, Naomi. 2007. *Reading in Detail: Aesthetics and the Feminine*. Forward by Ellen Rooney. London and New York: Routledge.

Paranoid pleasure: surveillance, online pornography, and scopophilia

Chris Vanderwees

ABSTRACT

This article explores the implications of paranoid pleasure and pornography in contemporary technocultures from a psychoanalytic perspective. If new media technologies not only interpellate desiring subjects as Peeping Toms, watching, stalking, and looking at each other, the author contends that subjects also live with the anxiety of being peeped, perhaps especially when engaged in private acts such as the consumption of online pornography. The author suggests that the contemporary viewer of online pornography might be best situated as a mediatized extension of Sartre's man looking through the keyhole, whereby scopophilic pleasure is sustained through anxieties around the Other's voyeurism, the self's shameful and narcissistic objectification of its own self. Here, the author argues that online pornography frequently portrays, encourages, and requires that the subject's jouissance be derived from the interplay between fantasies of looking and being looked at through the keyholes of technology. Ultimately, the article contends that the pleasure of online pornography in terms of production and consumption is inextricably linked to shifting, circulating, and conditional referents of the Other's gaze within the scopic regimes of post-9/11 technoculture.

Introduction

[Pornography] is, on account of its very 'shamelessness', probably the most utopian of all genres: it is properly 'Edenic' insofar as it involves the fragile and temporary suspension of the barrier that separates the intimate/private from the public. (Žižek 1997, 227)

At the intersection of post-9/11 internet technologies, corporate and government surveillance programmes, and the revelations of Edward Snowden, is there any question that our social imaginary is not organized explicitly or implicitly, consciously or unconsciously, through the fear that someone out there might be watching our every move? Contemporary technoculture certainly invites paranoid phantasies around the camera's eye and the Other. There are also growing social concerns around a supposed 'epidemic of narcissism' amongst the millennial generation that stems from the intersection of new technologies, celebrity culture, and neoliberal capitalism (Twenge and Campbell 2009). According to recent news coverage and several bestselling psychology texts, this epidemic is more prevalent than ever before.[1] Authors frequently employ the rhetoric of disease and infection to suggest that narcissistic personality disorder is spreading across the globe. Kristen Dombek nicely summarizes this attention to narcissism:

> many psychologists, journalists, and bloggers have, over the last ten years, argued that a personality disorder once used to describe those who could not fit in or deal with the rest of us is now, increasingly, the best label for most of us, that NPD [narcissistic personality disorder] is no longer markedly different from the expectations of our culture, but our culture exactly. (2016, 18)

Claims that a neoliberal form of narcissism is on the rise intersect with the current cultural paranoia perpetuated through ongoing developments in computer technologies. Dombek actually proposes a new entry for the *Diagnostic and Statistical Manual of Mental Disorders*, 'narciphobia', which would include a composite of narcissistic and phobic symptoms that appear to be fostered through the subject's immersion in digital communication networks.[2] The global spectacle of President Donald Trump's grandiosity, impulsivity, hypersensitivity to criticism, aggressiveness towards others, and use of social media, for instance, might function as a sketch for such an entry when understood alongside a social imaginary organized through what Hal Niedzviecki refers to as the contemporary subject's immersion in 'peep culture', a term that designates the individual's experience of being caught in a digital media matrix which provides a gratifying and anxious mix at the nodal point of seeing and being seen:

> Today we're all happily peeping away, seemingly free of social approbation. Governments, corporations, friends, and family all tell us (for different reasons) that it's okay to peer over the fence and see what's going on with the neighbors, particularly if what the neighbors are up to could in any way be construed as scandalous, scurrilous, seditious, or sexual – something entertaining enough to attract the millions of viewers up for grabs. Meanwhile, the neighbors are doing what they are doing precisely because they know that they are being watched. Just as we are willing voyeurs – no one forced us to look – they are willing performers. The voyeurs (us) and the people watching (us) are two groups acting together in cybernetic harmony, each one encouraging the other, neither stopping to think about what's happening and why. (Niedzviecki 2009, 19)

Subjects openly exchange personal information with others across social media platforms, thinning boundaries between publicity and privacy. Not only can personal search histories, emails, social media interactions, and GPS coordinates be exposed to corporate and state surveillance as a way of regulating, policing, and profiting from individuals, but subjects are told that cameras and microphones on every device might be hacked and operated as a kind of Peeping Tom's periscope, allowing the most private and intimate details of one's life to be recorded and consumed by unknown individuals.[3] There is the technological paranoia surrounding Russian hackers tampering with the 2016 American election, the government information leaks, the wire taps, the 'fake news', the 'alternative facts', the deluge of malware and computer viruses.[4] Undoubtedly, the cultural atmosphere under Trump's presidency has provoked much ongoing discussion amongst those in the 'psy' professions around social intersections between narcissism and paranoia in contemporary technoculture.[5]

Here, I am interested in exploring an extension of this phenomenon in the subject's encounter with online pornography. In this article, I examine some of the implications of paranoid pleasure and pornography in contemporary technocultures from a Lacanian psychoanalytic perspective. If new media technologies not only interpellate desiring subjects as Peeping Toms, watching, stalking, and looking at each other, I contend that subjects also live with the anxiety of being peeped, perhaps especially when engaged in acts that one may want to keep private, such as the consumption of online pornography. I also suggest that the contemporary viewer of online pornography might be best situated through an adaptation of Jean-Paul Sartre's understanding of subjectivity, using his classic example of the man spying through a keyhole whereby scopophilic pleasure is sustained through anxieties around the self's shameful and narcissistic objectification of its own self to the voyeurism of the Other. I argue that online pornography frequently portrays, encourages, and requires that the subject's jouissance be derived from the interplay between phantasies of looking and being looked at through the keyholes of technology. I circle around a central question: if we live increasingly with the technological evocation of the Other, what does this mean for the subject? Drawing from several cultural and philosophical examples involving anxieties around pornography and the Peeping Tom, I consider that the subject's encounter with online depictions of sex is always already bound to the paranoia and enjoyment of being watched, or perhaps to the reverse narcissistic anxiety that nobody is actually watching. I explore how online pornographic phantasies intersect with paranoia as fetish where the devices we use to peep are also shown or expected to be peeping on us with malicious intent. Ultimately, I contend that the pleasure of online pornography in terms of its production and consumption is inextricably linked to shifting, circulating, and conditional referents of the Other's gaze within the scopic regimes of contemporary technoculture.

A note from the classroom

I am recalling a lecture that I gave in a college classroom on digital technologies and surveillance. The students read David H. Price's (2014) article, 'The New Surveillance Normal', which describes a radical shift in the social acceptance of corporate and state intrusions into previously protected domains of private life. Price writes about a rapid decline of ideological resistance towards US government-sanctioned hacking and spying operations, corporate information-gathering campaigns, and the metadata and biodata catalogued and analyzed to grow capital and maintain control of citizens. Price argues that surveillance has become the technocultural background of everyday life:

> [T]he Internet's architecture, a compromised judiciary, and duplexed desires of capitalism and the national security state are today converging to track our purchases, queries, movements, associations, allegiances, and desires. The rise of e-commerce, and the soft addictive allure of social media, rapidly transforms U.S. economic and social formations. Shifts in the base are followed by shifts in the superstructure, and new generations of e-consumers are socialized to accept phones that track movements, and game systems that bring cameras into the formerly private refuges of our homes, as part of a 'new surveillance normal'. (2014, 47)

Classroom discussion of the article began innocently enough. Students debated distinctions between public and private spheres, and thought more about what might be at stake personally and politically under current scopic regimes. The conversation, however, took on an ambience of paranoia as students became more aware of themselves as objects of the technological gaze. This paranoia seemed to spread between students through looks and glances, murmurs in small groups. Several students made jokes about how the microphones dangling from the ceiling and the camera at the front of the classroom were not really used for distance education purposes after all. This instance now reminds me of Ariella Azoulay's comment that 'the camera [has an] ability to create a commotion in an environment merely by being there … in a state of temporary rest' (2011, 72). The subject's awareness of the camera is always an awareness of the Other's gaze. Upon further discussion of the article, one student anxiously posed a personal question after arriving at a realization: 'Wait a minute, could we say that if I have visited "certain websites" that there is a record of that somewhere? Is it possible that somebody can see that or have access to that information, know my search history?' This student was reluctantly referring to the consumption of online pornography and a fear that some Other might be able to record and view the history of one's pornography consumption. It should be unsurprising that a discussion around online privacy would produce anxieties about what one does with their privates. The student's fear was that someone might be able to gain an impression of an individual's private phantasies from monitoring online activity. Another student associated with an even more unsettling thought: 'And what if the camera on the laptop is live and someone is watching you visit those websites without you even knowing?' Students chuckled uncomfortably or shifted in their seats at this remark. These technological anxieties in the classroom actually highlight a circulating media narrative and social phantasy at the intersection between contemporary technocultures of surveillance and the subject's consumption of online pornography.

Technocultural voyeurism and the pornographic gaze

Hardcore pornography often situates the subject in the position of the voyeur who sees everything. Commonly found online, this genre, for instance, makes no effort to hide or cover parts of the sexual act, relying on the supposedly pure transparency of the actions it presents. Pornography offers a portrayal of what might otherwise be forbidden. Despite the hardcore film clip's laying bare of the scene for the spectator, 'porn is not so much realist', writes Cindy Patton (1991, 377), 'as it is a mirror for activities we imagine but cannot observe ourselves engaged in'. The subject is often between the pleasure in looking and the shame in having looked. Psychoanalysts, of course, traditionally interpret the subject's pornographic voyeurism in terms of childhood scopophilic and exhibitionistic conflicts. In this sense, the subject's interaction with online pornography might be theorized in terms of unconscious identifications and projections, which is sometimes understood as the subject's attempts to master or control the earlier trauma of the primal scene.[6] Online pornography providers offer this control through automated and categorized portrayals of sexual experience for the subject who experiences desire through fetish and repetition compulsion. Robert Stoller refers to pornography as 'a daydream in which activities, usually but not necessarily overtly sexual, are projected into written or pictoral material to induce genital excitement in an observer' (1970, 490). This excitement stems not simply from some projective transgression in the performance of the sexual fetish in the pornographic scene, but from the camera's inclusion of the subject as a witness to the sexual act. Here, the camera allows the subject to act as voyeur, exposing what might usually be understood as a private or intimate act between participants for the pleasure of the viewer. The camera allows for the pleasure of looking, but simultaneously conditions the subject's own paranoia of exposure to the gaze. 'This is why one is ashamed to look at it directly', writes Slavoj Žižek (1997, 227), 'one avoids the gaze emanating from the pornographic scene; it is this gaze which makes the scene obscene and shameless ... it is the spectator, not the object, who feels ashamed'. There is ambivalence in the subject's relation to pornographic material in terms of seeing and being seen since this image is always structured through the gaze of the Other.

It is in this sense that I suggest the subject's identification with the pornographic image on the screen might be partially understood through Sartre's theorization of subjectivity and looking in *Being and Nothingness*. Sartre ([1943] 1992) provides the useful example of the stereotypical Peeping Tom who observes another's body or sexual experience through a keyhole.[7] To be sure, this is a male and heterosexual gaze; the man stoops at the keyhole to look at a woman. It is also a perverse act of aggression since the very lock that is supposed to create a barrier for privacy is manipulated for spying into the private space. Sartre also admits that this act of looking involves an affective motivation as the subject may be 'moved by jealousy, curiosity, or vice' and a cognitive dimension where the subject is 'alone and on the level of a non-thetic self-consciousness' ([1943] 1992, 347). In other words, the subject's sense of self has not yet been registered through an Other. 'This means', writes Sartre, that 'there is no self to inhabit my consciousness, nothing therefore to which I can refer my acts in order to qualify them' ([1943] 1992, 347). The subject spying through the keyhole waits in a state of pre-reflective or preconceptual consciousness, immersed in the visual scene. The subject anticipates the possibilities of the forbidden spectacle in its emergence. Sartre's subject, however, becomes aware of its own objectivity in a reflexive sense through the signal of the Other's gaze. In Sartre's portrayal of the Peeping Tom, the subject looking through the keyhole recognizes its own objectivity at the implication of the Other in the sound of footsteps in the hallway:

> But all of a sudden I hear footsteps in the hall. Someone is looking at me! What does this mean? It means that I am suddenly affected in my being and that essential modifications appear in my structure – modifications which I can apprehend and fix conceptually by means of the reflective *cogito* ... I now exist as myself for my unreflective consciousness ... I see myself because somebody sees me ... [T]he person is presented to consciousness *in so far as the person is an object for the Other*. ([1943] 1992, 349; original emphasis)

While looking at the forbidden scene, the subject becomes aware of its transgression through the gaze of the Other, the self's externalization of itself as Other when the footsteps are heard. Sartre emphasizes the subject's superego injunction through its becoming object to the Other in this example, which may result in feelings of shame or embarrassment. For Sartre, shame does not necessarily constitute the subject's feeling of becoming a guilty object, but rather is an affective structure where the subject becomes aware 'in general of being *an* object; that is, of *recognizing myself* in this degraded, fixed, and dependant being which I am for the Other' ([1942] 1992, 384; original emphases). Shame always supposes the fundamental formula of the subject recognizing itself as exposed and a vulnerable object before the Other.

Sartre provides a triangulation for consideration: subject (man at the keyhole), object (woman behind the door), and Other (gaze). The subject looks at the object and falls under the look of the Other. Lacan (1977) draws from Sartre's theorization in the *Four Fundamental Concepts of Psycho-Analysis* to suggest that the subject is always already seen by the gaze of the Other through the subject's own projection. In other words, the gaze is always the gaze of another subject, but it is also always the subject's ability to see itself as Other:

> The gaze sees itself, the gaze of which Sartre speaks, the gaze that surprises me and reduces me to shame, since this is the feeling he regards as the most dominant. The gaze I encounter – you can find this in Sartre's own writing – is, not a seen gaze, but a gaze imagined by me in the field of the Other ... [at] the moment when he has presented himself in the action of looking through a keyhole. A gaze surprises him in the function of voyeur, disturbs him, overwhelms him and reduces him to a feeling of shame. (Lacan 1977, 84)

Along with Sartre, Lacan argues that the gaze is not simply a form of sensory perception in terms of the individual's ability to look, but is also located in the individual's perception of the Other's ability to look back. He refers to the capacity of the external gaze to turn the individual who is looked at into a kind of picture, an object of the Other's desire. The self experiences itself as an Other through the external gaze whereby the subject of the gaze continuously tries to recuperate an incomprehensible lack. In Lacan's terms, the subject identifies with itself through the externalized gaze as the *objet petit a*, the inassimilable object that structures desire. Not unlike the child's experience in the mirror stage, the subject becomes reducible to the object of desire, identifying with itself as this object, but also experiencing alienation through this identification. This split between eye and gaze structures the subject's scopophilic desire in relation to pornography and the Other. As Lacan argues, Sartre's Peeping Tom is in a paranoid position in the field of the Other's look as projection. It is in this sense that the subject actually becomes a vulnerable object for the pornographic scene, which produces its own look through the subject's externalization of the gaze.

I suggest that this philosophical and psychoanalytic approach to the gaze lends itself especially well to conceptualizing the subject's paranoid and narcissistic relation to pornography. Several scholars actually already suggest that the camerawork of pornography frequently offers a keyhole perspective on the scene of the sexual act since body parts appear deprived of unity as partial objects, cropped and framed for the viewing subject's pleasure (Kaite 1995, 84; Warburton 2009, 61). The subject's identifications are sutured to the camera's point of view, which substitutes for the keyhole.[8] Despite the camera allowing the subject to look at the sexual scene, the subject remains excluded, at a loss, since the camera can never capture the totality of the scene. Part of the subject's jouissance is derived from this exclusion. The image's vanishing point leaves a blind spot that motivates desire. The subject's identification with the camera's presentation of the hardcore scene may move between voyeurism and narcissism, between a controlling gaze over objects represented in the pornographic scene and the identification with the same object.

The fifth look

Traditionally, scholars of visual media outline four possible looks, which are also relevant for an understanding of online pornography and desire: the look of the camera; the look of the subject towards the image; the looks exchanged between the people depicted in the image; and the look that a given person may direct towards the camera, which becomes a look towards the viewer (Mulvey 1975; Burgin 1982, 148). Drawing on Lacan's theorization of the subject, Žižek (1997) emphasizes the fourth look in the context of pornography, locating the traumatic kernel of the sexual scene in the subject's exposure to its own objectification when the object (the individual who displays their sex to the camera) looks back. Žižek importantly points to an anomaly in pornography whereby the camera's evocation of an Other or third party (as the externalized gaze of the subject, the subject's objectification of itself) does not ruin the subject's jouissance, but actually engenders it. This, again, is the fourth look, which structures a paranoid perversity that is fundamental to the subject's encounter with online pornography:

> For this reason, the pornographic position is untenable: it cannot last too long, since it relies on a kind of magic suspension of the rules of shame which constitute our social link … [T]he very elementary structure of sexuality has to comprise a kind of opening towards the intruding Third, towards an empty place which can be filled in by the gaze of the spectator (or camera) witnessing the act. The elementary pornographic scene (a woman, twisted in an anamorphic way, displaying her sex to the camera as well as looking at it) also confronts the spectator with … the split between the eye and gaze at its purest. (Žižek 1997, 227–228)

Here, I might establish a fifth look as an extension of the fourth through Sartre and Lacan's understanding of the gaze. The fourth look extends and displaces into a fifth look as it not only manifests in the pornographic object's reversal of the subject's voyeurism, but also through the subject's paranoid phantasy that the Other may also be watching through a webcam or some alternative technological keyhole attached to the very device that provides the stream of pornographic content. This fifth look emerges from the webcam that is separate from the pornographic scene, lodged above the computer's screen or somewhere on the preferred device. Similar to the fourth look, the fifth look (the webcam's gaze) objectifies the subject in the act of looking, echoing the subject's paranoid phantasy of the Other catching the subject at the keyhole. Part of this phenomenon involves a drastic shift towards do-it-yourself production methods where the same devices used to produce and record pornographic content can now be used to view that same content (Tarrant 2016, 43). Amateur pornography flourishes online where users upload sexual content directly to public accounts from their webcams and smartphones. The Pornhub Network, for instance, categorizes content with designations including 'Homemade', 'Webcam', 'Live Sex Cam', and 'Behind the Scenes'. Although viewers of online pornography may assume their own webcam is dormant, this reflexive aspect of contemporary technology invites a paranoid and narcissistic sense of being watched while watching. Without the camera ever necessarily recording anything in actuality, the camera's presence posits the possibility of recording everything in virtuality. Certainly, for Sartre, to be caught or recorded in an object-state of naked vulnerability or masturbatory pleasure before the gaze of the Other would symbolize the terror of original shame. The subject sustains jouissance at the tension of looking with the fear of being seen most especially in pornographic content that directly incorporates variations of the Peeping Tom through aesthetic and narrative premises of hidden cameras, hacked webcams, or CCTV footage.[9] Pornography that provides the impression of a hacked webcam, whether it is actually hacked or manufactured to provide this aesthetic, allows the subject to engage in a phantasy where the primal scene becomes a deferred action, a displacement. The subject observes the Other through the keyholes of technology, allowing for the exclusion from the primal scene to be surpassed in voyeuristic transgression. At the intersection of pornography and digital surveillance, subjects become objects to themselves through a paranoid phantasy of being able to observe private sexual scenes through the keyholes of technology, the same keyholes that may look back.

Recommended for you: technocultural paranoia and pornography

With over 10 million registered users uploading amateur and homemade content for the free consumption of more than 60 million visitors per day, Pornhub collects and analyzes data on its visitors like any large internet company. One of the most popular websites on the global internet, Pornhub maintains a massive digital archive of amateur and professionally produced pornographic videos. Due to the website's mass popularity, there is a media narrative that situates the Pornhub Network (including RedTube, YouPorn, Tube8, and XTube) as a watchful eye. Drawing from Google Analytics, Pornhub is able to sample traffic from its millions of daily users in order to explore correlations between age, gender, nationality, search histories, and time spent on pages. Beyond featuring this information on its statistics blog, Pornhub collects these data from subjects for individually targeted content delivery and advertising purposes.[10] The implication is that the company knows each individual user's fetish preferences in order to distribute content based on subtle variations of the self-same in order to provide consistency of narcissistic identification. In *The Pornography Industry*, Shira Tarrant describes Pornhub's mobilization of data:

> The company … uses algorithms to create a highly curated, personalized site based on a user's keyword search history, location, and even time of day they log on. Another way of looking at this business model is that it spoon-feeds a limited range of content to unsuspecting online porn users who do not realize their online porn-use patterns are largely molded by a large corporation. (2016, 44)

These algorithms target the subject's narcissistic pleasure as pornographic content and marketing become directly matched with the fetish preferences of users.[11]

Pornhub's information-gathering practices contribute to a media narrative that shapes a social imaginary of the gaze whereby the subject's online patterns and perversities are vulnerable to hacking and surveillance. The subject's projection of the big Other as a phantasmatic, authoritative, and knowledgeable power structures this paranoid phantasy at the intersection of new technologies, surveillance, and pornography. The subject may externalize the big Other as radical alterity, as an overdetermined eye looking back through the webcam. Further, this data collection also gives the subject the paranoid impression that the big Other knows and records object fetishes, which are usually linked to transgression of a social taboo, something subjects generally may want to keep hidden or private. Pornhub, however, openly reveals that its algorithms gather data around the IP addresses of users, providing a specially developed category based on the analytics of each individual's search history: 'Recommended for You'. Journalists for major newspapers including the *Atlantic*, the *Independent*, and *Vice* respectively explore concerns around corporate and state data collection and the possibility of individual pornography preferences being leaked and exposed in a public forum for the eyes of the Other (Friedersdorf 2013; Merchant 2015; Griffin 2017). In their *Huffington Post* article, for instance, Greenwald, Grim, and Gallagher (2013) report on a document that surfaced through the Snowden leaks, which reveals the National Security Agency to have 'been gathering records of online sexual activity and evidence of visits to pornographic websites as part of a proposed plan to harm the reputations of those whom the agency believes are radicalizing others' and that these personal vulnerabilities 'can be learned through electronic surveillance, and then exploited to undermine a target's credibility, reputation and authority'. The article appeals to the subject concerned with the global neoliberal liquidation of civil liberties since the growth of technocultural surveillance and the beginning of the War on Terror. The emphasis, however, on the exposure of the subject's pornography consumption also appeals to the self's externalized gaze, fear that the Other might be witness to one's transgressive phantasies. In response to learning about Pornhub's data collection practices for advertising purposes, Martin Daubney (2014) declares in an article for the *Telegraph* that '[w]e are all of us mere pawns in the hyper-capitalized world of porn' and that '[e]very single porn user is being used, manipulated and watched'. Here, the Other is voyeuristic, manipulative, exploitative. Certainly, it is always the phantasy of the Other's malicious gaze that is evoked in recent paranoia inducing headlines including 'Who's Watching You When You're Watching Porn?' or, perhaps more simply put, 'Your Porn is Watching You' (Merchant 2015; Hawkins 2017).

These media narratives surrounding the corporate–state–media nexus and its apparent ability to monitor, analyze, exchange, and circulate the pornographic search history of subjects also manifest in social and individual fears of being monitored in real time through the webcam of a laptop or smartphone. This is the paranoia of the fifth look beyond the screen. The NSA, for instance, made headlines for expanding its abilities to remotely hack a subject's webcam and record the video feed for surveillance purposes without the camera notifying its active state through an indicator LED (Massoglia 2014). Popular media manufacturers also circulate stories about advancements in cryptovirology, the study of software or techniques for bypassing computer antivirus programs to perform 'trapdoor' or secret one-way operations on a subject's computer that only the virus' developer can undo. Often called remote administration tools or 'ransomware', this form of malware sometimes targets the unsuspecting subject's computer webcam or microphone, making it possible to wiretap audio and video, recording the content to a computer in another location for the purposes of extortion. This malicious software is developed with the purpose of gathering a victim's private information and threatening to publish or distribute it unless the subject delivers a ransom to the data thieves (Soltani and Lee 2013; Matthews 2017). In 2016, the National Crime Agency in the United Kingdom recorded more than 800 cases of cybercrime where subjects were extorted for recordings of private sexual acts over webcams, a number that doubled since the previous year. Several of these occurrences of extortion have also been linked to suicides in news reports, demonstrating one extreme reaction to overwhelming feelings of shame under the manifestation of the Other's gaze (Anthony 2016). Given this technocultural state of affairs, former FBI director, James Comey, recommended to the American public in an interview for the *Telegraph* that citizens should cover webcams with a piece of tape as a common-sense personal security measure:

> There's some sensible things you should be doing, and that's one of them. You go into any government office and we all have the little camera things that sit on top of the screen. They all have a little lid that closes down on them. You do that so that people who don't have authority don't look at you ... I put a piece of tape – I have obviously a laptop, personal laptop – I put a piece of tape over the camera. (Boult 2016)

The *New York Times* has also published a series of articles on personal security and new technologies that advocate this low-tech solution (Bromwich 2016; Rogers 2016; Chen 2017; Lohr and Benner 2017). 'I get a lot of strange looks because I put masking tape over the webcam on my computer', says cybersecurity reporter Nicole Perlroth, 'but the last thing I need is a hacker watching me' (Lehman 2014). Comey's remarks and a social media photograph of Facebook's CEO, Mark Zuckerberg, beside a laptop with tape over a webcam have generated significant media discussion around the technological gaze, which has become part of a new surveillance normal. Popular articles now suggest to users the best materials to employ for covering a personal webcam including Band-Aids, post-it notes, duct tape, and stickers (Brogan 2016).

Although personal security and privacy are important concerns, these social anxieties around being watched while watching pornography appeal to the narcissistic paranoia that someone out there must be peeping through the keyholes of technology. The digital Peeping Tom emerges as a fear and phantasy of the voyeuristic hacker hoping to catch subjects engaged in masturbation and other sexual acts. This media narrative regarding malicious digital voyeurs and the hacked webcam crystallize in the plot of 'Shut Up and Dance', an episode of Charlie Brooker's popular BBC and Netflix television show *Black Mirror* (2016). As the show's title suggests, *Black Mirror* attempts to project a dark, uncanny double of our present technocultural scenario into the near future. Each episode features some familiar technological phenomenon taken to its fullest, terrifying limits in terms of state control, corporate greed, dehumanization, and social destructiveness. In this particular episode, teenage boy Kenny (Alex Lawther) is remotely recorded in front of his webcam while masturbating to pornography. Kenny receives a text message from 'Unknown', an enigmatic Other, who blackmails Kenny, forcing him to complete grim tasks, tracking his every move with GPS, and threatening to send the recording to his family and friends. The suspense and terror of the episode's plot relies on the possibility that Kenny's sex and sexual secrets could be exposed in public light. The audience identifies with Kenny's plight until learning in a shocking twist conclusion that this protagonist's secret is far more disturbing than it may have first appeared. When the unknown Other finally distributes the recording across the internet, Kenny receives a phone call from his mother who screams in disbelief at the realization that her son has been caught on video masturbating to child pornography. The police arrive to arrest Kenny as the credits roll. 'Shut Up and Dance' emerges through the circulation of a media narrative where the gaze of the Other is turned upon the subject's consumption of online pornography. Although this abject conclusion leaves the audience to recoil with disgust at the earlier identification with such a shameful protagonist, producing radical disidentification as a screen for the viewer under the gaze of the Other, the episode demonstrates the structure of a paranoid social phantasy at the junction of pornography and surveillance.

Pornography provides the subject with a narcissistic voyeurism that reduces the subject to an object-gaze, but the webcam that looks back on the computer disrupts this experience through the possibility of a paranoid realization that one could also be seen. What I am ultimately suggesting, here, is that the subject's consumption of online pornography is always already linked to the subject's relation to the gaze, the look from the Other, which enables jouissance between paranoid and narcissistic identifications. This gaze, however, no longer simply emerges for subject from one direction, but the Other's look is fragmented into multiples of overdetermined virtualities in contemporary technocultures. Zygmunt Bauman and David Lyon confirm this point when they write that

> modern societies seem so fluid that it makes sense to think of them being in a 'liquid' phase. Always on the move, but often lacking certainty and lasting bonds, today's citizens, workers, consumers and travelers also find that their movements are monitored, tracked, and traced. Surveillance slips into a liquid state … through … a globalized gaze that seems to leave nowhere to hide, and simultaneously is welcomed as such. (2013, vi–vii)

The subject's experience of a globalized and liquid gaze extends through online pornography as the threat of shame in the possibility of exposure to the Other. Nevertheless, there is some enjoyment or pleasure in the very look that shames the subject.

As I complete this article on a train returning to Toronto, there is a man sitting beside me. He types emails on his laptop. I can see that he has covered the computer's webcam with a Band-Aid. Certainly, at the intersection of this experience of 'narciphobia' there is jouissance. Narcissistic and voyeuristic pleasures of the ego are enhanced in the fifth look, not necessarily undermined by a paranoia-inducing experience of the technocultural gaze. If behind each desire is a lack, the moment this pretence collapses is the same moment when the subject may experience the Real as staring back. It is as if the webcam's gaze was also a small wound that must be covered in order to maintain the unlikely pretense and paranoid phantasy that somebody is actually watching.

Notes

1. See Twerge and Campbell (2009), Acocella (2014), Kluger (2014), Burgo (2015), Brooks (2016), Fishwick (2016), Remes (2016), and Williams (2016).
2. According to Dombek, narciphobia would include a 'pervasive pattern of paranoia (in fantasy or behaviour), splitting (organizing people, events, and the world into categories of good and evil, real and fake, deep and superficial, etc.), and catastrophizing, beginning by early adulthood and present in a variety of contexts' (2016, 137). She includes a list of nine symptoms of which the patient would have five or more. Each of these symptoms is obliquely connected to social anxieties revolving around contemporary technoculture's influence on the subject and social relations.
3. See Bromwich (2016), Rogers (2016), Biersdorfer (2017), and Chen (2017).
4. Goldman (2017) reports on the spread of the WannaCry 'ransomware' attack that compromised more than 200,000 computers across 150 countries.
5. See Buser and Cruz (2016), Greene (2016), and Friedman (2017).
6. Much psychoanalytic literature describes the subject's relation to pornography as a kind of repetition, displacement, and attempt to control the primal scene. Here, pornography becomes the subject's libidinization of early childhood attempts to make sense of initial exposure to sexual acts. For Freud, the primal scene is a trauma for the child that struggles to integrate the bewildering noises coming from mommy and daddy behind a closed door. Melanie Klein (1945) later posits that despite the child being overwhelmed by the primal

scene, the child's exclusion from the scene also results in a wish to know and possibly to see what it is that mommy and daddy are doing to each other. Freud suggests that the child's initial experience of the sexual scene, whether actual or imaginary, is violent, exciting, and enigmatic. The child's exclusion from the scene results in an encounter with something beyond understanding or comprehension. This is why, for Klein, the primal scene is about the subject's acquisition of knowledge. The primal scene structures a cognitive dissonance between the wish to see and not see what is forbidden to the subject. The subject experiences the primal scene phantasy as sexually arousing, but also as shameful and embarrassing. The phantasy of this scene may provide a glimpse of the Real.

7. The Peeping Tom has its roots in a thirteenth-century account of Lady Godiva's myth. Godiva's legendary status stems from her demand of her husband, Leofric, Earl of Mercia, that he lower the taxes for the common people. Leofric agrees to lower taxes, but only if Godiva will ride nude through the streets of Coventry on horseback. Taking his challenge, Godiva wraps herself in her long hair and asks the townspeople to remain inside their houses, to avert their eyes, as she makes her ride. Following Godiva's ride, Leofric lowered taxes for the people. In a seventeenth-century addition to this story, however, not all of the citizens closed their shutters out of respect for Godiva. A tailor named Tom looked through his window to gaze at the forbidden scene. In variations on the myth, Peeping Tom is blinded by Godiva's beauty, struck blind by God, or beaten and blinded by the townspeople as punishment for his imprudence (Seal 2001, 90). 'Peeping Tom', of course, becomes symbolic for the voyeuristic figure who intrudes on the privacy of unsuspecting individuals. Tom as voyeur commits a crime with his gaze, providing the subject with a transgressive fundamental phantasy of seeing what should not be seen in a sexual context. Depending on the variation of the story, this same voyeur is also struck with painful blindness, beatings, and deep shame dealt from the townspeople, God, or what Lacan might call the law or the symbolic. Freud (1910) refers to the myth of Godiva and the Peeping Tom in order to give representation to psychogenic disturbances of vision. Hysterical blindness, argues Freud, often occurs through a superego imposition following the repression of sexual pleasure in looking:

> [W]e are in the habit of translating the obscure psychical processes concerned in the repression of sexual scopophilia and in the development of the psychogenic disturbance of vision as though a punishing voice was speaking from within the subject, and saying: 'Because you sought to misuse your organ of sight for evil sensual pleasures, it is fitting that you should not see anything at all any more', and as though it was in this way approving the outcome of the process. (1910, 217)

Underlying the psychosomatic manifestation of blindness may be the superego injunction. The subject experiences guilt or shame from the repressed scopophilic pleasure in visual transgression. For Lacan, the subject's projection and externalization of the Other's gaze similarly results in feelings of shame.

8. This suture effect of the point-of-view camera takes on a new dimension with virtual reality technologies for pornography that provide an intensified identification and immersion with the image.

9. One homemade film from Pornhub user Sissymark (2017) conveys this tension between looking and the technological gaze at a threshold of representation. This film, entitled 'Secret Shame – Anonymous Hacked Webcam Perversions', features a hooded man wearing a Guy Fawkes mask, a well-known symbol of the computer hacking group Anonymous. This man looks at two monitors which uncannily display the same sexual scene as doubled on the screen. This sexual scene appears to be sourced from the hacked webcam of another computer. The two monitors cut to sexual scene after sexual scene as the man types at the keyboard, presumably hacking into webcam after webcam. Periodically, the man turns away from the monitors, aiming his look back towards the viewer, calling the viewer's act of viewing to consciousness. Here, the viewer is objectified in the act of looking. Despite the unlikelihood that the man is actually hacking webcams, the homemade film conveys a paranoid phantasy, a Deleuzian rhyzomatics of the gaze where one subject unsuspectingly views

another individual through a webcam, who unsuspectingly views another individual through a webcam, and so on.

10. Pornhub regularly publishes articles about the anomalies of global traffic porn trends on its blog, Pornhub Insights. The blog provides readers with graphs, charts, and images that present statistical variations and amusing correlations in national pornography consumption. Pornhub's traffic in a given country, for instance, will experience a significant drop during a solar eclipse or a national sporting event.

11. For Lacan, the fetish is an object that functions to veil loss or separation from the mother. A fetish may structure a dynamic or an image through signifiers that provide the operation of disavowal (a simultaneous denial and recognition of loss) whereby the presence of the fetish object becomes conditional and necessary for the achievement of sexual satisfaction. Referring to the mass distribution and individualization of sexually explicit content, Rudolph Bernet argues that pornography actually furthers the subject's repression of sexuality, whereby subjects 'increasingly allow themselves to be determined sexually by anonymous and prefabricated fantasms' (2004, 64). 'It is now possible', writes Bernet (2004, 64), 'to say more precisely that pornography is a form of objectivism that disavows the individual subject of sexual desire and replaces it with automated programs for stimulation'. In a psychoanalytic sense, Pornhub's use of data may narrow the overdetermined potential of desire through a repetition of self-same content based on the individualized search history of each subject.

Disclosure statement

No potential conflict of interest was reported by the author.

References

Acocella, Joan 2014. "Selfie." *New Yorker*, May 12. Accessed 22 January 2019. https://www.newyorker.com/magazine/2014/05/12/selfie.

Anthony, Sebastian. 2016. 'Reported Cases of Webcam Blackmail Double, are Linked to Four Suicides.' *Ars Technica*, November 30. Accessed September 4, 2017. https://arstechnica.com/tech-policy/2016/11/webcam-blackmail-cases-double-uk-suicides/.

Azoulay, Ariella. 2011. 'Photography: The Ontological Question.' *Mafte'akh* 2: 65–80.

Bauman, Zygmunt, and David Lyon. 2013. *Liquid Surveillance*. New York: Polity.

Bernet, Rudolph. 2004. 'Sexual Identification and Sexual Difference.' In *Lacan in the German Speaking World*, edited by Elizabeth Stewart, Maire Jaanus, and Richard Feldstein, translated by Elizabeth Stewart, 53–69. Albany: State University of New York Press.

Biersdorfer, J. D. 2017. 'Protecting Your Smart Devices.' *New York Times*, May 31. Accessed June 22, 2017. https://www.nytimes.com/2017/05/31/technology/personaltech/protecting-your-smart-devices.html.

Black Mirror. 2016. 'Shut Up and Dance.' Netflix, October 21.

Boult, Adam. 2016. 'Put Tape over Your Webcam, FBI Director Warns.' *Telegraph*, September 15. Accessed September 3, 2017. https://www.telegraph.co.uk/technology/2016/09/15/put-tape-over-your-webcam-fbi-director-warns/.

Brogan, Jacob. 2016. 'What's the Best Way to Cover Your Webcam?' *Slate*, September 15. Accessed September 4, 2017. https://slate.com/technology/2016/09/the-best-ways-to-cover-a-webcam.html.

Bromwich, Jonah Engel. 2016. 'Protecting Your Digital Life in 9 Easy Steps.' *New York Times*, November 16. Accessed September 12, 2017. https://www.nytimes.com/2016/11/17/technology/personaltech/encryption-privacy.html.

Brooks, Arthur C. 2016. 'Narcissism is Increasing. So You're Not So Special.' *New York Times*, February 13. Accessed June 14, 2017.

Burgin, Victor. 1982. *Thinking Photography*. London: Macmillan.

Burgo, Joseph. 2015. *The Narcissist You Know*. New York: Touchstone.

Buser, Steven, and Leonard Cruz, eds. 2016. *A Clear and Present Danger: Narcissism in the Era of Donald Trump*. Asheville: Chiron Publications.

Chen, Brian X. 2017. 'Here is How to Fend off a Hijacking of Home Devices.' *New York Times*, February 1. Accessed June 22, 2017.

Daubney, Martin. 2014. 'Porn Users Don't Realize They are Being Watched.' *Telegraph*, February 5. August 30, 2017. https://www.telegraph.co.uk/men/thinking-man/10619206/Porn-users-dont-realise-they-are-being-watched.html.

Dombek, Kristen. 2016. *The Selfishness of Others: An Essay on the Fear of Narcissism*. New York: Farrar, Straus and Giroux.

Fishwick, Carmen. 2016. 'I, Narcissist – Vanity, Social Media, and the Human Condition.' *Guardian*, March 17. Accessed June 16, 2017. https://www.theguardian.com/world/2016/mar/17/i-narcissist-vanity-social-media-and-the-human-condition.

Freud, Sigmund. 1910. 'The Psycho-Analytic View of Psychogenic Disturbance of Vision.' In *The Standard Edition of the Complete Psychological Works of Sigmund Freud, Volume XI: Five Lectures on Psycho-Analysis, Leonardo da Vinci and Other Works*, 209–218. London: Hogarth.

Friedersdorf, Conor. 2013. 'The NSA's Porn-Surveillance Program.' *Atlantic*, November 27. Accessed August 30, 2017. https://www.theatlantic.com/politics/archive/2013/11/the-nsas-porn-surveillance-program-not-safe-for-democracy/281914/.

Friedman, Richard A. 2017. 'Is It Time to Call Trump Mentally Ill?' *New York Times*, February 17. Accessed June 16, 2017. https://www.nytimes.com/2017/02/17/opinion/is-it-time-to-call-trump-mentally-ill.html.

Goldman, Russell. 2017. 'What We Know and Don't Know about the International Cyberattack.' *New York Times*, May 12. Accessed June 22, 2017. https://www.nytimes.com/2017/05/12/world/europe/international-cyberattack-ransomware.html.

Greene, Richard. 2016. 'Is Donald Trump Mentally Ill?' *Huffington Post*, December 17. Accessed June 15, 2017. https://www.huffingtonpost.com/richard-greene/is-donald-trump-mentally_b_13693174.html.

Greenwald, Glenn, Ryan Grim, and Ryan Gallagher. 2013. 'Top Secret Document Reveals NSA Spied on Porn Habits as Part of Plan to Discredit "Radicalizers."' *Huffington Post*, November 26. Accessed August 30, 2017. https://www.huffingtonpost.co.uk/entry/nsa-porn-muslims_n_4346128?guccounter=1&guce_referrer_us=aHR0cHM6Ly93d3cuZ29vZ2xlLmNvLnVrLw&guce_referrer_cs=2EQELRPP713-z8DlBG1TAg.

Griffin, Andrew. 2017. 'People's Internet Browsing Histories Including Porn Viewing and Drug Purchases Can Easily Be Bought Online.' *Independent*, August 3. Accessed August 30, 2017. https://www.independent.co.uk/life-style/gadgets-and-tech/news/porn-crime-internet-browsing-history-online-public-private-security-cyber-sold-a7875411.html.

Hawkins, Alex. 2017. 'Who's Watching You When You're Watching Porn?' *Huffington Post*, January 31. Accessed August 30, 2017. https://www.huffingtonpost.com/entry/whos-watching-you-when-youre-watching-porn_us_58903804e4b02c397c178bc5.

Kaite, Berkeley. 1995. *Pornography and Difference*. Bloomington: Indiana University Press.

Klein, Melanie. 1945. 'The Oedipus Complex in the Light of Early Anxieties.' In *The Writings of Melanie Klein Vol. 1, Love, Guilt & Reparation*. London: The Hogarth Press.

Kluger, Jeffrey. 2014. *The Narcissist Next Door*. New York: Riverhead Books.

Lacan, Jacques. 1977. *The Four Fundamental Concepts of Psycho-Analysis*, edited by Jacques-Alain Miller, translated by Alan Sheridan. New York: W.W. Norton & Company.

Lehman, Susan. 2014. 'How a Times Cybersecurity Reporter Protects Her Data. And What You Can Do to Protect Yours.' *New York Times*, September 22. Accessed September 4, 2017. https://www.nytimes.com/times-insider/2014/09/22/how-a-times-cyber-security-reporter-protects-her-data-and-what-you-can-do-to-protect-yours/.

Lohr, Steve, and Katie Benner. 2017. 'With WikiLeaks Claims of C.I.A. Hacking, How Vulnerable Is Your Smartphone?' *New York Times*, March 7. Accessed September 7, 2017. https://www.nytimes.com/2017/03/07/technology/cia-hacking-documents-wikileaks-iphones-tvs.html.

Massoglia, Dan. 2014. 'The Webcam Hacking Epidemic.' *Atlantic*, December 23. Accessed August 30, 2017. https://www.theatlantic.com/technology/archive/2014/12/the-webcam-hacking-epidemic/383998/.

Matthews, Lee. 2017. 'New Mobile App Lets Wannabe Cybercriminals Create Ransomware with East.' *Forbes*, August 25. Accessed August 30, 2017.

Merchant, Brian. 2015. 'Your Porn is Watching You.' *Vice*, April 6. Accessed August 30, 2017. https://motherboard.vice.com/en_us/article/539485/your-porn-is-watching-you.

Mulvey, Laura 1975. 'Visual Pleasure and Narrative Cinema.' *Screen* 16 (3): 6–18.

Niedzviecki, Hal. 2009. *The Peep Diaries*. San Francisco: City Lights Books.

Patton, Cindy. 1991. 'Visualizing Safe Sex: When Pedagogy and Pornography Collide.' In *Inside/Out, Lesbian Theories, Gay Theories*, edited by Diane Fuss, 373–387. New York: Routledge.

Price, David H. 2014. 'The New Surveillance Normal: NSA and Corporate Surveillance in the Age of Global Capitalism.' *Monthly Review* 66 (3): 43–53. https://monthlyreview.org/2014/07/01/the-new-surveillance-normal/.

Remes, Olivia. 2016. 'Narcissism: The Science Behind the Rise of a Modern "Epidemic."' *Independent*, March 11. Accessed June 16, 2017. https://www.independent.co.uk/news/science/narcissism-the-science-behind-the-rise-of-a-modern-epidemic-a6925606.html.

Rogers, Katie. 2016. 'Mark Zuckerberg Covers His Laptop Camera. You Should Consider It, Too.' *New York Times*, June 22. Accessed June 22, 2017. https://www.nytimes.com/2016/06/23/technology/personaltech/mark-zuckerberg-covers-his-laptop-camera-you-should-consider-it-too.html.

Sartre, Jean-Paul. [1943] 1992. *Being and Nothingness*, translated by Hazel E. Barnes. New York: Washington Square Press.

Seal, Graham. 2001. 'Lady Godiva.' In *Encyclopedia of Folk Heroes, 90*. Santa Barbara: ABC-CLIO.

Sissymark. 2017. 'Secret Shame – Anonymous Hacked Webcam Perversions.' *Pornhub*. Accessed September 3, 2017. https://www.pornhub.com/view_video.php?viewkey=ph58bf4c3615032.

Soltani, Ashkan, and Timothy B. Lee. 2013. 'Research Shows How MacBook Webcams Can Spy on Their Users without Warning.' *Washington Post*, December 18. Accessed September 6, 2017. https://www.washingtonpost.com/news/the-switch/wp/2013/12/18/research-shows-how-macbook-webcams-can-spy-on-their-users-without-warning/?noredirect=on&utm_term=.effb8547c7af.

Stoller, Robert J. 1970. 'Pornography and Perversion.' *Archives of General Psychiatry* 22: 490–499.

Tarrant, Shira. 2016. *The Pornography Industry*. New York: Oxford University Press.

Twerge, J. M., and W. K. Campbell. 2009. *The Narcissism Epidemic: Living in the Age of Entitlement*. New York: Free Press.

Warburton, Nigel. 2009. *Free Speech*. Oxford: Oxford University Press.

Williams, Zoe. 2016. 'Me! Me! Me! Are We Living Through a Narcissism Epidemic?' *Guardian*, March 2. Accessed June 15, 2017. https://www.theguardian.com/lifeandstyle/2016/mar/02/narcissism-epidemic-self-obsession-attention-seeking-oversharing.

Žižek, Slavoj. 1997. *The Plague of Fantasies*. New York: Verso.

A porn voyeur's discourse

Fan Wu

ABSTRACT

This lyric article manoeuvres through the potential pleasures of gay porn, both amateur and studio. The article's framework and formal inspiration is Barthes' *A Lover's Discourse*, and his idiosyncratic, particularly literary understanding of psychoanalysis. Its fragmentary form touches on topics such as edging, authenticity effect, and the pleasures of personal porn archives. At the same time, it diverges from Barthes' aversion to pornography – outlined in *Camera Lucida* – to claim a renewed appraisal of porn's pedagogies for our desire.

In *Camera Lucida*, Roland Barthes makes a hard distinction between the pornographic and the erotic as mutually exclusive categories:

> Pornography ordinarily represents the sexual organs, making them into a motionless object (a fetish), flattered like an idol that does not leave its niche; for me, there is no *punctum* in the pornographic image; at most it amuses me (and even then, boredom follows quickly). The erotic photograph, on the contrary (and this is its very condition), does not make the sexual organs into a central object; it may very well not show them at all; it takes the spectator outside its frame, and it is there that I animate this photograph and that it animates me. The *punctum*, then, is a kind of subtle beyond – as if the image launched desire beyond what it permits us to see: not only toward 'the rest' of the nakedness, not only toward the fantasy of a praxis, but toward the absolute excellence of a being, body and soul together. (1981, 57–59; original emphasis)

If the *punctum* is the 'prick' of the erotic that tears open a space beyond the photograph, then the pornographic image is bulldozed and flattened such that its surface is blunted, and no longer possesses the power to pierce. Worse, for Barthes, the pornographic image has no beyond: there is no suggestion of a world outside the frame to be filled by the imagination; what you see is what you get, thus suffocating spectatorial agency.

It is certainly true that so much of porn smothers any possibility of the erotic's expression under the weight of its formulaic aesthetics, its exhausting explicitness. The worst offender in the realm of 'gay porn' (we shall use this term provisionally, despite its many problematic features, as the genre of porn I will be involved with) is the shot of a penis thrusting in and out of an asshole – the 'meat grinder' shot, a black hole shot that sucks away all erotic potential. But here I want to offer a less absolutely pessimistic perspective on porn (although not the porn industry, which is its own beast), or at least cock a neutral eyebrow at porn, as something not always mutually exclusive of the erotic: instead, as a montage of surfaces that constitute an endless pedagogy for desire. (My discussion will be on digital porn, in all its accessibility and endless permutation – sadly leaving behind, for scope's sake, porn's various historical shifts across media and technologies.) The Barthes of *Camera Lucida* and *A Lover's Discourse* will be my formal inspiration and my agonistic foil (a pervert's project: to use Barthes' writing methods to defend a type of representation he had so totally dismissed). I wish to differ from Barthes on his terms; that is, by embarking on a project whose shape takes what Barthes called *mathesis singularis*: a non-systematic system that is generated through subjective, phenomenological, and ultimately singular perceptions. This is also the method most appropriate for porn; it would be dishonest of me to write without including the assemblage I make with the porn I watch. Locating the erotic and the amorous in the pornographic, I do not collapse porn into those other (more sacred) categories; rather, porn as porn can condition unique forms of the appearing of the erotic and the amorous.

The dream of this writing, then, is that while the examples from my erotic world may not stir you (always the voyeur is hypersensitive to the vagaries of taste: what leaves him ensorcelled may leave another cold), something of the abstraction that the examples point towards makes you go 'eureka!' (and, I confess, the writing of this article has a therapeutic aim: to begin to think about the pornographic representations that have so constituted, and so captured, my own sexuality). To write, then, not from the impetus of sharing knowledge or imparting wisdom, but the singular universality of desire.

Authenticity effect

(1) The surface structure of big-budget studio porn is boring; a pre-set sequence of shots (kissing → oral → anal → perhaps, if you are lucky, post-coital kisses to weigh against the awkward first kisses, in degrees of intimacy). The temporality of the scene is mechanical (each shot lasts two minutes or so, too long by half); the camera is a pure function of capture for that which is supposed to be sexy (it mistakenly believes genital representation is directly proportional to sexual arousal). What is shown is the play of negligible differences: it hardly matters if the scene starts by announcing the brokenness and straightness of the actors (as in Broke Straight Boys), or if it begins with them asserting a happy-go-lucky casualness with their sexuality (as in Corbin Fisher). What would have been difference is subsumed under mainstream porn's cinematic conventions, deadened by the scripted conventions of its camera's positions, its theatrical performances.

(2) Yet despite – or because of – what Barthes calls the 'unary' status of pornography, the erotic flashes out of the occasional fissuring of the unary. Pornography cannot foreclose the erotic; at most, it can repress it so deeply that it is indiscernible, to a given viewer, in the image:

> A few millimeters more or less and the divined body would no longer have been offered with benevolence (the pornographic body shows itself, it does not give itself, there is no generosity in it): the photographer has found the *right moment*, the *kairos* of desire. (Barthes 1981, 59; original emphases)

The photographer holds the power of the contingent accident, the being in the right place at the right time that makes the photograph erotic. But it is the porn voyeur who stumbles across the *kairos* of desire. The *kairos* is the neutral moment that passes you by, even as it offers you an irreparable pleasure. In porn, the *kairos* is never authenticity in itself: such a thing is indiscernible, unlocatable, some impossible piece of the Real. But the authenticity effect belongs to the voyeur's sense: that this must be the real thing: a groan less measured than the rest; the wayward flick of a wrist; a contorted expression lying at the ambiguous edge between pain and pleasure. Suddenly the script is derailed, the workmanlike boredom of the performances shattered. A little burst of intimacy appears that cannot be swallowed back up by pornography's boring routines.

(3)   Another unary photograph is the pornographic photograph (I am not saying the erotic photograph: the erotic is a pornographic that has been disturbed, fissured). Nothing more homogeneous than a pornographic photograph. It is always a naive photograph, without intention and without calculation. (Barthes 1981, 14)

Yes – but precisely this naivete, this lack of calculation, this dull homogeneity, prepares pornography for the geysering pleasures of the authenticity effect!

(4) The feet and the hands are the loci of the authenticity effect. Their feet curl and cup themselves around the intensity of being penetrated; the hands splay and splash around, vivid windows into a set of internal sensations to which we are otherwise insensate. (The close-up shot ruins the effect of the hands and feet 'doing their own thing' by muddling the involuntary twitches with a focused, directed cinematic intention). The extremities are the portals to a touching of pornography that unseats the dominance of porn's visual regime: I feel what for them must be an unwilled intensity. (So, when I 'confess' to being a 'foot fetishist', it is not the feet that are the object of my attraction, but the affects and impulses that materialize in the feet before cognition seizes hold and sculpts them.)

(5)   A proof *a contrario*: Mapplethorpe shifts his close-ups of genitalia from the pornographic to the erotic by photographing the fabric of underwear at very close range: the photograph is no longer unary, since I am interested in the texture of the material. (Barthes 1981, 15)

Barthes here overlooks that the genitalia can themselves reveal interesting textures; I register a prudishness in his insistence on the cover-up of what is shown in close-up. The genital close-up is certainly abominably dull in shots of penetration: pneumatics without affect, friction without pleasure. But the shot in which the penis leaks precum gives the genitals animation and, moreover, that elusive texture: the alternation of wetness and dryness; a forthrightness of disclosure; a lust whose precise aim or origin is never fully known. Again, it is the involuntary (my ability to invest belief in the precum's involuntariness) – the unconscious strata of the body's biological processes – that is illuminated, these gestures that soften my heart to the life at work behind the acting. (At the hyperbolic extreme of my masturbatory delirium, the authenticity effect, because it nurtures intimacy at the place where it seems ignored and abolished, evades – for the briefest moment – the capitalist exchange of bodies as objects that undergirds all porn. Intimacy is the 'bonus' that exceeds an economy of exchange whose currency is baldly called the money shot).

Figure 1. 'Jason Matthews & Skyler Daniels'. Brokestraightboys.com, 1 June 2013.

(6) In 'Jason Matthews & Skyler Daniels' (Figure 1) (the name Skyler somehow sends shivers down my spine: it belongs to the fantasy realm of proper names proper to porn, the Platonic form of the name of the sullen skateboarder), a video from BrokeStraightBoys.com (2013), the two boys begin by shaking hands with each other (a blunt symbol of their 'straightness'). Jason instigates the conversation; he is the top from the beginning, all the more enticing for his fringe of femmeness, playing (implicitly) the gay boy who leads Skyler, who flips him over (Skyler all the while bites his lip nervously, as a straight boy might). They get straight to business: no kissing at the beginning. But things heat up; the video becomes a blur of erotic signifiers: they blow each other with a not dispassionate fervour; Jason captures Skyler's eye contact for several moments before Skyler's gaze slinks away embarrassedly; two cumshots later, Jason draws Skyler down to kiss him; panting, Skyler acquiesces, his body melting down to the consistency of putty. Is it that Skyler is confused by Jason's (unidirectional) desire? Or does Skyler begin to feel something other than the duty of performance? The authenticity effect opens the scene up to erotic questioning (all the more erotic for their unanswerability) and spreads into a mess of the voyeur's projections.

(7) Amateur porn (insofar as it can certifiably be amateur – a whole other problem of authenticity we will not countenance here) parades its authenticity, leaving me with a feeling of cuteness at the back of my throat that is just shy of the erotic. There is a pleasure to the discovery of the authenticity effect that only the drudgery of studio porn, so inimical to the erotic, makes possible: where the erotic rips through the pornographic surface, as though it had lain there long dormant, waiting for the voyeur to unloose it.

Mormon performance

(1) I must contradict myself. The authenticity effect is not the sole node of eros in pornography. Sometimes it is the sheer performative surface of the pornography that arouses: sometimes the artificiality of the signifier inverts itself into an eros of the signified. Mormonboyz.com (2017), a predominantly daddy–son site, mimics the various stages of rituals that take place between the seniors and the new recruits of the Mormon faith, with names like 'Ordination', 'The Calling', and 'Setting Apart'. Such names are equally ripe with Christian connotation and pederastic euphemism; I need no knowledge of actual Mormonism to enjoy the implications of this pornified ritual. Everything is deliberately staged so a role play can unfold. Here the texture of the underwear (Figure 2), the starched-white dress shirts (undressed by

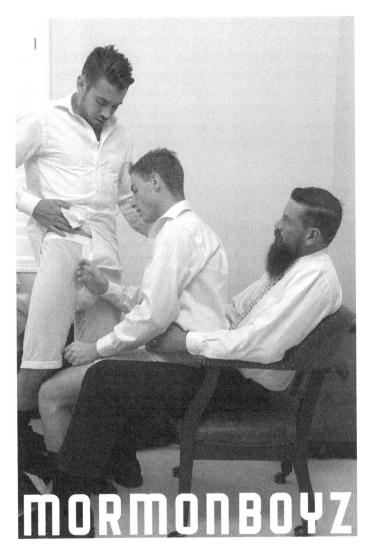

Figure 2. 'Elder Garrett & Brother Calhoun'. Mormonboyz.com, 26 July 2017.

the elder priest, of course), and the black socks kept on while fucking all contribute to the elaborate scenography; the overfullness of the scene makes it so my fantasy moves from what is seen (the signifiers) to the manifestations of power in sexuality, ordained by divine hierarchy (the signified). The fakeness of the scene is earnest (perhaps it is at that level of intention that an authenticity might be said to appear), and disarming in its earnestness; I relinquish myself to its utterly constructed pleasures.

Edged

(1) CumControl101's videos (2018) have an air of the ascetic to them. Captions such as 'Daniel is tied to the workout bench, gagged, edged and cums twice' and titles like 'Muscle stud edged to two loads' give you the factual overview, and concisely lay out for you the video's narrative scope. CumControl101 brings these men close to orgasm and pulls away, using an array of toys, techniques and – crucially – verbal commands: they must announce the edge when they near it, and they must thank him after he has granted them the privilege of the orgasm, lest they be punished with a raw rubbing at the nub. The power that underlies these videos is of two types: the classic masochistic contract, undersigned by both parties' consent (power is at once equalized and asymmetrical); and the power of the edge to prolong their own discomfort (an almost macho form of endurance) and hence their pleasure. A Stoic self-fashioning is at play in the restricted zone of orgasmic delay: you touch your extreme self at the limits of bearability.

(2) Barthes writes of the lover as one who is 'flayed' by love:

> I am 'a mass of irritable substance (Freud).' I have no skin (except for caresses) … the child who is off in the moon is not a playful child; I, in the same way, am cut off from playing: not only does play continuously risk bruising one of my exquisite points, but even everything the world finds amusing seems sinister to me; you cannot tease me without danger: irritable, hypersensitive? – Let us say, rather, tender, easily crushed, like the fiber of certain kinds of wood. (1979, 95–96)

For the lover, love must be without play, for only seriousness leaves undisturbed the flayed lover, sensitive to anything that could disrupt the image of their absolute love. But edging is play unto infinity, the kind of play that makes the body into a mass of nerves; it extends penile sensitivity throughout the whole body, turning all flesh into a shuddering head and shaft. But it is also a practice (again, the ascetic bells ring), insofar as the aim is to discipline the body to stay in the liminal, hypersensitive zone: the edge of orgasm. (No longer solely a voyeur, I participate: I edge myself alongside the video; I fend off the telos of orgasm until I can no longer; I inevitably show the hand of my impatience.) A practice whose documentation in pornography is at once meditative slow cinema and exhilarating action cinema, edging is a pedagogy in paradox, at once the suspension of the telos and an intensification of the telos: for when the orgasm comes at last, it is made more intense and unbearable.

(3) Yet the multipleness of the orgasms in CumControl101's videos (anywhere from two to five orgasms happen in each video) denies the orgasm the pure teleological

privilege it is given in the 'money shot' of mainstream porn. So CumControl101 opens onto Jean-Luc Nancy:

> Just as orgasm is a pleasure that is neither terminal or preliminary, but pleasure that is exempted from having to begin and end, similarly orgasmic sense is sense that ends neither in signification nor in the unsignifiable ... To have an orgasm is always to feel, and since to feel is always also to feel oneself feeling, thus presupposing an alteration and an alterity, to have an orgasm is to feel oneself through the other and in the other. (2008, 127)

Pornography, in the form of the edging video, is the cyborg circuit of sustain/release, in which orgasm is withheld to the point of all senses becoming orgasmic: although the videos end, it is easy to fantasize that they might go on forever; the climax is no longer a telos or an *arche* (origin) but a distributed sense, a *joui-sens*.

Crush of archive

(1) During a masturbation session, while I scan through the videos endlessly disgorged by the internet, I pause upon a boy for some reason or other of desire: a posture of the body (e.g. I 'like' the posture that falls somewhere between confidence and gangliness), or, often, a resemblance to someone I know (a doppelganger who smuggles reality into representation). I develop a crush; I drop everything; I attempt to search for and download every scene in which that actor appears. So, on my hard drive you will find the proper names of hundreds of porn actors, each stacked with a near-complete archive of their career performances. In this feeding frenzy of the crush 'I am dead to all sensuality except that of the "charming body"', as Barthes (1979, 174) writes in his chapter on 'The Ribbon': only that one body will charm. The erotics of pornography are displaced onto the erotics of classification, sorting, and a compulsion towards completion of the collection (always asymptotic). Under this will to possess, porn is cruising without disappointment, without stakes; this consumption is tinged with some sad utopic sentiment: what is desired becomes collectible. Yet porn confronts you with total disappointment: no quantity of videos would be enough to sate the desire; the hoped-for essence of the porn star scoffs at your attempt to seize it.

(2) Barthes' beautiful expression 'blind field' indicates the explosion of an outside to the image:

> Yet once there is a *punctum*, a blind field is created (is divined): on account of her necklace, the black woman in her Sunday best has had, for me, a whole life external to her portrait; Robert Wilson, endowed with an unlocatable *punctum*, is someone I want to meet ... The presence (the dynamics) of this blind field is, I believe, what distinguishes the erotic photograph from the pornographic photograph. (1981, 57)

The crush produces the blind field; that is, it spawns the unlocatable *punctum*, sometimes from the emergence of many qualities (a way of puckering the lips, a style of thirsty kissing), sometimes from a purely atopic, unqualifiable aura. I have a crush on this actor; I envision his life beyond the sterility of the porn studio, and each moment is charged with care for his pasts and futures (all virtual). There is always more that is left unseen, most of all his life outside the world of porn. Who is he when he is tying his shoes, or making meaning for himself in the world, or touching his nephew sweetly on the head?

(3) Derrida writes of the *archon*, that figure who guards the access to the archive:

> The archons are first of all the documents' guardians. They do not only ensure the physical security of what is deposited and of the substrate. They are also accorded the hermeneutic right and competence. They have the power to interpret the archives. (1991, 2)

The porn archive is the collection of things that makes possible my literacy over a history of desire. Every flash of desire is concomitant with a history of having desired precisely this moment of this person. Not only this, but porn also offers you an index for watching someone age: Skyler moves from prickly-twink to tan-lined jock: a whole montaged world could be conjured in the change of body types.

(4) 'There would be no archive desire without the radical finitude, without the possibility of a forgetfulness which does not limit itself to repression ... there is no archive fever without the threat of the death drive, this aggression and destructive drive' (Derrida 1991, 19). For the digital archive, the fever at its fringes is the threat of data collapse, of hard-drive malfunction: an event no less destructive than the library fire; or perhaps more so, because it denies you the pleasure of the spectacle of destruction (trading the illusory infinitude of the archival vaults for the sumptuous visual feast of the conflagration such that the destruction of art becomes, itself, art). One day I wake up and I find my porn archives wiped clean. It is only then that I realize: porn has functioned as a memory of desire, a collection of singularities to which I can return, singularities that proliferate without abandoning themselves to generality: this boy's hair flip, this boy's southern drawl, that boy's flinch when he is fucked on his back. Insofar as the death drive promises an encounter with rebirth, with a time before being, the archive's precarity offers a thrilling fantasy: if it all burnt down I could start my desire over again.

Porny proliferation

(1) The writing of this article made possible a discovery: the erotics of listening to, then recording, my friends' discourse around porn. From a dialogue with A:

> I never watch porn, nor do I need to. It's of no aesthetic interest to me, and because of my self-love practices, of no sexual interest either. I get home from a day of work in the field; then I'm *bestowed* an erection, and the sweat is rushing from my back, and I feel the hardness of my muscles, and my own health, and that's all I need for erotic fulfilment. (Original emphasis)

T calls it self-love: already this tells of a specific relationship to masturbation, the word resonant with both detachment from the corporeal and depth of care:

> Pornography is a means of fleeing from my own body (I do not have to pay attention to how it is my flesh that is taking pleasure); it is the arrest of fantasy (I do not even have to pay attention to what scenes my own mind generates).

T achieves an entirely self-reflexive pleasure built on sensation, not on image: is this not more philosophical (if we think philosophy with Deleuze as the continued reconstitutions of the logics of sense, against the cohesion and recognizability of the image)?

(2) For others, there is no amorousness to pornography. In dialogue with L:

> Pornography is pure authenticity effect, for me, to use your language. I never bookmark porn, let alone download it; I trawl through Xtube but it is never this or that body that obsesses me. I want to get off and so I do. There's no crush; the most crushing thing is my magic wand.

L instrumentalizes the authenticity effect: it ends just before the amorous begins, lasts just long enough for her to get off. For others, porn is a shameful prosthesis anchored not in pleasure but in necessity. In dialogue with O:

> I hate having to use porn to get off. No – rather, it's that I know when I'm using porn I'm in a bad place, I've scraped to the bottom of my imagination, I don't respect myself enough to rest patiently with my libido.

Porn is a litmus test for self-esteem. For others, porn has been foreclosed, and this foreclosure becomes the condition for the installation of a 'higher morality'. In dialogue with M: 'I was twelve when I stumbled on my first *PlayBoy* magazine. I knew then and there that it was *gross* and I never touched it again.' (Is there a sense of moral abjection specific to straight porn's grotesque, bald reflection of patriarchy?)

(3) At the beginning of *Camera Lucida*, Barthes admits to a (unpopular) desire:

> I was overcome by an 'ontological' desire: I wanted to learn at all costs what Photography was 'in itself,' by what essential feature it was to be distinguished from the community of images. Such a desire really meant that beyond the evidence provided by technology and usage, and despite its tremendous contemporary expansion, I wasn't sure that Photography existed, that it had a 'genius' of its own. (1981, 3)

There is something magnetic about essence, even though Barthes' very method of deriving a system from his singularity defeats the search before it begins (or conditions the search on the impossibility of finding that essence for everyone: at end, nothing but a partial essence, or, put harshly, a fetish for a form). Pornography is not technologically specific in the same way that photography was for Barthes a matter of the camera lucida; it cannot be a matter of an instrument, a fact or trick of light. Unbound by medium – locatable in the drawing, the photograph, the video, the dream – the category of the pornographic springs forth, and then proliferates, from the eye of the beholder: porn has an ontology that is speckled with, but not shackled to, its technological media. There is no search for the essence that does not pass through the desire of the subject and, in so passing, become distorted by that subjectivity. Porn's perhaps ultimate pleasure is in discourse: not a discourse of confession that pins people down to their porn habits, but a discourse of the experimentation with pleasure that is both manufactured by porn, and that leaves imaginative space open for a proliferation of erotic possibility on the slick, fissured surface of pornography.

Disclosure statement

No potential conflict of interest was reported by the author.

References

Barthes, Roland. 1979. *A Lover's Discourse: Fragments*, translated by Richard Howard. New York: Hill and Wang.

Barthes, Roland. 1981. *Camera Lucida*, translated by Richard Howard. New York: Hill and Wang.

BrokeStraightBoys. 2013. "Jason Matthews & Skyler Daniels." June 1. https://www.brokestraightboys.com/house/play/MTAwOA==/jason-matthews-&-skyler-daniels.

CumControl101. 2018. Accessed 1 October 2018. https://www.xtube.com/profile/cumcontrol101-27595042#videos.

Derrida, Jacques. 1991. *Archive Fever: A Freudian Impression*, translated by Eric Prenowitz. Chicago: University of Chicago Press.

MormonBoyz. 2017. "Elder Garrett: Brother's Oath." July 26. https://mormonboyz.com/elder-garrett-brothers-oath/?nats=MC4wLjEuMS4wLjAuMC4wLjA.

Nancy, Jean-Luc. 2008. *Dis-Enclosure: Deconstruction of Christianity*, translated by Bettina Bergo. New York: Fordham University Press.

Looking for Pei Lim's penis: melancholia, mimicry, pedagogy

David K. Seitz

ABSTRACT
This article considers the salience of Freud's account of melancholia – one that points to the constitutive role of loss in subject formation – for understanding the racialization of queer sexuality and its mediation in pornography. Scholars have long and insightfully demonstrated the value of melancholia as an interpretive lens for making sense of the dynamics of racialization in the context of the contradictions of liberalism in the Global North. Taking cues from such work, I seek here to trace how pornography might stage returns to inaugural scenes of repudiated desire, and how it might proffer insight into the specificities of racial melancholia for queers. To illuminate the potential of constitutive loss for thinking about race in queer porn, I turn to the figure of Lim Pei-Hsien, an artist, activist, and porn star with a storied but rarely acknowledged history in Canadian LGBTQ, AIDS, and anti-racist circles. I argue that sustained engagement with Lim's work positions him as a profoundly and perhaps instructively melancholic figure, one who might productively inform thinking on race, queerness, and pornography, particularly when read through a psychoanalytic lens.

Common and unique losses

This article considers the salience of Freud's (1955) account of melancholia – one that points to the constitutive role of loss in subject formation – for understanding the racialization of queer sexuality and its mediation in pornography. Scholars have long and insightfully demonstrated the value of melancholia as a theory of subject formation in general (Butler 1997), and a lens for making sense of the dynamics of racialization in the USA and Canada in particular (Cheng 2001; Eng 2010; Varghese 2017). Taking cues from such work, I seek here to trace how queer pornography centring racialized subjects might stage returns to inaugural scenes of repudiated desire (Georgis 2006), and what might be learned from such returns about pornography's role in mediating constitutive loss.

Throughout this article, I use 'constitutive loss' to refer to Freud's insight in 'Mourning and Melancholia'– that melancholia, which has been famously defined as mourning without end or the loss of loss itself, proffers a 'view … of the constitution of the human ego' itself ([1917] 1955, 247). The melancholic subject's relentless self-criticism of a part of his or her own ego, Freud observes, is not altogether discontinuous from 'the agency commonly called conscience' which is 'among the major institutions of the ego' ([1917] 1955, 247). This passing remark – that melancholia tenders insight into the role of loss in subject formation much more broadly, and indeed offers a helpful way of reading Freud's account of subject formation, the Oedipus complex – has informed a vast body of theoretical and clinical scholarship that is beyond the scope of this article to review. Suffice it to say, however, that the insight that we are constituted as social, psychical beings through loss – of repudiated incestuous ties, of a sense of continuity with ourselves and our environments – has proven particularly rich for analysts and social theorists interested in questions of alienation, difference, and power. Thus, Judith Butler (1997) argues that it is socially and linguistically organized foreclosure, and not merely repression, of a subject's desire that retroactively constitutes the distinction between a subject's interiority and external reality in the first place. In Butler's reading, 'Freud distinguishes between repression and foreclosure, suggesting that a repressed desire might once have lived apart from its prohibition, but that a foreclosed desire is rigorously barred, constituting the subject through a certain kind of preemptive loss' (1997, 23). Such 'rigorous' foreclosure involves a subject pivoting from sadism to masochism, redirecting incipient rage or disappointment at the lost object towards the ego itself, and incorporating and identifying with the force of social prohibition, which founds conscience. But here a question arises: if, psychoanalytically speaking, we are all melancholics, all inaugurated as subjects through foreclosed loss, does it necessarily follow that we are all inaugurated in the same way? One answer in the negative comes from Anne Anlin Cheng (2001), among the most prominent scholars to turn to melancholia to study race in the United States, who offers a formulation of melancholia specific to the experience of racialization. What Cheng calls 'racial melancholia', she explains, 'serves not as a description of the feeling of a group of people but as a theoretical model of identity that provides a critical framework for analyzing the constitutive role that grief plays in racial/ethnic subject-formation' (2001, xi).

In this article, I seek to draw on the insights of Freud, Butler, Cheng, and others to think about racialized sexuality and its mediation in queer pornography. To illuminate the potential of constitutive loss for thinking about race in queer porn, I turn to the figure of Lim Pei-Hsien (hereafter Pei Lim), an artist, activist, and porn star with a storied but rarely acknowledged history in Canadian LGBTQ, AIDS, and anti-racist circles (see McCaskell 2016). Born in 1953 to a large, middle-class Chinese-Malaysian family, Pei Lim left home at age 16 and came of age in part in Toronto. Active in gay, HIV/AIDS, and Asian-Canadian organizing in Toronto and Vancouver until his passing in 1992, Lim appeared with regularity in the work of prolific gay Trinidadian-Canadian filmmaker Richard Fung (1986, 1990, 2016). Yet the affective and political valences of his work have largely eluded scholars of race, diaspora, sex, and queer politics, in and outside Canada. One of my aims here is not so much to 'discover' or 'Columbus' Pei Lim, as to get scholars to attend with care to his underappreciated aesthetic, political, and intellectual contributions to queer and diasporic life in Toronto and Vancouver. Further, I argue that sustained engagement with Lim's work positions him as a profoundly and perhaps instructively melancholic figure, one who might productively inform thinking on race, queerness, and pornography, particularly when read through a psychoanalytic lens.

The article builds on a rich tradition of psychoanalytically informed cultural studies of race and sexuality, bringing that scholarship to bear on pornography in particular. It takes for granted that both the production and the consumption of porn are constitutively racialized (Miller-Young 2014; Nguyen 2014), and that psychoanalytically informed reading practices help scholars attend to both individual and collective histories of subject formation and (dis)identification, and to the ethical and political implications of those processes (Muñoz 1999). Still, certain risks attend to a turn to constitutive loss in the context of racialized pornography in particular. Depending on the reader's stakes and theoretical compass points, melancholia might seem an entirely appropriate or altogether incongruous choice of lens for interpreting pornography at all. Because Freud hints at the melancholic character of subject formation as such, such a turn might understandably invite questions about the hazard of slippage into a kind of 'post-racial' or pan-racial universalism – of losing sight of the specificities of racial melancholias. Alternatively, a focus on racialized queer loss might be regarded by some scholars and activists as politically deleterious, since it foregrounds vulnerability for subjects already burdened by the maldistribution of socially organized violence and by a dearth of pornographic representation. Such potential objections are worth anticipating and considering with care. I would reply that to focus on melancholia and its key role in subject formation is neither to fetishize racialized queer experiences of loss, nor to gloss over the historical and geographical specificities of such experiences. On the contrary, if inaugural trauma does indeed comprise part of what it means to be human, then a failure to contend with constitutive loss, even and especially for historically marginalized subjects, could itself prove profoundly dehumanizing. Indeed, as Butler (2009) has argued throughout much of her recent work, the question of which losses even register as 'grievable' at all is among the central questions of politics. Moreover, attending to historically marginalized experience of constitutive loss could open up insight into more emancipatory forms of life for living with loss; as Cheng points out, investigating 'the nature of racial fantasy and of racial melancholia must surely alter how we conceive of ethics and politics' (2001, 27; see also Georgis 2006; Muñoz 2014; Varghese 2017).

Finally, there remains the question of the conceptual lens. For indeed, among the vast conceptual repertoire of psychoanalytic thought, why turn to melancholia or constitutive loss in particular in thinking about racialized queer sexuality or pornography? Indeed, numerous scholars (for example, Diaz 2006; Eng 2010, 2016) have quite productively turned to object relations in the past decade or so to think quite fruitfully about the imbrication of race with sexuality. It is far from my aim here to privilege melancholia to the exclusion of other key psychoanalytic concepts, or to suggest that other psychoanalytic engagements with race and porn give short shrift to subject formation. Nor, indeed, do I aim to pathologize pornographic production or consumption; as Butler's reading of Freud suggests, melancholia is a natural response to loss, and, indeed, incipient in all processes of mourning. Rather, my interest in melancholia vis-à-vis pornography has to do with its centrality to subject formation itself. As I will demonstrate in the following, over the course of my study of Pei Lim as a pornographic and political figure, I have found that the question of subject formation, and the role of inaugural loss therein, has persisted, proving impossible to ignore.

Such a relentless return might well point to my own limitations as a reader of psychoanalytic texts, or to my own psychical investments. Yet such persistence also resonates in Slavoj Žižek's (1998) prescient, characteristically, and flippantly titled essay on the psychoanalysis of race, 'Love Thy Neighbor? No, Thanks!' In this essay, Žižek makes a full-throated case for constitutive trauma and loss in illuminating the psychodynamics of race, imploring scholars of race to 'give psychoanalysis another chance':

> The problem with earlier psychoanalytic accounts of racism was not their abstract-psychologistic approach (direct references to 'aggressivity' and the 'death drive,' which only *seem* to disregard concrete social and cultural conditions), but their all too hasty pseudoconcrete application of specific clinical categories (paranoia, compulsive neurosis) to racist phenomena. I contend here that if one is to account for the uncanny logic of racism, one needs the exact opposite of this pseudoconcreteness. One must instead begin with the subject's elementary relationship to the traumatic kernel of jouissance structurally unassimilable into his or her symbolic universe. Racism confronts within us the enigma of the Other, which cannot be reduced to the partner in symbolic communication; it confronts us with the enigma of that which, in ourselves, resists the universal frame of symbolic communication. (1998, 154; original emphasis)

Rather than apply a particular psychoanalytic concept or category to the study of race and racism, Žižek argues for interpretive engagement with psychoanalytic theories of subject formation. Although Žižek's ostensible focus in much of the rest of the essay is the psychic life of a racist subject, presumed but unmarked as white, he also suggests that attention to constitutive loss – framed in the Lacanian formulation of 'the subject's elementary relationship to the traumatic colonel of jouissance structurally unassimilable into his or her symbolic universe' (1998, 154–155) – productively extends to the psychic lives of racialized subjects, who may well themselves be both targets and perpetrators of racism. What I want to do in the space that remains is provide just a few examples of how I think Pei Lim's work and the representations of his life and insight that survive him might speak to contemporary currents in cultural studies at the intersection of psychoanalysis, race, and sexuality. Engaging Lim's political, sexual, and aesthetic itineraries, I argue that his work points to the primacy of constitutive loss for thinking about race and queer sex in porn.

Dancer on the dock

This article in a sense begins with a story about how my object of research has migrated from church to porn. It emerges out of my longstanding interest in a figure who inhabited and haunted the archive of my previous project, which examined the psychic and political life of the Metropolitan Community Church of Toronto, Canada, a large predominantly LGBTQ congregation that has a rather storied history of activism around religious homophobia, police brutality, HIV/AIDS, anti-discrimination laws, and more (citation redacted). The minister of that church, Rev. Dr Brent Hawkes, appears quite a lot in Harry Sutherland's (1982) documentary film *Track Two: Enough is Enough*, which chronicles rioting and organizing by Toronto gay activists and their allies in response to the infamous February 1981 raids on gay men's bathhouses by Toronto Police that resulted in over 300 arrests. Yet repeated viewings and close readings of *Track Two* directed me to another figure (Seitz 2017), one whose creative response to violence concludes the film. Throughout the documentary, interview subjects make a vociferous case for coalitional organizing across race, religion, ethnicity, gender, and sexuality as the most effective and most broadly emancipatory form for confronting police violence and excess in a wide range of marginalized communities. As if to punctuate or illustrate that claim about multiracial coalition, the film's final image is a dance performance by Malaysian-Canadian artist and activist Lim

Pei-Hsien, who carries a gay liberation pink flag and struts his stuff on the shores of Lake Ontario. When I first saw *Track Two*, I thought Lim was cute, but I also worried about the implications of his appearance in the film, wondering whether Lim's appearance comprised a kind of racialized tokenization or instrumentalization of his performance. Much as Robyn Wiegman (2012) writes that the very idea of intersectionality functions to soothe Euro-Atlantic feminist anxieties and promises relief from injustice, the film's conclusion, which hails coalition and intersectionality, cedes the figural stage to a queer Asian-Canadian man. The stage, but not the microphone – Lim says nothing, and although his dance may be taken to symbolize a great deal, I initially felt a certain degree of surety that, once again, to recall Gayatri Spivak's (1988) insight, the subaltern could not speak.

I can now say in hindsight that I subjected the use of Lim's dance to what Eve Sedgwick ([1997] 2003) famously called a 'paranoid' reading. For of course, and as Spivak would remind us, while 'subaltern' is currently bandied about with the same looseness often associated with 'queering' or 'decolonizing', it in fact refers with far more precision to those who cannot enter the space of self-representation. In that sense, it turned out that Pei Lim, while certainly marginalized by racism, xenophobia, homophobia, and the stigma surrounding HIV, represented himself prolifically and with verve. Perhaps a year or two after first watching *Track Two*, I attended a retrospective on Trinidadian-Canadian filmmaker Richard Fung's body of work, which I had long used to teach queer diaspora and queer geographies. It was then that I put together that the silent dancer who concluded *Track Two*, credited therein simply as 'Lim', had been something of a polymath. As Fung's partner Tim McCaskell (2016, 238) recalled: 'Lim was a renaissance man: a professional dancer, registered nurse, martial artist, and graphic designer' – and, as McCaskell added in correspondence with me, a porn star.

In part because he passed away at such a young age (not yet 40 years old), Pei Lim himself might be taken to figure as a kind of melancholic lost object. Fung's films *Fighting Chance* (1990) and *Re:Orientations* (2016) respectively chronicle Lim's life with HIV/AIDS, and look back with longing at his memory. This melancholia might understandably be regarded as most explicit in *Re:Orientations*, which is itself a retrospective, revisiting Fung's interlocutors in his first film *Orientations: Lesbian and Gay Asians* (1986) some three decades after its making. Lim is among the three subjects in the original film who have since passed away, all of them listed at the Toronto AIDS Memorial in Cawthra Square Park and given a tribute in the film.

But we might also take Lim himself as a kind of melancholic interlocutor. Indeed, both *Orientations* and *Re:Orientations* showcase 'Never Again', a dance choreographed by Lim and shown in *Track Two*. But Fung's films include a portion of the same dance rather different from the proud, triumphant conclusion seen in *Track Two* – a portion that stages a kind of Fanonian (Fanon [1952] 2008) drama of (mis)recognition. Lim begins the dance bound in rope and wearing a white mask, and as the dance proceeds, contorting in struggle with the rope, ultimately liberates himself, first from the rope and finally from the mask. Lim explains:

> Originally, the rope simply means some kind of bondage, oppression, and the white mask just simply means life in the closet – no tan, white, and lifeless, no color. And when I'm performing for gay Asian[s], I re-choreograph it somewhat and it has a deeper meaning for me. Basically, it means an Asian wearing a white mask, an Asian in North America or Asian in general in a

white-dominated world. And taking off the white mask, reclaiming who you are, and celebrating that, along with gay liberation. (Fung 1986)

The valences of Lim's piece reverberate strongly, indeed perhaps even didactically, with the writings of anti-colonial revolutionary and psychiatrist Frantz Fanon ([1952] 2008), particularly his thinking on the psychical dynamics of colonialism and racism, as well as with Herbert Marcuse's (1955) linkages between sexual and political liberation.

For Fanon, both colonizer and colonized are enlisted in a bad, asymmetrical Hegelian dialectic of recognition, one requiring investment and participation from both actors. Fanon links the resuscitation of desire for the colonized subject to resistance from the colonizer, and suggests that mutual recognition of conflicting desires is a key condition of a more egalitarian mode of relationality. The absence of conflict is what makes formal decolonization so limited for Fanon, particularly when independence is constructed as a 'gift' from benevolent colonial powers. Conflict, then, becomes central to any possible future without racism. Lim's dances in *Orientations* and *Re:Orientations* figure such a conflict by centring a racialized subject who casts off his white mask. Removing the mask – which we can read as a critique not only of colonial independence but Canadian settler multiculturalism – suggests a subject working through melancholia into mourning, perhaps finally ready to repudiate a lost object that had long been incorporated and idealized.

Yet although the dance tells a hopeful story – one of a passage from melancholia into mourning – it might be asked whether the dialectic of recognition, in this case between white and Asian gay men, might evince a melancholic attachment to its traumatic inauguration into the very racial hierarchy it decries. For indeed, racial melancholia recurs in Lim's initially optimistic accounts of sexual play in BDSM communities. Consider his account of the comparative openness but also the persistent race and class hierarchy of the Toronto leather scene in the 1970s and 1980s:

> I found that within the gay community, somehow, amongst the people that are into leather, raunchy sex, that are more open to different kinda people – height, weight, skin color, whatever. It doesn't matter. They're into play. If you're hot and if you turn them on, they want to play with you.
>
> But, you know, don't get me wrong – 'the leather scene is grand,' and whatever – because I have friends who also experience things that they, they consider racism, which is related, also to class. For example, one of the things they're into quite a bit in the leather scene is muscle, a good body. But this guy is a Vietnam refugee working in a restaurant, being exploited. He doesn't have the time or money to go to a gym to pump up his tits. So even though I could lend him all my costume – he's into leather – and [he could] wear it, but he doesn't have muscle. So what is he gonna do? [Lim gives a shrug of resignation] (Fung 1986)

Here, it might well be asked whether reading Lim through racial melancholia on its own would adequately account for some of the nuances of his wide-ranging political, aesthetic, and sexual practice. One possible interpretation of Lim's account might draw on the psychoanalytic concept of play, particularly in the work of Donald Winnicott, to consider the conditions for what might be thought of as 'good enough' racialized object relations (see Eng 2010, 2016). For Winnicott (1953), play describes a state of creative engagement with so-called transitional phenomena, located neither purely in a subject's internal object world nor exclusively in external reality. As anthropologist Margot Weiss (2006, 239) elaborates, Winnicott's work on play has received a fair bit of engagement in BDSM communities and scholarship, because 'play mediates between the external and the internal, it is a way of creatively negotiating, constructing and communicating the gaps between the self and the other/external world'. In Lim's account, the promise of play for thinking about racialized queer sex is that it loosens, although certainly does not do away with, racialized identitarian referents, privileging other, more fluid, polarities of difference and power. He intimates that leather cultures – which as Michel Foucault (see Halperin 1995) so famously put it, 'degenitalize' and re-territorialize bodily pleasures and thus unmoor essentialized sexual identities – likewise loosen the stratified racialization of queer bodies and scenes.

Yet the full account of BDSM that Lim proffers is far from univocally celebratory. He also readily decries the profoundly classed character of the kind of musclebound ascesis that queer theorists like David Halperin (1995) are perhaps too quick to praise as integral to leather culture. Moreover, Lim's analysis of racialization in queer communities does not stop at what one might, on Lauren Berlant's (2008) terms, think of as a kind of middle-class queer of colour complaint, but synthesizes political economic critiques as well. Lim explicitly links race and class, and anticipates by decades critiques that have only recently come to the fore in the academic world of the conviviality between white supremacy, neo-liberalism, BDSM, and polyamory cultures (Weiss 2006). Most significantly for my purposes, on psychoanalytic terms, the story Lim tells about his friend, 'a Vietnam refugee', is strikingly melancholic, presenting us with an attachment to a beloved object ('he's into leather') that is not simply repressed, repudiated, or rejected, but foreclosed ('I *could* lend him my costume … but he doesn't have muscle … So what is he gonna do?'; emphasis added) (Fung 1986). The inaugural trauma at play here is not even or necessarily one of a man who goes to a leather bar or a dungeon only to be refused, ignored, or ridiculed, but of a man who sees the writing on the wall, who has in some sense incorporated norms and prohibitions of white North American BDSM culture, even as he cannot afford to embody them. 'Eligible for melancholic incorporation', Butler writes, 'power no longer acts unilaterally on its subject … Social power … effects a melancholia that reproduces power as the psychic voice of judgment addressed to (turned upon) oneself, thus modeling reflexivity on subjection' (1997, 198–199). As we will see, however, even as melancholic incorporation maintains complicity with the power that impels it, it can also serve as 'sites of rearticulation, conditions for a "working through", and potentially, a "throwing off"' (Butler 1997, 191).

Of mimicry and moaning

As we have seen, Lim's accounts of his sexual practice, even at their most playful and confident, also refers back, with varying degrees of directness, to the trauma and the loss inaugurated by initial (and vicarious) encounters with sexual racism. Another account that bears a trace of this inaugural loss comes second-hand from Tim McCaskell, Fung's long-time partner in an open relationship, who recalls Lim as an important sexual pedagogue:

> We were fuck buddies for a while when Richard [Fung] was in South America in 1981. He taught me to make noise when I came. Although he had a noticeable Malaysian accent, when having sex, he sounded completely Midwestern U.S., since he'd learned all that vocabulary from porn videos. (personal correspondence, 17 September 2014)

In this educational scene, a Chinese-Malaysian-Canadian man entrains a white man from Ontario in the conventions of the masculine, corn-fed Aryan fantasies that dominate a vast swathe of US and Canadian gay porn. Here we might recall Homi K. Bhabha's reformulation of Jacques Lacan's concept of mimicry as a necessarily ambivalent strategy for colonized and postcolonial subjects. Bhabha argues that when colonial discourses enlist racialized subjects as proxies, intermediaries, or avatars, the speech of the colonized 'mimics' – both mutes and amplifies – the contradictions inherent in colonial logic, making it difficult to differentiate between mimicry and mockery. Ironically, the colonizer's desire for mimicry on the part of the colonized:

> … reverses 'in part' the colonial appropriation by now producing a partial vision of the colonizer's presence; a gaze of otherness … . [T]he look of surveillance returns as the displacing gaze of the disciplined, where the observer becomes the observed and 'partial' representation particulates the whole notion of identity and alienates it from essence. (Bhabha 1994, 48–49)

Ironically, Lim's repetition of the conventions of sexual fantasy and performance he learned from normatively white US gay pornography – his mimicry, even – puts McCaskell in the position of student who needs schooling, for it is Lim who in some respects surpasses McCaskell in the performance of white US gay sexual conventions. Even though this scene is recounted from McCaskell's point of view, it follows Lim's gaze, directing us to earlier encounters with both lovers and with pornography, to 'a partial vision of the colonizer's presence' (Bhabha 1994, 88). In this way, Lim's ordinary practice of repetition or mimicry refers back to his own inauguration into the sexual conventions of normatively white gay men's culture in Canada and the United States in the 1970s and 1980s, and might even be read as offering 'suppressed criticism' of those experiences (Ferenczi 1949, 226). As Butler (1997, 190) expounds on Bhabha, 'melancholia contests the ideality of authority precisely by incorporating it. Authority's ideality is incorporable elsewhere, no longer tie in any absolute sense to one figure of the law'.

Such an inauguration, and the trace of Lim's experience of traumatic self-discontinuity left behind through the break in accent, must be understood as not simply racialized, but geographically contingent, playing out not only of the visual (racialized bodies, colonial gazes) but also the aural (accents, enunciations, utterances). As Suzanne Yang writes in her essay 'A Question of Accent', accent comprises:

> … the shuttle by which a primal configuration makes its way out to the surface, finding there a geographical and linguistic specificity. Accent indicates a source and designates the place by which the subject is spoken—an accent of that moment when the child encounters the implantation of the signifier as Other. Indeed, *encounter* describes the situation of accent, where the voice meets the signifier in discordant strangeness and in its transmission through speech. (1998, 146; original emphasis)

Yang's insight into accent as palimpsestic, revealing one's histories of encounter with strangeness – including one's own – suggests Lim's sexual pedagogy proves yet even more profound here. Indeed, Lim's investment in performing a Midwestern accent speaks to Lacan's (1999) observation that language itself can be an object of libidinal investment and jouissance. In entraining McCaskell's desire, Lim reveals, however briefly, not simply the normative whiteness of North American gay men's porn, but the structural work of fantasy itself. 'Fantasy', Žižek observes, 'underlies the public ideological text as its unacknowledged support, while simultaneously serving against the direct intrusion of the real' (1998, 162). If we understand pornography to both open up a space of fantasy and to entrain fantasy as a 'public ideological text', Žižek suggests, such fantasies prove crucial to making it possible for people to encounter one another sexually. In other words, Lim's sexual pedagogy is not simply one that bears traces of a traumatic encounter with normative whiteness or the conventions of North American gay pornography, but one that points to the structural centrality of fantasy as fundamental to the experience of sex itself. 'Here', Žižek elaborates:

> we encounter the Lacanian maxim *'il n'y a pas de rapport sexuel'* at its purest: Even in the most intense moment of bodily contact with another human being, we cannot simply 'let ourselves go' and immerse ourselves into 'that' – a minimum of narrative support is always needed, even if this narrative is not always announced. (1998, 162)

Lim thus might help us to begin to differentiate between structural and contingent experiences of constitutive loss – between those defences against the real that are part and parcel of racism, and those without which relationality itself would be unbearable.

'The/beginning of my love affair/with others/and myself'

Butler writes that 'Survival is a matter of avowing the loss that inaugurates one's own emergence' (1997, 195). Importantly, then, dialectics of recognition with whiteness, or traces of initial traumatic encounters with it, are far from being the only melancholic scenes in Lim's interviews or work. Indeed, Lim's recollection of his early sexual experiences in Malaysia points to a milieu characterized by cross-class and perhaps interracial intimacy, but one in which whiteness was rather differently positioned, as Malaysia declared independence from Great Britain when Lim was a toddler:

> I grew up in a rather big family, with five sisters and three brothers, and I always hang out with my sisters. I didn't like men at all. I thought they were boring, and women were lots of fun. But it wasn't until I was around ten, eleven, my body start changing, the hormones start going, I start looking at men, particularly the workers around the house – the gardener, the [shelver?] – you know, when they walk around, with bare chests and sweat glowing on hard muscles. And I start realizing that I am getting really turned on by men. So that is when I start exploring it – and, well, start doing it with them. (Fung 1986)

Before Lim's memories of the Midwestern accents of white American porn stars, then, are other desires, differently racialized object-choices. Without indulging a white North American viewer's prurient curiosity or colonial gaze, Lim implicitly reminds the viewer of the geographical contingency of white supremacist hierarchies of desirability, while at the same time avowing the losses that constitute him as a sexual subject. Although Lim recounts these moments of incipient desire, he does not mention how his family bore witness to that desire, how they reacted. In *Fighting Chance*, Fung's (1990) follow-up to *Orientations* focused on HIV in gay Asian-North American communities, Lim elaborates on that latter question, describing the structural impossibility of disclosing his HIV status to his parents, on terms that speak to the limitations of translation:

> I'm in the process of sharing with my family my HIV status. It's a big family, and I told one, and I'm on my way home, and I will be sharing with my brothers and sisters. I've chosen not to tell mom and dad – out of love, not self-hatred or homophobia. My dad is turning eighty. So is my mom. Their health is not well. And I want them to have quiet, peaceful old age. I'm not sharing with them also because I have a language problem. I left home when I was sixteen. All my gay experiences and HIV stuff are in English. They only speak a dialect that very few people speak, and I find it really hard to express myself when I'm talking about HIV or AIDS stuff. (Fung 1990)

In contrast to his mimicry of the accent and narrative conventions of white North American gay porn, Lim finds that his queer and seropositive experiences are structurally inadmissible and inassimilable to his parents' symbolic universe (Žižek 1998, 155). Dina Georgis (2006) argues that diaspora itself, in its renounced relationship to home and parental ties, might be thought of as queer. How might such inassimilable queer desire recur or resurface in the space of pornography? What might prove generative, productively excessive about engaging such loss?

In 'Looking For My Penis', Fung (1991) famously laments the alternating desexualization and fetishistic exoticization of Asian men in North American gay men's porn. Thus, we might take it as a kind of good surprise that Lim appears in the 1980 book *Men Loving Themselves*, a softcover softcore porn book edited by the psychologist and sex therapist Jack Morin. In addition to spreads of about a dozen photographs of each model jerking off, models contribute narratives and even poetry about their early sexual experiences and how specifically they prefer to fantasize and masturbate. Lim's section is anchored by a brief poem recounting a teenage sexual experience with 'a distant cousin', one which Lim fondly recalls as 'the/beginning of my love affair/with others/and myself' (Morin 1980, 51). A kind of 'loss' that is also an inauguration, this early, queer experience makes no reference to whiteness or to the specifically racialized dimensions of melancholia, yet there nevertheless is a bittersweetness to its description that illustrates melancholia as a process of sexual subject formation. It is in this regard that considering Lim's pornographic work in the context of the broader archive of his life, activism, and sexuality proves so important. The tiny Lim archive I have sought to bring together and present in this article – the interval that emerges between Lim's experiences in Malaysia and those in Canada – helps bring into view the difference that the experience of racialization makes in experiences of constitutive loss, and to highlight the specificities of racial melancholia alongside the constitutively melancholic character of subject formation more broadly. What makes Pei Lim's interventions and contributions so remarkable in contesting the white hegemony that Fung critiques, then, is not merely the fact of his presence as an Asian-Canadian, nor his reclamation of Asian queer masculinity, but the insightful, melancholic vulnerability with which he framed his own sexuality and subjectivity.

Acknowledgements

The author thanks Dina Georgis, Natalie Kouri-Towe, Ricky Varghese, and two anonymous reviewers for their feedback on this manuscript, and Richard Fung and Tim McCaskell for sharing their work and memories of Pei Lim.

Disclosure statement

No potential conflict of interest was reported by the author.

References

Berlant, Lauren. 2008. *The Female Complaint: The Unfinished Business of Sentimentality in American Culture*. Durham: Duke University Press.
Bhabha, Homi K. 1994. *The Location of Culture*. London and New York: Routledge.
Butler, Judith. 1997. *The Psychic Life of Power: Theories in Subjection*. Stanford: Stanford University Press.

Butler, Judith. 2009. *Frames of War: When is Life Grievable?* London: Verso.

Cheng, Anne Anlin. 2001. *The Melancholy of Race: Psychoanalysis, Assimilation, and Hidden Grief*. Oxford: Oxford University Press.

Diaz, Robert G. 2006. 'Melancholic Maladies: Paranoid Ethics, Reparative Envy, and Asian American Critique.' *Women & Performance: A Journal of Feminist Theory* 16 (2): 201–219.

Eng, David L. 2010. *The Feeling of Kinship: Queer Liberalism and the Racialization of Intimacy*. Durham: Duke University Press.

Eng, Drantz L. 2016. 'Colonial Object Relations.' *Social Text* 34 (1): 1–19.

Fanon, Frantz. (1952) 2008. *Black Skin, White Masks*. New York: Grove.

Ferenczi, Sándor. 1949. 'Confusion of Tongues between the Adults and the Child.' *International Journal of Psycho-Analysis* 30: 225–230.

Freud, Sigmund. [1917] 1955. 'Mourning and Melancholia.' In *The Standard Edition of the Complete Psychological Works of Sigmund Freud*. Translated by James Strachey, 239–260. London: Hogarth Press.

Fung, Richard, dir. 1986. *Orientations*. Canada. Toronto: V-Tape

Fung, Richard, dir. 1990. *Fighting Chance*. Canada. Toronto: V-Tape.

Fung, Richard. 1991. 'Looking for My Penis.' In *How Do I Look?: Queer Film and Video*, edited by B. Object-Choices, 145–168. Seattle: Bay Press.

Fung, Richard, dir. 2016. *Re: Orientations*. Canada. Toronto: V-Tape.

Georgis, Dina S. 2006. 'Cultures of Expulsion: Memory, Longing and the Queer Space of Diaspora.' *New Dawn: The Journal of Black Canadian Studies* 1 (1): 4–27.

Halperin, David. 1995. *Saint Foucault: A Gay Hagiography*. Oxford: Oxford University Press.

Lacan, Jacques. 1999. *The Seminar of Jacques Lacan: On Feminine Sexuality, the Limits of Love and Knowledge, Vol. XX*. Edited by Jacques-Alain Miller, translated by Bruce Fink. New York: W. W. Norton & Co.

Marcuse, Herbert. 1955. *Eros and Civilization: A Philosophical Inquiry into Freud*. Boston: Beacon.

McCaskell, Tim. 2016. *Queer Progress*. Toronto: Between the Lines.

Miller-Young, Mireille. 2014. *A Taste for Brown Sugar: Black Women in Pornography*. Durham: Duke University Press.

Morin, Jack. 1980. *Men Loving Themselves*. San Francisco: Down There Press.

Muñoz, José Esteban. 1999. *Disidentifications: Queers of Color and the Politics of Performance*. Minneapolis: University of Minnesota Press.

Muñoz, José Esteban. 2014. 'Wise Latinas.' *Criticism* 56 (2): 249–265.

Nguyen, Hoang Tan. 2014. *A View from the Bottom: Asian-American Masculinity and Sexual Representation*. Durham: Duke University Press.

Sedgwick, Eve Kosofsky. [1997] 2003. 'Paranoid Reading and Reparative Reading, or, You're So Paranoid, You Probably Think This Introduction is About You.' In *Touching Feeling: Affect, Pedagogy, Performativity*, 123–151. Durham: Duke University Press.

Seitz, David K. 2017. *A House of Prayer for All People: Contesting Citizenship in a Queer Church*. Minneapolis: University of Minnesota Press.

Spivak, Gayatri Chakravorty. 1988. 'Can the Subaltern Speak?' In *Marxism and the Interpretation of Culture*, edited by C. Nelson, and L. Grossberg, 271–313. Urbana: University of Illinois Press.

Sutherland, Harry, dir. 1982. *Track Two: Enough is Enough*. Canada. Toronto: Sutherland Communications Corp.

Varghese, Ricky. 2017. 'Black Queer Grief in Michèle Pearson Clarke's *Parade of Champions*.' *Esse* 91: 48–49.

Weiss, Margot D. 2006. 'Working at Play: BDSM Sexuality in the San Francisco Bay Area.' *Anthropologica* 48 (2): 229–245.

Wiegman, Robyn. 2012. *Object Lessons*. Durham: Duke University Press.

Winnicott, Donald W. 1953. 'Transitional Objects and Transitional Phenomena.' *International Journal of Psycho-Analysis* 34: 89–97.

Yang, Suzanne. 1998. 'A Question of Accent: Ethnicity and Transference.' In *The Psychoanalysis of Race*, edited by C. Lane, 139–153. New York: Columbia University Press.

Žižek, Slavoj. 1998. 'Love Thy Neighbor? No, Thanks!' In *The Psychoanalysis of Race*, edited by C. Lane, 154–175. New York: Columbia University Press.

Pornography, psychoanalysis and the sinthome: ignorance and ethics

Katie Goss

ABSTRACT

This article conjoins pornography and the radical ethics of psychoanalysis to attend to the Real ignorance that pornography generates. Rather than a pathological symptom of the impossible sexual relation or a relativistic enjoyment assimilable to capitalist and patriarchal paradigms, Lacan's seminar on the sinthome informs an approach to pornography as that which has the potential to undo regimes of phallocentric knowledge and form new bonds between fantasy and social reality, symptom and artwork, jouissance and ethical (sexual) relationality. I will explore the sinthomic potential of pornography in a selection of films and texts that represent the radical deconstruction of knots that solidify meaning and signification, and perform the creative elaboration of subjective knowledges tending towards substantialization. I demonstrate how the 'savoir-faire' that pornography supports and can engender – an absolute unknowability that exposes our essential ignorance – holds unique possibilities for creative appropriation of the Real in modes of artistic and ethical sexual practice.

(K)not-knowing pornography

For psychoanalysis, ignorance is immanent to sexuality. The axiom that 'there is no sexual relation' is not intended to dismiss the symbols and laws, fictions and fantasies, impulses and encounters that we are immersed in and recreate, nor to refuse the possibility of ethical sexual practices. Rather, this lack amounts to an absence of coherent (sexual) meaning. The impossibility of a sexual act that could guarantee complementarity between or full intelligibility of sexuated subjects (even apparently self-evident and stable masculine and feminine positions) is precisely that which makes space for the over-abundance of meanings, 'the multiplication and overlap of incompatible knowledges' (Berlant and Edelman 2014, 8) of symptoms that bind us to language, fantasy and acts of sublimation. The contingency – and frequently contempt, embarrassment or ambivalence – that inspires and disrupts attempts to define or discuss pornography, to discern, prohibit or prescribe its features, function or value, is undoubtedly characterized by this ineradicable uncertainty of the meaning of sex, as well as the sexual nature of meaning that this uncertainty belies.

The site of subjective construction from internal division, replete with gaps, contradictions and irresistible connections to meaning, is articulated in the topography of the Borromean knot. In *Seminar XXIII* on the sinthome, Lacan states that 'two are loose from one another is the very definition' ([1975–76] 2016, 38): the (k)not-knowing of sexuated subjectivity, where Symbolic formalization and Imaginary processes never fully correspond, is how we become bound to meaning in symptoms and jouissance. The sexuated subject as a knot is formed by kinds of knowledges (in the Real) that are both a solution and an error, symptoms that resolve contradiction in the Symbolic and Imaginary registers of meaning while simultaneously bearing witness to their incommensurability.

Pornography is frequently invoked as a symptom in terms of being both the cause and effect 'of our modern cultural decline' (Miller-Young 2015, 10) situated at a fraught convergence of the law, social reality and psychic life. Indeed, if there is no sexual relation then pornography, as the most 'explicit' articulation of the infinite permutations and disjunctions of meaning arising from this absence, cannot exist as a coherent or singular entity. To align pornography with the potential for a creative and ethical sexual mode, rather than pathologically deviant or purely relative enjoyment, is to attend to its generation of Real ignorance – an impossibility of knowing in language, fantasy or materiality – that is central to the radical ethics of psychoanalysis. With pornography you do not always 'get' what you see – pornography which does not conform with one's own fantasy can be comical, inane, traumatic or thoroughly devoid of eroticism. Many critics argue that pornography is always an unsatisfactory image for the 'act itself' – there is always something more to experience than the image can show – and thus denigrate pornography as a simulation lacking in substance. Yet the clamorous and conflictual world of censorship laws attests to the fact that one does not always see or understand what one 'gets' (off on) – the uncontrollable appearance of the pornographic as an unexpected partial element or contaminating agent in words, images and acts threatens to supersede and eclipse the social and aesthetic codes that build them.[1]

These competing interpretations situate the Real on one side or the other – in the emptiness of the sign or the excessive/invading fantasy – revealing the paradoxical antagonism/interdependence between Symbolic and Imaginary registers that pornography substantializes. We cannot be un(k)not-ed: certainty as to what pornography is and its effects brings about strange inversions in political discourse. Laura Kipnis notes: 'suddenly cultural conservatives start sounding like ardent feminists ("Pornography exploits women!"), feminists start sounding like autocratic patriarchs ("Women in the sex industry are incompetent to make informed career choices"), and staunch free-marketeers become anti-big business' (1999, xi). These distortions reflect the need to reform coherency at the point of insecurity pornography situates, but we can see that ignorance is a purely oppositional term (rather than constitutive element) by which absolute knowledge is confirmed, of what 'is best' for women or what 'is really' damaging society. Certainty also announces itself as perverse disavowal: Justice Potter Stewart's infamous 'definition' of pornography – 'I don't know what it is, but I know it when I see it' – exemplifies how the ignorance integral to the encounter with jouissance cannot be fully erased but merely displaced and installed in an ego-driven relativism.

The consistency of social reality, from whatever point of view, depends upon the Real that ties the Symbolic and Imaginary together despite the fact that they are not 'extensions of one another' (Dean 2000, 39). Although an encounter with the impossibility of the Real is commonly conceived as a traumatic rupture or psychosis, in Lacan's discussion of the sinthome he wonders how the experience of symptoms that simultaneously secure and undo us in this space (the hole in each order and the gap that persists around and between them) can be substantialized through creative processes:

> How can an art target in an expressly divinatory way substantialization of the sinthome in its consistence, but also in its ex-sistence and in its hole … to the point of getting as close as it is possible to get? ([1975–76] 2016, 28)

Today we are more accustomed to conflating pornography with the modality of commodity capitalism, as a lure of proximity to, and certainty of, the object of desire, that removes us from the ambiguities of how desire is generated by conflicting and unstable forces. Yet I would suggest that pornography offers possibilities for close encounters with a Real ignorance that our symptoms bear witness to, the impossibility of guaranteed relations and a jouissance that lies beyond the apparent consistency of our sexual proclivities, phallic cultural orders and practices of representation. Drew DeVeaux asserts: 'Porn is the medium through which sexual culture is both reflected and reshaped' (2016, 151). What is at stake in changing our conception of pornography and its potential contribution to subjective and social life is a change in (sexual) culture, from obsessive pathologization, instrumentalization, exclusion or disavowal of relative knowledges to a sinthome that makes way for creative and ethical treatment of the Real in artistic and subjective sexual practices.

XXX-istence

The Freudian conception of sexuality as proliferation of meaning was fundamental to the 'liberation' of the subject in modernity. Today we see this has been co-opted by a neoliberal framework seeking to situate all choices within a flexible and homogenized field, the injunction of which Slavoj Žižek (1989) describes as the demand to 'enjoy your symptom'. In the internet phenomenon of 'food porn' or 'shoe porn' we see that 'porn' acts as a signifier for the arbitrariness of the (absent) object of language/desire and an excessive enjoyment instrumentalized as a prosthetic supplement. In this instance, the relation of 'porn' to its content is a link in the simplest sense, fusing the Imaginary and Symbolic by way of an enjoyment that represses unknowability, circumvents ambivalence and reinforces the symptom as the construction of the individual. This 'parasitic' form of power (Lacan [1975–76] 2016, 44) is also a regulatory function, simultaneously indulging and attempting to rehabilitate the Real of sexuality to generate cultural capital and stimulate virtual economies through the masturbatory relation with the commodity (the Imaginary phallus par excellence).

Jacques-Alain Miller describes:

> … the twenty-first century is seeing the vast spread of what is called 'porno,' … coitus on show in a spectacle that is accessible to anyone on the web … we have not only passed from prohibition to permission, but to incitation, intrusion, provocation, and forcing. What is pornography but a fantasy that has been filmed with enough variety to satisfy perverse appetites in all their diversity? (2016)

While pornography's excessive variety breaks from a repressive modality (where suppression of jouissance constitutes meaningful cultural practice) to a permissive one, the violence Miller identifies at work in this perverse economy suggests that both of these regimes deny the impossibility of the sexual relationship. Steve McQueen's *Shame* (2011) features a protagonist who shuns long-term relationships, friendships and even the affection of his one and only sister as 'unrealistic' or 'parasitic dependency'. As Lacan ([1963] 2016) concludes in 'Kant with Sade', McQueen (2011) shows the fantasy of liberation from prohibition to be exactly that – a fantasy which confirms the eminence of the Name of the Father as a phallic paradigm in a perverse imaginary. The 'freedom' from conventional relationships that Brandon 'enjoys' is shown to be enslavement to the claim of an absolute pleasure that forces, incites and provokes him to compulsively fill his work hard drive with pornography, stalk the city looking for sexual encounters and, when that fails, to engage the services of sex workers in virtual and physical exchanges. McQueen's bleak vision of sex addiction is an excellent example of the tendency in much contemporary thinking to cast pornography as an individual symptomatic defence against a fragmenting social realm.

Tim Dean asserts that, 'Unlike consumer culture, psychoanalysis provides a space in which desire is taken seriously rather than exploited' (2000, 202). To situate pornography's unique contribution to culture and psychic life, without restricting its significance to consumer-capitalism or exploitative patriarchal paradigms, it is vital to appreciate how seriously it takes desire and the validity it bestows to parts and forms of sexuality that meaning usually misses despite constant delegitimization. The Audiovisual Media Services Regulation 2014 imposed censorship on pornographic representation in the United Kingdom, specifically targeting BDSM practices (including spanking and penetration by an object 'associated' with violence), and the feminine body. The prohibition of highly self-conscious performances of BDSM 'scenes' to protect social reality and the abjection of feminine fluids (such as female ejaculation) in the name of women's liberation indicates a Real of pornography that cannot be dispelled from a permissive neoliberal framework – that no one of us is 'free' to choose what we 'are into' and neither does the given language and cultural imaginary, from the human sciences to Hollywood, provide the means to understand and access jouissance; we must create our own.

Mireille Miller-Young points out that the 'abiding injustice of sexual criminalization' rests upon a function of prohibition that upholds the law precisely through unelaboration of the uncertainty and contradictions that pornography generates:

> … the sex panic around porn is, of course, convenient. It distracts from the more complex questions of what kind of sexual morality should be embraced … why so many people choose to work in the sex industry … and how exactly youth come to gain an education about sex and sexuality. (2015, 10)

It is vital to acknowledge that the suppression, policing and stigmatization of pornography is not the protection of a fragile innocence from corrupting sexual knowledge, nor the preservation of stable and fulfilling human relationships in 'real life' against the deviant fantasies or impulses opposing them. Lee Edelman asserts that the mythical Child 'whose innocence solicits our defence' (2004, 2), so often invoked in anti-pornography legislation, subtends a logical modality that covers the energies of the Real with a Law that must remain empty. This function, the Name of the Father, is also reflected in the designation 'R' (for 'Restricted') – the empty signifier of prohibition marks that which exceeds regulatory social norms of sex and the norm by which desire is generated through an exterior obstacle/enabler of the Law.

The repression/liberation dichotomy that so often organizes pornography debates attests to the phallic monopoly on meaning that psychoanalysis and feminism also grapple with. Addressing the pro/anti-sex split that emerged within feminist debates during the 1970s and 1980s, Julia Creet describes how 'both the charge of repression … and the charge of replicating masculine desire … carry with them the symbolic weight of the father' (1991, 138). Yet taking this ambivalence as her central theme, Creet explores desires that are 'absent rather than prohibited' such as lesbian S/M fantasy, arguing that 'it is precisely in the internal struggle, within ourselves and within the feminist movement, that I see evidence of a new loci of power' (1991, 138). Pornography is also frequently designated XXX – crossed out in the same way as the barred subject or Other, implying an inability to represent that which goes beyond the limit of Symbolic prohibition. This universal short-hand gestures towards the 'ex-istence of sex' as 'something from which we cannot [always] derive jouissance' (Lacan [1975–76] 2016, 47) and 'a point of arrest' ([1975–76] 2016, 38) in the interdependency of Symbolic and Imaginary that exceeds and unites their operation.

Verity in *Variety*

The release date of Bette Gordon's *Variety* (1983) contextualizes the film in the explosion of pornography onto the market in the mid-1970s thanks to VCR technology and the accompanying denunciation by anti-pornography feminists of this commodity, which at the time was made almost exclusively by men for men, as 'the essential sexuality of male power' (Dworkin 1981, 35). Yet Gordon's artistic practice situates pornography as a source of radical uncertainty that, while produced within definitively patriarchal social conditions, nonetheless contains the radical potential to exceed a phallic monopoly on meaning, of sex and of cinema. 'Variety' – the name of the porn theatre where Gordon's protagonist, Christine, sells tickets – evokes a free-market or a spectacle of sordid appetites and objects. Janet Maslin's (1985) disparaging review upon its release attests to one viewer's disappointment that this lure does not live up to its promise: 'the idea that Christine might develop a growing fascination with voyeurism and pornography, while provocative, is something that Miss Gordon is almost entirely unable to articulate in visual terms'. However, this 'failure' is presupposed by the impossibility of any apprehension of pornography that appeals to visibility and truth as operating together; Gordon's *Variety* reformulates fetishistic expectations through emphasis on the pornographic generation of ignorance rather than the satisfaction of desire. While dated, my choice of this film aims to demonstrate how, in the current debates around porn and its conditions of production and dissemination, we must pursue the continuation of feminist work to divest ourselves from the limited localizations we are provided within homogenizing phallic functions and seek more possibilities in what pornography can offer through enigmatic and ambivalent encounters with the absence of the sexual relation these functions are intended to conceal.

The obsessive desire of phallocentric culture, to see and to know, is also the 'fear of what might remain unknown, inaccessible, in the dark' (Cohen 2015, xi). Gordon depicts Christine's emergent relationship with pornography as a neo-noir, embedded within a cinematic tradition and social realm relentlessly homogenized by the visual regime of the phallic imaginary which Laura Mulvey (1975) called the 'male gaze'. From the romantic interests who interrogate her knowledge as a means of articulating their own fantasies – 'do you watch the films?' – to customers who watch her through the window of the ticket kiosk (Figure 1), the banality of phallic jouissance in everyday life is an unending imposition that erects transparent screens in order to project desire from a comfortable distance. While Lacan's gaze is non-gendered, Mulvey's conceptualization of a male gaze highlighted how in patriarchy there is a social complicity with individual attempts to refuse our lack. Pornography is often perceived to be seamlessly continuous with the scopic drive as an exercise of power, where seeing and knowing are co-terminous. In this phallic paradigm, Woman (the representation of what is negated by and confirms masculine self-identity) and pornography are both situated as a symptom or spectacle, 'the bearer of meaning and not the maker of meaning' (Mulvey 1975, 7) and therefore responsible for fulfilling our fantasies and bearing this lack. Today we still see subjects (often women) who participate in pornography conflated with superficial constructs and instruments of patriarchal power. However, the objectification of sex workers and codification of all forms of pornography in these terms reinforces the coherency of masculine desire in social reality, when there is nothing but the 'paradox of phallocentrism' (1975, 8). In his commentary on Seminar XXIII, Moncayo explains:

> The homogeneity of the Imaginary and the Real ... in the knot of three also leads to false consistencies since we suppose an ego where the Real makes a tie and construct a self where there is no self. (2017, 48)

In psychoanalysis it is the feminine subject who most intimately relates to the Real of desire, not as our own but 'of the Other', and confronts the opacity of the (imagined) self and the inconsistency of any totalizing system of meaning. At stake in Christine's relationship with pornography is a recognition that the 'being-there-to-be-looked-at' (Gordon 1990, 418) which women and porn share when situated within a consistent phallic imaginary always escapes apprehension and creates new kinds of meaning and significance.

Lacan reminds us that 'there is a centrifugal dynamic of the gaze' ([1975–76] 2016, 70) usually excluded from perception as the place of unseeing that allows us to 'know' what we are looking at. Gordon places mirrors in frame throughout *Variety* and the multiple observational positions induce a topographical knotting of gazes. Christine's face is reflected back to the viewer as she is observed by the male gaze, but the intrusion of the dark shape of her shoulder indicates something inaccessible which defies exclusion from perception (Figure 2). Just as Mulvey does with her concept, Gordon objectifies the male gaze in the viewer's observation of its operation, pre-empting Christine's voyeuristic pursuit of the man. In 'Variety: The Pleasure in Looking', Gordon (1990, 421) cites Paul Willemen and asserts that pornography contains the possibility of a 'fourth look' which is usually excluded from the three gazes (between characters, camera and viewer) of mainstream cinema. In *Variety*, 'a woman in a porn store represents the fourth look and so makes men uncomfortable' (1990, 421). Christine's voyeurism in illicit masculine spaces is not just an external source of prohibition 'catching him in a taboo act' (1990, 421), but substantializes the male gaze as an object and insinuates the possibility of looking at pornography in a different way. This 'fourth term' (Lacan [1975–76] 2016, 28) as an unimaginable feminine imaginary has a different but consistent relationship to the Real, not just relative but transformative.

Figure 1. Christine is observed by the male gaze, which then prompts her voyeuristic pursuit of the man into the criminal underworld. Still from *Variety* (Gordon 1983).

Kipnis suggests that to 'regard pornography more creatively' is to consider 'how it regards us' (1999, xiii). In *Variety*, pornography is brought to bear upon the gaze to regenerate the blind spot that undoes the security of the masculine imaginary. Instead of the 'normal distortion of vision wherein we think that images come from the outside' (Moncayo 2017, 48), pornography is always parallax: it does not exist as an objective entity but a change of subjective perspective enacts an ontological shift in the object itself. The gaze of the subject is always already inscribed into that which is perceived to be pornographic, what is 'in the object more than the object itself' (Žižek 2006, 17) and remains an unknowable constituent that looks back at us. When Christine searches her target's bag, finds a porn magazine and carefully flicks through the pages, the male gaze is a blemish on the images as an invisible stain of phallic jouissance. The relative consistency of the masculine imaginary, supported by pornography as a symptom which offers straight-forward comprehension, is undermined by the feminine gaze as a fourth term. As Creet asserts, for the feminine subject to position herself not as the object of masculine desire but as a subject of desire (for another woman) is precisely 'unimaginable within this [phallocentric] framework, thus absent rather than prohibited' (1991, 137). The jouissance derived by Christine is not self-affirming pleasure against prohibition that objectifies pornography, but the ambivalent or enigmatic desire of the desire of the (non-existent) Other that is subjectivizing and impossible. As well as representing the variability of symptoms (the male gaze being one kind of 'truth' that confirms a patriarchal logic), her relation to porn also expresses the necessity, substance and belief, a kind of 'verity' (Lacan [1975–76] 2016, 52), in the inarticulate consistency of the Real that induces our relation with what exists beyond and within the visible.

The inconsistency of the Imaginary revealed by the Real consistency of Christine's relationship to pornography, the substance implied by the symptom's verity, also appears in her sudden descriptions of vivid pornographic scenes:

' … Smooth, smooth stories … Smooth black slip against her skin. … She … he strokes himself … Slowly, slowly the slippery fabric. Sex smell fills the room … ' 'Why are you telling me this?' 'I'm telling you about my life.'

These instances of increasing intensity challenge the interrogation and touches of the men with the unassailable contours of an act of saying. At one point she speaks for five long minutes as a man stoically plays a pinball machine. One cannot see or know whether he is listening, but as Lacan ([1975–76] 2016, 9) points out, ' … because it has orifices, the most important of which is the ear because it can't be sealed, shut, or closed off … there is a response in the body to what I have called the voice'. Talking about pornography makes us uncomfortable and thus has a pornographic dimension of its own because of the sensitivity of the body to a fact of saying. The sound of the voice as a Real is excluded from meaning and interferes in intelligibility but also what creates the significance suturing imaginary and unconscious knowledge as 'j'ouïs-sens' ([1975–76] 2016, 58) in hearing and meaning. Because the speaking of fantasy is taboo in culture, the 'language of desire is male' (Gordon 1990, 421), but Kathy Ackers' exquisite writing, the voice of actor Sandy McLeod, and the viewer's own bodily and psychic sensitivity to the Symbolic and the Real contribute to and participate in the construction of Christine's fantasy as she utilizes language of desire on her own behalf.

Christine's emergent relationship with pornography only comes into view through schism between the gaze as an object and the object of the gaze, between the voice that speaks and the body which receives it, which threatens the Imaginary sensibilities through which we understand the world and carrying significance of the Real:

> … Christine's description of and reaction to porno films raises the question of individual sub-jectivity: the viewer interprets and gives meaning to the representations, which are far from uniform despite the conventions of culture. (Gordon 1990, 422)

The homogony of phallocentric imaginary shifts to heterogeneity of Imaginary and Real in the enigma of Christine and the viewer's pornographic encounters and creative practice. Willemen also suggested that the fourth look 'marks itself in the light from the projection reflected back on to the faces of the audience and constitutes the viewer as visible subject' (1994, 107). In one of the final scenes, the first time we see Christine take a seat in the theatre, the screen shows a pornographic alternative ending to a 'real' encounter that occurred earlier in the film (see Figure 2).

The frame within a frame does not 'reflect' desire projected onto it, but redoubles the alienation from the Other and illuminates the reshaping and unknowability of Christine and the viewer's respective fantasies, which still remain in the dark. While *Shame* lays bare (and harshly lights) Brandon's sex life to demystify the lure of absolute gratification, there is nothing remotely sexy about it – he is an object of the Other's will to enjoy, holding at bay an oppressive Symbolic Law inexorable in its emptiness. In *Variety*, the viewer cannot claim a position of exteriority from the symptom's failure but must participate in and assume the subjective variety generated by pornography, in their readings of Christine's enigmatic desire and in their own responses to her fantasy. This is sinthomic – despite troping the subject's 'truth', Christine and the viewer retain their own subjectivity. The Name of the Father moves from Symbolic censorship or a purely phallic jouissance to the Real impossibility seeing or knowing the other's desire exemplified by pornographic

Figure 2. Christine watches a pornographic encounter that includes herself 'caught in the act' of searching the man's bag. Still from *Variety* (Gordon 1983).

blindness of perception and half-saying/over-expressiveness speech. Phallic apprehension and mastery give way to verity and creativity which tend towards substantiation in acts of seeing and saying that remain resistant to definitive interpretation.

Frisking the (w)hole

Integral to Lacan's proposition of the sinthome is the process of formation at the level of creative practice, not simply embodiment in a single work of art. James Joyce, who Lacan found exemplary of the sinthomic appropriation of the symptom, made a name for himself in society despite the 'failing of the father' (Lacan [1975–76] 2016, 80) and simultaneously transformed culture with the very jouissance that is usually prohibited as a socially acceptable pleasure and resists symbolization. There has always been something pornographic about Joyce's sinthome – obscenity trials and highly publicized sexual fantasies are indissociable from his literary creations – but this is frequently neutralized in academia or dismissed as a sordid underside of the genius. Yet Joyce explicitly announced his intention to 'keep the professors busy for centuries' (as quoted in Ellmann [1959] 1982, 573). While some critics continue to treat his works and author-God Joyce himself as a symptom containing a secret codified knowledge awaiting one intellectually potent enough to discover it, surely it is time to acknowledge and embrace the way the academy collectively 'gets off' on its own ignorance, supported by Joyce's jouissance in sinthomic artistry.

Kipnis writes that 'we're devoted to keeping art and pornography so discursively sequestered exactly because aesthetics and perversion are so contiguous (and perhaps, contagious)' (1999, 83). The mutual exclusivity that must be constantly reconstructed between forms of sublimation and enjoyment which have such radically different statuses reveals the fragility of aesthetic and social codes in an encounter with the Real that sustains them. The pleasure principle is a limit on enjoyment – sexuality and the forms of 'jouis-sens' (significance without definitive meaning) it engenders are not driven by pleasure but the drive as 'nonproductive, nonteleological, and divorced from meaning making'

(Berlant and Edelman 2014, 11) which achieves satisfaction by not achieving its aim. The inhibition of drive is not an exterior obstacle or prohibition but internal to its activity, which holds 'the place of what meaning misses in much the same way that the signifier preserves ... the meaningless substrate of signification that meaning intends to conceal' (Edelman 2004, 10). The correspondence of drive with the emptiness of the signifier (rather than a biological instinct opposed to culture) situates the Real in the Symbolic as the inhibiting and excessive jouissance which give symbols purchase on subjectivity.

Joan Copjec finds the 'commonplace misconception about sublimation [is] that it substitutes a more socially respectable or refined pleasure for a cruder, carnal one' (2002, 29). Exemplifying the shift in queer artistry since the late twentieth century, to resist the cleaning-up of sexuality while simultaneously refusing to locate queerness as an 'outside' that revalorizes heteronormative culture, Dennis Cooper's *Frisk* confounds the mutual exclusivity between artistry and sexuality by invoking the Symbolic as Real in the dimension of wholeness which 'negates the possibility of any meta-dimension, any meta-language' (1991, 94). Cooper not only situates pornography at its most extreme, obscene and threatening, but does so to stage the conflictual interdependence of symbolic representations of sex and the pornographic Real-ity – that which impedes and instigates creative representational practices out of the impossibility of positivization.

Two descriptions of a series of photographs precede and follow the main narrative of *Frisk*, the first of which is implicated as the object-cause of the protagonist Dennis' morbid sexual obsessions and violent narrative events to come:

> ... His eyes ... reflect the front of a camera ... His ass sports a squarish blotch, resembling ones that hide hardcore sexual acts ... Five. Close-up. The blotch is actually the mouth of a shallow cave ... the sort ocean waves carve in cliffs ... At the centre's a pit, or a small tunnel entrance, too out-of-focus to actually explore with one's eyes, but too mysterious not to want to try. (Cooper 1991, 3–4)

Emphasizing the desire at work in symbolizing systems that are always in consort with readers 'especially in illicit moments' (Kaite 1995, viii), Cooper's description simulates the motion of the camera from the 'first ... medium shot' to the close-up of the lethal wound. The metonymic displacement – from the enigma of the blotch that censors/arouses to poetic clichés of ocean waves – seduces the reader by implicating a repressed signifier 'at the centre' and promising a 'mysterious' hidden meaning beneath the 'shallow' surface of language.

Berkeley Kaite characterizes the pornographic photograph as a 'published dream' where the 'illusion of a private "phantasmatic" (secret, privileged view at the keyhole) is contradicted by the acknowledgment of the mass circulation' (1995, viii). Cooper's elaborate contouring of the penetrable void contradicts its status as an anonymous utterance without symbolic construction, and exposes precisely how the reader enjoys the snuff-porn – we 'know' the photographs are not 'real' but simultaneously make the presumption of a symptom within signification, while the pornographic Real-ity exists 'beyond' or 'behind' the text. Lacan finds that 'the symptom's articulation with the symbol ... [is] a false hole' ([1975–76] 2016, 15). The falsity of this hole – which Cooper substantializes in the wound made of 'dyed cotton glued on' (1991, 30) – is that the symptom and the symbolic that represents it can be separated without a cut. However, *Frisk*'s dismembered structure confronts the reader with the multiplication of cuts, contradictions and inconsistencies that present the Real pornographic dimension of Cooper's aesthetic dissimulation.

The uncertain status of the 'truth' of Cooper's fiction (reinforced and undermined by the first-person narrative and epistolary form of a protagonist that shares his name and is also a writer of perverted fictions) and the excess enjoyment of the reader which parallels Dennis' sexual technique of attempting to read the body from the inside, disintegrates the boundaries between fiction and the Real-ity of its cause/effects. Indeed, the Real as the limitation on words and images appears in *Frisk* as what 'makes them relative to one another' and presents 'an alternative possible or impossible world beyond either of them' (Moncayo 2017, 46). The empty signifier fails to fully express the symptom qua the wanting to say, but because of this representation is able to 'grasp hold of some excess, some surplus existence … over what it signifies … ' (Copjec 2002, 96). Cooper's text does not implicate this Real existing 'beyond' the schism of words and images, the exquisite prose and obscene depictions, as the unknown unconscious content of the author's symptom. Rather, the very inadequacy or 'self-imposed impotence' (2002, 95) of the drive and empty signifier substantializes and enables the reader's excessive enjoyment obtained from the unconscious 'known' in reading experience, but about which we know nothing. To frisk is to search for something concealed, usually a weapon or contraband, without trespassing on the boundaries of the social 'decency' and over-exposure. As well as the hole in the Symbolic that allows for the Real excess of drive to bind representations to reality, 'language is tied to something that makes a hole in the real … [it is] impossible to consider how it is handled' (Lacan [1975–76] 2016, 21). Cooper's pornographic depictions of Dennis' sexual deviancy contradict the delicacy of this gesture, yet the disgust/enjoyment of the reader's jouissance is a kernel of the Real that would be unthinkable without the symbols cohering around it *ex nihilo*, shaped by the artist.

The continuity of the holes of Symbolic and the Real in artifice 'is a form of making that eludes our grasp … which far exceeds the jouissance we can derive from it (Lacan [1975–76] 2016, 50). Cooper's 'savoir-faire' is not a repressed impulse 'beyond' the reader's comprehension, but the pornography of representation (excess enjoyment beyond meaning/pleasure and rawness of symbols) as the hole that divides and creates cohesion between fictional representation and Real-ity which creates artistic significance. In the final series of photographs, the pornographic element is not contained within a hidden depth but is an entirely surface entity marked by traces which invite a reading but which cannot be entirely grasped:

> His eyes … each reflects a little camera and part of a hand … his ass crack is covered with something that vaguely resembles a wound when you squint … Five. Close-up. The 'wound' is actually a glop of pain, ink, makeup, tape, cotton, tissue, and papier-mâché sculpted to suggest the inside of the human body … it's a bit out of focus. Still, you can see the fingerprints of the person or persons who made it. (Cooper 1991, 128)

Moncayo describes how the 'False hole is a form of deception, the true hole is a new invention' (2017, 64). The two pornographic descriptions that supplement the main narrative as origin and destination are entitled '∞', implicating something mathematical, topological and impossible which encircles the (w)hole significance of the text and circumscribes the locus of what cannot be symbolized.

For Lacan, the division between the symbol and the symptom and continuity of the false self and signifying chain of the unconscious structured like a language is an 'infinite straight line' ([1975–76] 2016, 67) that cuts through the holes of Real and Symbolic and a mobius strip that guarantees the continuity of the subject. Miller (2016) opposes pornography to creativity by asserting that 'masturbators' are now 'spared from the task of having to produce their own waking dreams' because they find them 'readymade'. Yet the object of drive as an inherent inhibition and the subject as a mobius strip exemplify how that which is most intimate to us is often radically externalized, just as we always find something irreducibly foreign in our depths. This extimacy of the Real means that the significance of pornography is always contingent and encountered in what ties the symbol and symptom together and what necessitates their pulling apart. Queer artists like Cooper are often accused of 'really' being pornographers, contaminating and degrading the legitimacy of symbolization with sexual significance. But the pornographic savoir-faire of *Frisk* presents the possibility that it is our own fetishization of art behind the tired attempts to preserve it from the drive and negativity that give purchase to representational practice. Cooper gestures towards a reformulation where artistic processes do not desexualize the Real of the drive, and the Real-ity of the pornographic does not eviscerate representation, but brings us into a relation with the transformational quality of jouissance in art that is someone else's porn.

What's your Real name?

Moncayo explains that 'A relationship to the Name has to be established in order to retain a Real immeasurable dimension beyond image and word that functions within the Borromean knot' (2017, 16). Cooper re-appropriates his own name for pornographic purposes, undoing the assumption of the ego of the author where the jouissance of the symptom/artwork ties the Real and Symbolic, and introducing the split that nomination designates, pertaining to the hole that substantializes the impossible dimension of representation and its irresistible purchase on subjectivity. Adult film workers, both behind and in front of the camera, are far more 'available for dismemberment in the public eye' (Nova 2015, 123) than famous writers like Cooper. Jiz Lee writes: 'Coming out as a porn star has critical consequences for one's relationships, one's sense of self … one's livelihood and social mobility. Coming out means risking everything' (2015, 11). Pornography and psychoanalysis align in their focus upon non-conforming sexual fantasies which would usually endanger the public reputations of those who participate in discourse or practice (Moncayo 2017, xv) and which also shift privacy to a more essential dimension of unknowability in subjective experience.

Conner Habib's (2015) 'The Name of Your First Pet and the Street You Grew Up On' invokes the forms of naming in pornography, usually associated with an evasion of symbolic authority or compartmentalized 'dark-side' of the self, as a practical necessity in an intolerant culture that nonetheless emerges as a creative strategy. The well-known formula from which Habib derives his title is not mathematical but sinthomic in the sense of that 'which concentrates in itself the singularity of the case and the universality of a structure that belongs to all' (Morel and Végső 2016, 68). Habib's epiphany implies a process of nomination coming from the Real, retaining an interdependency between the symbols that sustain imaginary self-hood and fantasies that guarantee the persistence of social reality:

> Instead of being reborn in my birth name 'after' porn, I will be reborn into my porn name after my birth. My porn name, anyone's porn name, may now just be the name of a braver self, one that's not afraid to be open.

> … I was asked to give an autograph as Conner, but I had no idea what that signature would look like. … [I] saw the frenetic symbols tilted into the same gestures as Andre Khalil. They shared the same loops and the same dot on the 'i' just before the end. It was as if the name was there all along. (2015, 106)

Instead of a cipher that can be discarded to restore a lost origin or neatly separate the self, Habib posits an 'i' that refers to instantaneous, unknowable and infinitely permuting interdependency between the Real of nomination, the symbolic, the body and the subject that it perpetually transforms and is sustained by. Geneviève Morel and Roland K. Végsö find that the sinthome 'proposes an alternative to the Name-of-the-Father by generalizing the power of separation that has been conceptually reserved for it' (2016, 69), symbolically linked to filiation, economic interest and the common inheritance of a community, but also an imaginary function of a stop-gap for lack in the subject. For DeVeaux, the alternative identity that is a necessity for the porn performer creates a separation with which to repair the subjective dissonances incurred in patriarchal society: 'by creating and getting to know Drew, I've been able to give myself the space (from myself) … to effect change in how I relate to my body' (2016, 49). The name as sinthome, or the sinthome as a name, is a singular invention, a sexual (not just sexuated) identity and a re-appropriation of the name in a different way (Morel and Végsö 2016). The porn name as a cipher of protection or alienation from culture is foiled by its circulation as a non-signifiable identity or unknowability that produces self-symbolization in artistic-sexual subjectivity.

Linda Williams ([1989] 1999, xi) asserted that 'to be moved by pornography is not to be uncritical'. The sinthome contributes towards a continued understanding of how we can be moved by pornography without delegitimizing it. It is not that pornography as a legal definition, genre, rhetorical device, pastime or profession can ever simply conform to what psychoanalysis, or any other discourse or subject, says it is. But it can and should be conjoined with the ethics of psychoanalysis, feminism and queer theory to untie prescriptive modes that pertain to uncover, pin-down or expose the 'truth' of sexuality. Miller and others are eager to identify pornography as the perverse symptom of the absence of the sexual relation, but perhaps risk colluding with criminalization by lawmakers and homogenizing phallic paradigms that structure both repressive and perverse regimes. The only way to simultaneously denaturalize and depathologize sexuality is to attend to how ignorance is constitutive of sex and meaning itself. Identifying with the contours of our (k)not-knowing reveals our symptoms as something of our own production that we can take responsibility for in creative savoir-faire. Signalling jouissance in the impossibility of totalizing relations and meaning, pornography does not have to disguise but can creatively expand this. Undoing and retying the different contributions of the Real, Symbolic and Imaginary and substantializing the enigmatic bonds that produce significance, the Real of pornography remains unnameable and unknowable and can be used for constructive and artistic purposes.

Note

1. Kirby Dick's documentary *This Film is Not Yet Rated* (2006) offers a brilliant insight into the Real inconsistency at the heart of the film ratings system in the United States.

Acknowledgements

The author thanks Kris Beaghton, for their infinite conversations, inspiration and support for all things psychoanalytic and pornographic.

Disclosure statement

No potential conflict of interest was reported by the author.

ORCID

Katie Goss (iD) http://orcid.org/0000-0002-4522-6025

References

Berlant, Lauren, and Lee Edelman. 2014. *Sex, or the Unbearable*. Durham: Duke University Press.
Cooper, Dennis. 1991. *Frisk*. London: Serpent's Tail.
Cohen, Josh. 2015. *The Private Life: Why We Remain in the Dark*. Berkeley: Counterpoint.
Copjec, Joan 2002. *Imagine There's No Woman: Ethics and Sublimation*. Cambridge: MIT Press.
Creet, Julia. 1991. 'Daughter of the Movement: The Psychodynamics of Lesbian S/M Fantasy.' *differences: A Journal of Feminist Cultural Studies* 3 (2): 135–159.
Dean, Tim. 2000. *Beyond Sexuality*. Chicago: University of Chicago Press.
DeVeaux, Drew. 2016. 'Coming Out Again (and Again).' In *Coming Out Like A Porn Star: Essays on Pornography, Protection, and Privacy*, edited by Jiz Lee, 141–151. Berkeley: ThreeL Media.
Dick, Kirby. dir. 2006. *This Film Is Not Yet Rated*. USA.
Dworkin, Andrea. 1981. *Pornography: Men Possessing Women*. New York: Putnam.
Edelman, Lee. 2004. *No Future: Queer Theory and the Death Drive*. Durham: Duke University Press.
Ellmann, Richard. [1959] 1982. *James Joyce: New and Revised Edition*. Oxford: Oxford University Press.
Gordon, Bette. dir. 1983. *Variety*. USA.
Gordon, Bette. 1990. 'Variety: The Pleasure in Looking.' In *Issues in Feminist Film Criticism*, edited by Patricia Erens, 418–485. Bloomington: Indiana University Press.
Habib, Conner. 2015. 'The Name of Your First Pet and the Street Your Grew Up On.' In *Coming Out Like A Porn Star: Essays on Pornography, Protection, and Privacy*, edited by Jiz Lee, 103–106. Berkeley: ThreeL Media.
Kaite, Berkely. 1995. *Pornography and Difference*. Bloomington: Indiana University Press.
Kipnis, Laura. 1999. *Bound and Gagged: Pornography and the Politics of Fantasy in America*. Durham: Duke University Press.
Lacan, Jacques. [1963] 2016. 'Kant with Sade.' In *Écrits*, Translated and edited by Bruce Fink, 645–668. New York: W. W. Norton.
Lacan, Jacques. [1975–76] 2016. *The Sinthome: The Seminar of Jacques Lacan, Book XXIII*, edited by Jacques-Alain Miller, translated by. A. R. Price. Cambridge: Polity Press.
Lee, Jiz. 2015. 'How to Come Out Like a Porn Star: An Introduction.' In *Coming Out Like A Porn Star: Essays on Pornography, Protection, and Privacy*, edited by Jiz Lee, 13–20. Berkeley: ThreeL Media.
Maslin, Janet. 1985. 'Screen: Variety, by Bette Gordon.' *The New York Times*, March 8. Accessed August 1, 2017. http://www.nytimes.com/1985/03/08/arts/screen-variety-by-bette-gordon.html.
McQueen, Steve, dir. 2011. *Shame*. USA.

Miller, Jacques-Alain. 2016. '*The Unconscious and the Speaking Body*.' Xth Congress of the WAP, Rio de Janeiro, April 25–28. Translated by A. R. Price. Accessed April 15, 2017. https://www.wapol.org/en/articulos/Template.asp?intTipoPagina=4&intPublicacion=13&intEdicion=9&intIdiomaPublicacion=2&intArticulo=2742&intIdiomaArticulo=2.

Miller-Young, Mireille 2015. 'Foreword.' In *Coming Out Like a Porn Star: Essays on Pornography, Protection and Privacy*, edited by Jiz Lee, 9–12. Berkeley: ThreeL Media.

Moncayo, Raul. 2017. *Lalangue, Sinthome, Jouissance, and Nomination: A Reading Companion and Commentary on Lacan's Seminar XXIII on the Sinthome*. London: Karnac Books.

Morel, Geneviève, and Roland Végső. 2016. 'The Sexual Sinthome.' *Umbr(a): Incurable* 1: 65–83.

Mulvey, Laura. 1975. 'Visual Pleasure and Narrative Cinema.' *Screen* 16 (3): 6–18.

Nova, Cyd. 2015. 'The Mechanism of Disappearing to Survive.' In *Coming Out Like a Porn Star: Essays on Pornography, Protection and Privacy*, edited by Jiz Lee, 118–123. Berkeley: ThreeL Media.

Willemen, Paul. 1994. 'The Fourth Look.' In *Looks and Frictions: Essays in Cultural Studies and Film Theory*, 99–113. London: British Film Institute.

Williams, Linda. [1989] 1999. *Hard Core: Power, Pleasure and the 'Frenzy of the Visible'*. Berkeley: University of California Press.

Žižek, Slavoj. 1989. *The Sublime Object of Ideology*. London: Verso.

Žižek, Slavoj. 2006. *The Parallax View*. Cambridge: MIT Press.

'Bodies that splutter': theorizing jouissance in bareback and chemsex porn

Gareth Longstaff

ABSTRACT
This article explores associations between the psychoanalytic theory of jouissance and representations of bareback and chemsex between cis-gendered men in gay porn. It uses the concept of 'bodies that splutter' to focus on how tensions allied to the definition and interpretation of jouissance can be used as a foundation to interpret and reposition a queer and psychoanalytic politics of bareback and chemsex as porn. In so doing, the article will suggest that pornographic practices of bareback and chemsex in the output of UK director Liam Cole and US website RawFuckClub.com attempt to frame these practices of gay male desire as phallic jouissance. Working with the notion of 'bodies that splutter', the article will transpose Judith Butler's concept of performative bodies that matter and Tim Deans' unconscious bodies that mutter to consider a dialogue between pornography and jouissance where bodies also 'splutter'.

Introduction

The pornographic work of UK-based director Liam Cole and the increased popularity and visibility of websites such as RawFuckClub.com belong to a specific genre of cis-gendered gay male porn predominantly identified as bareback. Recent work examining this (Ashford 2015; Scott 2015; Mercer 2017) places emphasis on the increasing complexity and paradox involved in both its production as pornography and its critical discussion within the emergent and interdisciplinary arena of porn studies. Yet the potentials of aligning it to psychoanalytic theory have yet to be fully developed. This article aims to explore these potentials and in so doing explore how problems of phallocentric jouissance for gay male bodies that attempt to lay claim to the phallus on Lacanian terms may energize other perspectives on jouissance and pornography.

In the psychoanalytic context, jouissance is often aligned to Jacques Lacan's register of the Real and understood as a phallic, pre-Symbolic, orgasmic, and ejaculatory form of pleasure, yet it can also find a Symbolic genus in non-phallic expression, most famously explored by Lacan's theory of feminine jouissance in *Seminar XX Encore: On Feminine Sexuality, The Limits of Love and Knowledge 1972–73* (Lacan 1999). Whilst many aspects of Lacanian jouissance may be heavily reliant on a cis-normative and gender binary understanding of pleasure/desire mapped onto the phallus, Lacan also offers up a form of 'jouissance [that is] wrapped in its own contiguity' (Bowie 1991, 149) to 'offer momentary respite from the severity of signifying law' (1991, 202) whilst concurrently remaining an effect of the signifier. The possibility of aligning jouissance to the visual politics of bareback and chemsex porn drives it towards an ideological, political, and subjective limit, and in this way it is stripped (just like the pornographic representations it haunts) of its enigmatic flexibility and resilience to interpretation and analysis. This wrench between jouissance and language (Fink 1995), between identity and desire (Dean 2000, 2009), and between a 'drift from "pleasure" to "bliss" [that] indicates queer theoretical values and investments' (Bond Stockton 2017, 104) also underpins its power as 'provocatively sexy, intimate, scandalous and bodily' (2017, 102). Alongside Lacan, other key theoretical interventions and accounts of jouissance such as Roland Barthes' (1975) *The Pleasure of the Text* position jouissance liminally between forms of language and desire that simultaneously 'wound or seduce me' (1975, 38).

Furthermore, much of the power that jouissance yields is located through this seductive wounding. Jouissance has ideological, political, and subjective interpretations and, in this way, remains difficult and unruly. Just as it is often discussed through the signification of the phallus and phallic jouissance, here it also begins to resist definition or representation, and the subsequent ways in which it is theorized call into question the critical nature of what jouissance may be in relation to desire. It is worth noting here that the use of 'phallic' has often been misconstrued as something that pertains to distinctly masculine, patriarchal, and dominant tropes. In fact, the critical point, which Lacan was striving to emphasize, was that the phallic and the phallus are fragile and fallible. As Bruce Fink observes, 'one cannot take the failure out of the phallus' (2002, 39), so that when this notion is plugged into how the signifier and jouissance are both theorized and articulated in terms of cis gay male bareback and chemsex porn, something like the provisional and intersectional nature of a phallic 'cis gay male bareback and chemsex' ontology is exposed. To say that jouissance is only phallic is to foreclose and confine its locality only to a phallic Imaginary. Lacan suggests that the *objet a*, or that signifier which causes jouissance rather than that which attempts to sustain it, has its most obvious or explicit grounding in a materiality connected to jouissance's cause; in other words, a pleasure that reaches a particular point, but a point that ultimately brings jouissance to an end. In this way, 'the signifier is what brings jouissance to a halt' (Lacan 1999, 24). Here, and in an attempt to express it as a pornographic jouissance, we find an erratic tension at work in this structure, one which locates jouissance as both a cause of or spur to desire and a stop or terminator of that desire.

In light of these tensions there may be challenges within bareback porn that arise due to its distinctly phallic formation of jouissance. Tim Dean's (2009) *Unlimited Intimacy: Reflections on the Subculture of Barebacking* is perhaps regarded as the seminal text on barebacking practices and its critical steer is towards axioms of queer theory and ethnography. Articles which employ psychoanalytic frameworks, such as Christien Garcia's (2013) 'Limited Intimacy: Barebacking and the Imaginary', explore 'the subjective tensions between experience and representation' (2013, 1031) but do not move beyond the Lacanian frameworks of Imaginary narcissism and fantasy. Perhaps more provocatively, Leo Bersani and Adam Phillips suggest that barebacking is analogous to psychoanalytic notions of 'sexual desire as indifferent to personal identity, antagonistic to ego requirements and regulations [...] and inferences about the unconscious' (2008, 43), which in turn begins to energize considerations of bareback and pornography, and the potentials of linking them to jouissance. As something more specifically allied to bareback and chemsex, jouissance is something that they (vis-à-vis Dean) assimilate and recognize. Here the malevolent dismissal of bareback as 'mindless fucking' bound to the ethical, legal, and medical discourses (and inherent dangers and risks) of HIV and AIDS is also 'deeply invested with meaning [… that] signals profound changes in the social organization of kinship and relationality' (2008, 46) and how desire might be invoked and expressed.

Furthermore, in recent work such as *Gay Pornography: Representations of Sexuality and Masculinity*, John Mercer (2017) places emphasis on the representational and visual politics of bareback and chemsex porn. Here, tensions between an aesthetics of realism, authenticity, and documentary 'truth' are traversed by 'the extraordinary, the extreme and the excessive aspects of sexual play' (2017, 141). Like jouissance there is an ethical implication to the drug and cum-fuelled orgies where endless pleasures seem to take place and, in this way, bareback differs from earlier iterations of practices of sex between gay men without the use of condoms. From the mid to late 1990s, the shift away from practices of 'unprotected anal sex' (Rofes 1998, 196) between cis gay men towards practices of condomless sex (Scott 2015) developed to construct bareback sex. This is sex which relies upon the transmission and abjectly pleasurable ejaculation and/or 'breeding' of semen (also variously referred to as 'cum', 'seed', 'load', 'dump', 'juice') to fortify and enhance a 'heightened erotic charge, cultural cachet and recklessness', also problematically underpinned by the practices of 'men transmitting HIV at its heart' (Ashford 2015, 195). As a way to buttress these key epistemological and ontological features of barebacking and chemsex, it is clear that both inside and outside of this genre of gay pornography this '"transmission" of seminal fluid from one partner to another not only deposits genetic material, but serves to breach the membrane of hygiene and "good gay" sex that the homonormative and contemporary sex education seeks to prescribe' (2015, 196). Here, porn inflected by bareback and chemsex also fosters a mediated 'site where the taxonomy of objective/subjective representation collapses in on itself' (Garcia 2013, 1038) and goes some way towards capturing the 'visual conflation of reality and fantasy' (McNamara 2013, 233) in a range of ideological, political, and aesthetic ways.

Greteman also argues that the barebacker (in porn) exists within 'a contested "empirical reality"' (2013, S22) which forces cis gay men, and, perhaps more pertinently, queer theory and the range of non-cis genders and sexualities it overarches, to reposition the tensions between sexual regulation, assimilation, and normality. This forges an ambiguous kind of crossing point or schism in which the tripartite of bareback–chemsex–HIV/AIDS might offer 'a particular promise of a queer lifestyle' (2013, S25) in response to 'the pale of bourgeois respectability' (Dean 2009, 84–85) that phallocentric gay masculinity, same-sex marriage, and the commodification of gay culture has led us to. In other words, there may also be scope to suggest that by reorganizing and/or renegotiating the phallic, moral, ethical, and political implications of bareback–chemsex–HIV/AIDS, an alternative and transgressive configuration of kinship, bonding, and affirmation may be possible. In sync with jouissance, bareback is difficult to define. In his introduction to a special issue of the journal *Sexualities*, 'Bareback Sex and Queer Theory across Three National Contexts', Oliver Davis positioned bareback 'in its most minimal acceptance' as 'anal sex between men without using condoms and in cognizance of HIV/AIDS' (2015, 120). More specifically and in this article, this cognizance (Berg 2009) situates this shifting epistemology of bareback to chemsex and cis gay masculine pornographic representation. By also aligning this to the psychoanalytic concept of jouissance, the article aims to identify some of the tensions aligned to our knowledge of bareback sex and pornography in both theoretical and ideological frames. To do this in relation to jouissance requires that the affective and representational spaces of the body in porn are addressed. In the next section this is positioned through a consideration of the discursive limits of bodies and sex via bodies that have performatively 'mattered' and unconsciously 'muttered' such they might be reconceptualized so that they also 'splutter'.

Bodies that matter, bodies that mutter, bodies that splutter

Tim Dean states that in her 'rhetoricalist' account of psychoanalysis Judith Butler fails to see how jouissance and the subject are always underpinned by a 'desire [that] is predicated on the incommensurability of [that] body and subject' (2000, 200). In this way, Dean suggests that Butler misconstrues the unconscious ego as a 'bodily ego' aligned to conscious, anatomical, and biological sexual difference, and as a result fails to develop how egos 'occlude – rather than manifest – desire' (2000, 200). Using this contention, Dean (2000, 202–205) renovates Butler's concepts allied to bodies that performatively 'matter' into bodies that now unconsciously 'mutter'. Dean's muttering body is one demarcated by a limitless jouissance because it cannot be rationalized or demarcated through an ego or a body that 'matters'. What is also central to Dean's critique of Butler is hinged on the restrictive ways in which we, as desiring subjects, misapprehend and, in many ways, misrepresent desire in terms of an Imaginary, identifiable, personalized, and bodily 'other' as opposed to one riven through Lacan's conceptual registers of the Symbolic Other and the Real.

Here, the body is one that is mindful of its 'mattering' and materiality but unaware of the 'muttering' possibility of desire. Or, in other words, the mattering body is one that accounts for 'subjects of the signifier and not subjects of desire' (Dean 2000, 187). From the confines of the Imaginary signifier, the mattering body fails to recognize desire, and, more so, jouissance beyond the constraints of the ego and the materiality of that ego. For instance, the Imaginary cis gay male body that is represented, read, looked at, and thus embodied through bareback and chemsex porn can only be re-represented, re-read, and re-interpreted through its own disembodiment that mutters as a form of diffuse and disruptive jouissance which is Real. This muttering body also serves to emphasize the failures and limits of a cis gay male ego that 'obscures the subject of desire', to formulate that 'while the ego matters, the body mutters' (2000, 202). Whilst Dean conveys this in terms of an Imaginary ego that matters and a Real body that mutters, it is also within this formulation that the notion of a Symbolic body that splutters is, on the one hand, neglected and, on the other, beckoned in. If this is the case, the alignment of 'mattering' and 'muttering' could be realigned to suggest that when the cis gay male body operates through jouissance, and is excessively signified in pornography, it Symbolically splutters. This spluttering relies upon the Symbolic Other and a cultural signifier (the body, an object, an image, a series of images) but also follows Dean's claim that 'the difference between muttering and speaking [mattering] concerns the distinction involved in the notion of desire as something in language but not itself linguistic' (2000, 203).

Spluttering occurs in this gap between mattering and muttering. Here, bodies must splutter through the force and peril of the Symbolic Other before they can capture and relinquish the notions of 'mattering' or 'muttering' through jouissance.

Building on both Butler and Dean, this new construction of spluttering, which in this instance is aligned to cis gay masculinity in porn, forms a 'contingent foundation' (Dean 2000, 205) of how to read jouissance, in that it locates this gay male spluttering body and its precarious phallic jouissance between bodies that matter and mutter. Whilst muttering is 'struggling to be heard' (2000, 203), the 'spluttering' bodies in bareback/chemsex porn are not necessarily struggling. They are repetitively activating desire through the process of spluttering – here the spluttering body produces a Symbolic form of anxious phallic jouissance that will only splutter because it is torn between a body that matters and a body that mutters. In this case, the gay male pornographic subject of the Symbolic is spluttered, a subject who is both alert and naive to the constraints and the limits of Imaginary and Real modes of jouissance. This body that splutters is located between the mattering and muttering self, and the spluttering that is activated in this space is done so intensely, indeterminately, and repetitively, like the process of bareback penetration and ejaculation it awkwardly underpins. In this setting, spluttering is continuously realized retroactively through a gap, an excess, or a slippage between mattering and muttering. This spluttering involves processes of bodily and egotistical expulsion that falter, stumble, and hesitate to express the nature of phallic jouissance and simultaneously undermine and distress the pornographic signifier. In any pornographic image, the subject can only express themselves through a series of representational constructions that rely upon impersonal and metonymic contiguity, and in so doing they begin their own practices of spluttering. Through this process, the ego and the associations that it has with an Imaginary Other fails to articulate desire and, in so doing, shifts the potentiality of how jouissance can be realized to the Symbolic and the Real.

Jouissance, barebacking, and chemsex

It is clear that jouissance is a psychoanalytic concept that deliberately resists and subverts; it does not clearly translate from French into an English definition or word and, as a result, is balanced on the inscrutable threshold of its own perplexing signification and meaning. Yet Jacques Lacan ([1960] 2003) first elaborates on the concept of particularly phallic jouissance in 'The Subversion of the Subject and the Dialectic of Desire in the Freudian Unconscious' by stating that 'the erectile organ comes to symbolize the place of jouissance, not in itself or even in the form of an image, but as a part lacking in the desired image' ([1960] 2003, 353). This lack riven into the phallus is relevant to jouissance and how it is (and ultimately is not) expressed and represented in bareback and chemsex porn that relies upon both phallic and anal desire to express this lack as jouissance. In its resistance to definition or representation, the critical nature of what jouissance may be in relation to the disruptive tensions between pleasure and lack also forms a conundrum between the politics of bareback and chemsex representations within cis gay male porn and their practices outside and beyond porn. Potentially, in all pornographic representation jouissance is circumscribed as a form of visual and textual desire that shifts and sways between pleasures, excesses, and, ultimately, barriers to itself. Here the attempts that pornography makes at citing and fulfilling jouissance always destabilize that jouissance, and more so in sexual practices allied to bareback and/or chemsex where this works in a double-bind or even a deadlock. On the one hand it invigorates how 'sex can function as an arena in which the most basic of barriers – including those of disgust and shame – maybe negotiated or overcome' (Dean 2009, 137), yet on the other it also remains vulnerable to the potentially reductive and 'pernicious ideology of safety' (2009, 211) and stigma allied to key discourses of disease, risk, and shame around HIV and AIDS.

Here, the UK director Liam Cole's attempts to authenticate and visualize jouissance as it might be understood through the combination of bareback and chemsex demands some attention. His work with Paul Morris's Treasure Island Media has become synonymous with pornography that is inscribed with the spontaneity, rawness, and urgency of pure documentary film, yet is also clear that this technique is still structurally and ideologically contained as a pornographic mode of production. Rather than an authentic way to represent the complex movements and intersections between the bodily and subjective states that bareback and chemsex catalyze and inhabit, Cole aligns them to a performatively inscribed discourse of hyper-masculine bareback and chemsex that controls what these practices might be or could be as jouissance. In porn, this discursive naming and citing of signifiers is somehow inevitable in that the Imaginary and the Symbolic orders 'need to be named via the Other, or otherwise no subjectivity is possible' (Geldhof and Verhaeghe 2017, 212–213), but in this way and through the pornographic reproduction of bareback and chemsex we find that 'the attempts to define something undefinable show us how radically we are cut off from it' (2017, 215). For instance, as Cole exploits 'the 'real' settings of the apartment/sex club/hotel chain' he also forces them to 'operate as liminal spaces due to their banality and anonymity' (Mercer 2017, 141), thereby miscarrying the 'real' veracity of what bareback and chemsex might be. In this way, and when the mutability of jouissance (phallic or not) is attached to the pornographic signifier, it unfetters the consumer and viewer of porn from the stimulating risks, traumas, and transgressions that bareback and chemsex actually contain. Porn sanitizes and regulates these practices so that the strategically amateurish and documentary aesthetic of Cole functions as an attempt to connect jouissance to a Symbolic order which cannot contain it.

Still, in Cole's work this paradox is visualized to such an extent that the excessive practices of drug-taking and unprotected sex between cis gay men sublimates and repositions the trauma of HIV/AIDS and/or crystal meth addiction into affirming and transformative practices. Here the pornographic subject is neither on the side of objectification nor on the side of subjectification; rather, they and the practices aligned to their (dis)embodied states of desire 'splutter jouissance' so that the subject/object bifurcation unravels towards, but never attains, jouissance. Here, the ejaculatory climax (and purpose) of cumming in the anus which is enmeshed in breeding, seeding, spreading, and gifting relies on an 'erotic pleasure [that] can be gained by means of retention and release' (Arundale 2017, 78) clustered around the risky potentials of sharing fluids, drugs, and, ultimately, HIV, so that within 'a simultaneously lateral and vertical kin relation' (Dean 2009, 85) the possibilities of subverting and relocating discourses of phallocentrism, heteronormative and homonormative conception, and marriage in a queer frame are also articulated.

The attempt to splutter and embark on a re-evaluation of kinship in which cis gay men volitionally and deliberately transmit and infect other men with HIV moves these practices towards a queer mode of desire explored by Dean in the following ways:

[The] man whom one infects with HIV becomes his sibling in the 'bug brotherhood' at the same time that one becomes his parent or 'Daddy', having fathered his virus. If this man also happens to be one's partner or lover, then by 'breeding' him one has transformed what anthropologists call a relational affine into a consanguine; one's 'husband has become one's 'brother' via a shared bodily substance. (2009, 85–86)

Here the conflation of impersonal sex with brothers, with husbands, and the queer potentials that might come from renegotiating these kernels of sexual and bodily pleasure and exchange fits into both the discursive and psychoanalytical conflations of the virus (and its correlation to disease and death), drug use, jouissance, and the communion of 'a piece of himself inside of me; his cum, like the sex itself, [that] has a psychological value far beyond anything physical' (O'Hara 1997, 69 as quoted in Dean 2009, 87). However, it is also these affective urgencies, intensive thrills, and extreme levels of sexual and bodily arousal that also extinguish jouissance. The phallic and cis-gendered gay porn scene simultaneously facilitates and undercuts the mattering body, and in so doing urges it towards a muttering one to renegotiate and search for spaces in which a doxa of bareback and chemsex that has been cultivated by figures such as Cole also splutters.

Whilst this amalgamation of men phallically impregnating one another's anuses is 'invested with woman's power to conceive [whereby …] the rectum becomes the procreative womb' (Bersani and Phillips 2008, 45), it is also (as Bersani famously asserts) here that the 'barebacker's rectum is [also] a grave' (ibid.). Through this act the potential for a queer inversion of reproductive sex as the giver of life into the non-reproductive transmission of a potential death allows the cis gay male barebackers to move towards a form of jouissance that comes close to the 'essential insanity' of bareback and chemsex that Bersani, Dean, and Liam Cole all recognize on their own conceptual and representational terms. More so, and as pornography, the subversive and transgressive potentials of jouissance are obscured if not obliterated in an attempt to contain it within the signifying chain of tendencies which might be more broadly situated through neoliberalist and late capitalism consumerism.

In *Homosexual Desire*, Guy Hocquenghem uses the notion of the sublimated anus to claim that 'sublimation is exercised on the anus as on no other organ' ([1972] 1993, 96). Writing in an era which preceded HIV and AIDS by almost a decade and one which might now be regarded as an historical moment allied to gay liberation, Hocquenghem sees both its function and its desirability as primarily private and personal. Barebacking, and more so the commodified value and power of Liam Cole's pornography in work such as *Slammed* (2012), *Overload* (2013), *Hard Cuts I* (2014) and *Hard Cuts II* (2015), transforms, inverts, and re-routes this sublimation of the anus into an unstintingly visual politics of anal visibility and accessibility. The cum-drenched anus so central to Cole's work functions as an impersonally public and open space of desire cleaved and 'gashed by bliss' (Bond Stockton 2017). In a paradoxical contrast to the technical scrutiny allowed by the close-up of the wet, gaping, and convulsing arsehole in this genre of pornography, Hocquenghem's claim that 'there is no anal pornography [...] the anus is over-invested individually because its investment is withdrawn socially' ([1972] 1993, 97) is upturned. The exposure and parting of the anus for anyone and everyone to enter forces us to re-engage and re-evaluate how the anus that 'forms the division between society and the individual' is transposed so that the anus becomes a communal site. To rephrase Hocquenghem's claim that 'the anus is overinvested *individually* because its investment is withdrawn *socially*' ([1972] 1993, 97; emphases added) to now read 'the anus is overinvested *socially* because its investment is withdrawn from the *individual'* brings us closer to its potential as a space whereby the cis gay male subject productively embraces both desire and anxiety in parallel towards a queer model of jouissance that splutters between phallic and anal inter-subjectivity.

Both inside and outside Liam Cole's pornographic textuality, Bersani's claim that 'the community engendered by barebacking is completely nonviable socially and politically' (Bersani and Phillips 2008, 49) also resonates. This is precisely because it is increasingly commodified and trapped between the possibilities of anti-egoistical acts of self-subordination and affirmative impersonality, whilst always being anchored to a rhetorical politics of 'hypermascilinised ego, the grotesquely distorted apeing of reproductive values, [and] the all-too-visible appeal of an eroticized militarism which in turn positions it as a perpetuation of homo and heterosexual hegemonic and dominant masculine values' (2008, 51). In barebacking and chemsex, the spluttering cis gay male subject attempts to connect, implicate, and haunt the other but they are still barred from the jouissance of his own subjective experience. Barebacking and chemsex, and more so the signification and expression of how it 'feels' in porn, could be seen as a queer attempt to renegotiate this barrier or limit. Here, the tensions of a psychoanalytic identification which fails overlap with queer identifications that partially connect the subject with the other through a complex milieu of sex, death, risk, regulation, and transgression. Through these practices and their situational intent, the impersonality of the self and the repositioning of what the narcissistic possibilities of that impersonality may be are where the truly affirmative and genuine possibilities of jouissance are located. This is a non-representational politics which moves beyond the bodily politics and archetypes of gay porn actors and the partiality of the visual signifiers which are all too familiar. In a search for jouissance outside identity politics and ideological networks of mediated desire it may be that the politics of bareback and chemsex lie beyond the pornographically mediated and/or liminal spaces of the orgy or gangbang as well the porn actors who continue to maintain and repeat an embodied rhetoric of hyper-male, phallic, and cis-gendered gay male signifiers such as tattoos, cropped and shaved hairstyles, piercings, jock-straps, and military jackboots. Porn of this type paradoxically undermines and confines the potential of the subject's diffuse, joyous, unconscious jouissance and how it might relate to the stimulating epistemological and ontological potentials of spluttering bodies and the self-led shattering of the subject's own narcissistic ego.

The problem with narcissism! Shattered, suave, and spluttering bodies

A concept like bodies that splutter may also allow the cis gay male and potentially all queer subjects and subjectivities to get closer to a form of jouissance that is both sustained and disavowed by the Symbolic in language. These faltering and spluttered significations are the ones that can only be partially expressed via the Symbolic and jouissance. They also form the splutters which position the aimless, random, and obtuse ejaculations into the anus that 'come/cum' close to how jouissance can only be incompletely expressed both metonymically and impersonally in bareback and chemsex porn. This approach to jouissance as an expression of the impersonality of identity and ego can also be found in the critical reconsiderations of the narcissistic cis gay man in Lee Edelman's (1994) concept of 'narci-schism' and Leo Bersani's (1987, 1995; Bersani and Phillips 2008) enduring exploration of impersonal narcissism, which push cis-gendered gay masculinity towards practices of narcissism outside of the gay male ego and its Imaginary other.

For instance, Edelman understands that there is an Imaginary relation between the narcissistic gay subject and the mirror as constitutive of gay male subjectivity, and, in turn, gay desire. Yet, as Edelman argues, this is also the foundation for an alternative notion of gay subjectivity or activism that would involve a self-disciplined depersonalization of narcissism as 'narci-schism', so that 'the luxurious "passivity" derided as "narcissism", that signifies the erotic indulgence of the [cis-gendered gay male] self that always threatens to undo the "self"' (1994, 10), is either undermined or removed. In this instance, 'narci-schism', which is assimilated from the 'erotic mode of the dominant subject' (1994, 10) as self-disciplinary, has the potential to simultaneously reposition the gay male narcissist and his capacity as a 'mirror bound narcissist[s] reviled for a passivity' (1994, 108) as a 'narci-schisist'. That is, the subject who moves beyond his Imaginary ego and the metaphors of gay identity towards a way of expressing his subjectivity (and jouissance) Symbolically and impersonally.

In this way, the potential ruptures that the 'narci-schisist' and 'narci-schism' impart can also contribute to considerations allied to narcissism and the Imaginary subject of desire seen in Bersani's (1987, 222) theory of a 'self-shattering' of the ego and subjectivity. This shattering can be understood as a conceptualization of the 'self' that Bersani recognizes via Freud's assertions that the narcissistic 'sexualizing of the ego is identical to the shattering of the ego' (Bersani and Phillips 2008, 66). By aligning a shattering of the ego to a spluttering of the body in bareback and chemsex porn it is also useful to think about how, in his early use of the terms, Bersani used shattering as a device to imagine gay masculinity 'in which [...] the self is exuberantly discarded' (1987, 217–218). It is here and through the self-shattering of the ego, and through the ego's own struggles with narcissistic and 'narci-schisistic' desire, that something Bersani constitutes as '"impersonal narcissism" begins to make its own insensible sense' (Bersani and Phillips 2008, 92). On the one hand, this stands if we literalize and invest in the pornographic images on the basis of an identifiable 'bareback/chemsex culture' and 'bareback/chemsex gay male subject' existing through personalizing, inclusive, and tangible forms of desire and identity. Yet, on the other, if we approach these images as traces of the depersonalized, exclusionary, and intangible desires they endlessly reproduce, we also begin to see them as close to a queer combination of 'narci-schisistic' and shattered jouissance.

This connects to a spluttering body that also relies upon the conflicts rather than the failure 'to distinguish others from Others' (Dean 2000, 187) in its search for jouissance. In pornography that claims to capture and represent bareback and chemsex practices this can only be a vulnerably phallic body that splutters; a body that Dean might also position as 'suave' (2000, 187). This 'suave body' is situated as the body that has been rehearsed, smoothed over, repetitively copied, and 'so completely rhetoricalized' that it is effectively 'devoid of desire' (2000, 187). This is the body as a pornographic text whose devolution of desire is desire itself, a desire activated by its own loss of desire. On RawFuckClub.com this intersection of spluttering and suaveness facilitates a form of phallic jouissance that is always strategized, constructed, and manipulated and is 'not in any way liberated or liberating' (2000, 187), so that the 'suaveness' becomes an indicative part of how phallic jouissance as spluttering is expressed. For instance, in several 'gangbang' scenes such as 'Alex Mason's Birthday Gang Bang' (2016, https://www.

rawfuckclub.com/), the close-up representations of bareback sex and/or allusions towards chemsex present us with a spluttering and suave subject who can only be identified through the limits of cis-gendered gay masculinity and its alliance to the pornographic text. Here, the enigmatic nature of this spluttering underpins and undermines the discursive bodies' 'mattering' because of its pornographic representation as suave. This allows the performatively phallic and mattering body's Imaginary ego from within the explicit porn image to fall into impersonal modes of sexual representation that Symbolically splutter and strive towards jouissance because they are suave.

More problematically, we also see that the sexual pleasures of the suavely spluttering subject are embedded in a level of phallic power that is lacking, missing, or remains frustratingly disavowed in both the Imaginary and the Symbolic. Through the Real, a muttering body is inaudible whilst a spluttering body is one that can be partially understood. For example, if we consider the notion that bareback bottoms such as Alex Mason possess an Imaginary ego that 'matters', we see that bareback pornography does something to position that subject as a subject. In the tagline for this particular scene, the viewer as consumer is told that 'Alex Mason gets the gangbang of his life when six studs tear the slutty bottom apart. They fuck, double fuck and breed his hungry hole … all in real time! This is as close as you're gonna get to being there' so that cis gay male identity, personality, and sexual desire remain tethered to Symbolic 'meaning as a substitute for sexuality' (Dean 2000, 188) that disproportionately splutters. Yet, in turn, this is configured through the metonymic potential of a jouissance that splutters and the stimulating impossibility and impersonality of a pornographically mediated 'body that splutters' as a substitute for that meaning. Whilst the Real body of Alex Mason that mutters may be the limit and the actual place of jouissance, we also see in signification and via the signifier that, because the Symbolic 'Other is lacking' (2000, 205), the subject's phallic jouissance is most powerfully realized as a form of spluttering.

In pornographic representations such as this which could be aligned to bareback and chemsex as 'mainstreaming and normalizing', the mattering body 'eroticizes the performance of hypermasculinity through sex acts that foreground danger, risk and abandonment' (Mercer 2017, 139). Here the potential of phallic jouissance is always obscured by the pornographic signifier, unwittingly and negligently limiting jouissance to Imaginary othering. This pornographic subject of the signifier is tethered to a mattering body that is locked into a materiality by the signification of a bodily ego or, as Dean's argument claims, one restrained by the Imaginary (and always to an extent the Symbolic) registers. It is clear that websites such as RawFuckClub.com produce a regulated and commodified representational space where egotistical 'bodies that matter' attempt, yet also fail, to capture and release the inherent anxiety tethered to desire, the phallus, and jouissance. Yet it is within this failure to express jouissance that the body begins to splutter, so that the imprudent preservation of gay male narcissism instilled through an Imaginary Other gives way to a cis-gendered gay subject that is both controlled and restricted by the Symbolic Other whilst remaining aroused and exasperated by jouissance.

Conclusion

Perhaps to grasp jouissance and/or compound it to bodies that splutter, one must understand that 'it is [the] barriers or limits to jouissance that 'permit the full spectrum of desire'

(Dean 2000, 91). In terms of the cis gay male subjects or bodies that we see in bareback and chemsex porn, it is the practices themselves and their attempts to superficially allow 'unlimited access to jouissance that permits desire to flourish' (2000, 91). Yet it seems that to begin to articulate something, indeed anything, of jouissance and its inference in bareback and chemsex porn we must connect to how language always instils a limit to the subject's jouissance as an unconscious pleasure and also allows us to access and gain (temporary) pleasure from it. In light of this, what phallic jouissance alerts us to are the gaps (*failles*) that Lacan claims exist between self and Other. These gaps can be identified as a form of desire that demands. That is, a desire which is never exacting or sufficient but, rather, one that acts as a ceaseless and selfish cathexis; never giving up on its jouissance or, as Lacan states, 'demanding it (*ne cesse pas*)' (1999, 5).

Bruce Fink suggests that it is precisely because desire and pleasure are inadequate that our 'knowledge begins with a deficiency of jouissance' (2004, 155). A lot like the amplification of sexual pleasure and arousal that is represented in bareback and chemsex porn, this leaves both the spectator/consumer as well as porn actors/barebackers wanting more. We/he/they want to see or take another dick deep in a raw, widened, and pulsating hole and then 'we/he/they' want it again, and again, and again. This endlessness and transgressive level of phallic pleasure also seems to locate bareback, pornography, and indeed jouissance close to Lacan's ideas around the *objet a* or 'object as *cause* of desire' (Fink 1995, xiii; original emphasis). This object of desire as its cause will never fulfil desire and meanders through formations of jouissance that endlessly cause 'aporias, paradoxes and conundrums' (1995, xiii). Just as the bodies that splutter do so because of the Symbolic, they also splutter in response to a jouissance that perpetually 'upsets the smooth functioning of structures, systems, and axiomatic fields' to form 'another kind of pleasure' which [is] where the failure of signification to express this cause of desire is always 'decompleted by the alterity or heterogeneity it contains within itself' (1995, xiii).

In this way, it may be beyond the restrictions of market-driven pornography and through self-representational and non-cis-gendered modes of sexual desire that the new possibilities of bareback and chemsex can be situated. The self-representations which have emerged through 'selfie culture' and which encompass a far more amateurish, objective, and raw representation of these practices may be where we next need to relocate our emphasis. The ethnographic processes and 'real' practices that Cole attempts to capture, that Rawfuckclub.com commodifies, and that Dean (2009) narrates have been remediated onto vast, limitless, and potentially queer social media platforms. Here and through processes of self-production and self-representations, the bareback and chemsex so prevalent on Tumblr blogs, Grindr, and Gaydar profiles, and in Snapchat and WhatsApp groups, suggest that there is another layer of representation emerging to reposition the subjective and unconscious vectors of jouissance and bodies that splutter their jouissance through bareback and chemsex.

A lot like the pursuit of jouissance, the production and use of pornography is a search for something transgressive and affirmative. Bareback and chemsex as porn may be responses to the assimilatory and morally repressive discourses of cis-gendered gay men as acceptable others, less marginalized, and now commodified. Perhaps as a way of renegotiating the mattering, spluttering, and muttering potentials that (when compounded) push the body to its own point of subversion of legal, moral, ethical and moral discourses. Pornographies of bareback, and more explicitly their convergent nature in the work of someone like Liam Cole, open up the possibilities that modes of phallic jouissance and bodies that splutter may contain in their capacity to splutter. By reconsidering what cis/gay/male pornography might be in light of jouissance may also allow for new forms of spluttered jouissance to exist as states of productive incoherence and excitement. At once instantaneous and ejaculatory, abject and enigmatic, the spluttering body and the jouissance through which it is torn apart seem to splutter together as impersonal traces of one another.

Disclosure statement

No potential conflict of interest was reported by the author.

References

Arundale, Jean. 2017. *Identity, Narcissism and the Other: Object Relations and Their Obstacles*. London: Karnac Books.
Ashford, Chris. 2015. "Bareback Sex, Queer Legal Theory, and Evolving Socio-Legal Contexts." *Sexualities* 18 (1/2): 195–209.
Barthes, Roland. 1975. *The Pleasure of the Text*. New York: Hill and Wang.
Berg, R. C. 2009. "Barebacking: A Review of the Literature." *Archives of Sexual Behavior* 38 (5): 754–764.
Bersani, Leo. 1987. "Is the Rectum a Grave?" *October* 43: 197–222.
Bersani, Leo. 1995. *Homos*. Cambridge: Harvard University Press.
Bersani, Leo, and Adam Phillips. 2008. *Intimacies*. Chicago and London: University of Chicago Press.
Bond Stockton, Katherine. 2017. "Jouissance, the Gash of Bliss." In *Clinical Encounters in Sexuality – Psychoanalytic Practice and Queer Theory*, edited by Noreen Giffney and Eve Watson, 101–122. Earth, Milky Way: Punctum Books.
Bowie, Malcolm. 1991. *Lacan*. London: Fontana Press.
Cole, Liam. 2012. *Slammed*. USA.
Cole, Liam. 2013. *Overload*. USA.
Cole, Liam. 2014. *Hard Cuts I*. USA.
Cole, Liam. 2015. *Hard Cuts II*. USA.
Davis, Oliver. 2015. "Introduction – A Special Issue of *Sexualities*: Bareback Sex and Queer Theory Across Three National Contexts (France, UK, USA)." *Sexualities* 18 (1/2): 120–126.
Dean, Tim. 2000. *Beyond Sexuality*. Chicago and London: University of Chicago Press.
Dean, Tim. 2009. *Unlimited Intimacy: Reflections on the Subculture of Barebacking*. Chicago and London: University of Chicago Press.
Edelman, Lee. 1994. *Homographesis – Essays in Gay Literary and Cultural Theory*. London: Routledge.
Fink, Bruce. 1995. *The Lacanian Subject: Between Language and Jouissance*. Princeton: Princeton University Press.
Fink, Bruce. 2002. "Knowledge and Jouissance." In *Reading Seminar XX – Lacan's Major Work on Love, Knowledge, and Feminine Sexuality*, edited by Suzanne Barnard and Bruce Fink, 21–46. Albany: State University of New York Press.
Fink, Bruce. 2004. *Lacan to the Letter: Reading Ecrits Closely*. Minnesota: University of Minnesota Press.
Garcia, Christien. 2013. "Limited Intimacy: Barebacking and the Imaginary." *Textual Practice* 27 (6): 1031–1051.
Geldhof, Abe, and Paul Verhaeghe. 2017. "Queer as a new Shelter From Castration." In *Clinical Encounters in Sexuality – Psychoanalytic Practice and Queer Theory*, edited by Noreen Giffney and Eve Watson, 211–221. Earth, Milky Way: Punctum Books.
Greteman, A. J. 2013. "Fashioning a Bareback Pedagogy: Towards a Theory of Risky (Sex) Education." *Sex Education* 13 (S1): S20–S31.
Hocquenghem, Guy. [1972] 1993. *Homosexual Desire*. Durham and London: Duke University Press.

Lacan, Jacques. 1999. *The Seminar of Jacques Lacan – Seminar XX Encore: On Feminine Sexuality, The Limits of Love and Knowledge 1972–73*. New York: Norton.

Lacan, Jacques. [1960] 2003. *Ecrits: A Selection*. London: Routledge.

McNamara, Michael. 2013. "Cumming to Terms: Bareback Pornography, Homonormativity, and Queer Survival in the Time of HIV/AIDS." In *The Moral Panics of Sexuality*, edited by Breanne Fahs, Mary L. Dudy, and Sarah Stage, 226–244. London: Palgrave MacMillan.

Mercer, John. 2017. *Gay Pornography: Representations of Sexuality and Masculinity*. London: I.B Tauris.

O'Hara, S. 1997. "Viral Communication: There's Life Beyond Condoms." *POZ* (November): 69.

Rofes, Eric. 1998. *Dry Bones Breathe: Gay Men Creating Post-AIDS Identities and Cultures*. Binghamton, New York: Harrington Park Press.

Scott, Stuart. 2015. "The Condomlessness of Bareback Sex: Responses to the Unrepresentability of HIV in Treasure Island Media's *Plantin' Seed* and *Slammed*." *Sexualities* 18 (1/2): 210–223.

A psychoanalytic ethics of the pornographic aesthetic

Alison Horbury

ABSTRACT

In his seminar on ethics, Lacan examines how certain forms of art reveal desire to us in ways that allow us to affirm and better handle it in our lives, and positions a psychoanalytic ethics in opposition to traditional ethics – what he describes as 'the cleaning up of desire', through 'modesty', and 'temperateness'. This article asks: can this psychoanalytic ethics be applied to a pornographic aesthetic? Within the vast array of production and performance modalities that shape pornography in the digital era (including the digitized back catalogue), I argue something at once particular and universal in the pornographic aesthetic might be distinguished and articulated prior to any categorization of it being 'good,' 'bad,' or 'better'. Where this aesthetic animates something of the Freudian revolution it may be thought of as an artefact of the libido – our partial drives and erotic life – in ways that differentiate it from other screen cultures. This aesthetic is ethical, I suggest, for refusing to substitute or displace its libidinal origins; here I draw on Barthes' theory of the punctum to consider how the intractability of this aesthetic may 'prick' our symbolic identifications and ideals to generate a more honest engagement with the (libidinal) truth of our desire.

Introduction

In this article, I want to make a claim for the significance of pornography as an ethically aesthetic project that speaks to the concerns of a psychoanalytic praxis. In many ways, it is a simple and seemingly obvious claim, specifically, that a pornographic aesthetic produces an affective experience that invites us to learn something of the reality of human existence in ways that affirm the real drives so often elided, distorted, or co-opted by the world of work and socio-symbolic political ideals. In this, I suggest, a pornographic aesthetic may offer an ethical experience that approximates some of the work done in analysis. This follows the project for ethics outlined in Lacan's (1997) seventh seminar, where the work of art and aesthetic practice is likened to the work of the psychoanalytic clinic in which the subject works to untangle the inhibitions that have been erected, imposed, or imagined as barriers to desire and thus, in removing them, reduce suffering. This ethics is premised on the Freudian revolution: its discovery of the unconscious, the mapping of the libidinal life of the subject through the development of partial drives, and the pleasure-seeking foundation of the ego where, for Freud, 'the sexual instinct does not originally serve the purposes of reproduction' but, rather, seeks 'particular kinds of pleasure' from 'infancy' onwards, where 'it attains its aim of gaining pleasure not only from the genitals but from other parts of the body (the erotogenic zones)' (Freud [1908] 2001, 188). In her seminal work on pornography, Williams (1999, 3 and 6), takes cinematic pornography as a Foucauldian artefact of 'knowledge-pleasure' emanating from a range of socio-cultural and political forces that needs to be understood through the discursive power structures – patriarchy, and the political economy – of its time, nominating feminist discourse as the most logical mode of analyzing the 'symptomology' of this artefact (1999, 5). In contrast, I aim at understanding how the pornographic artefact animates a truth of the Freudian revolution, and submit the pornographic film for analysis as an aesthetic arte-fact of the libido to consider what ethical possibilities may emerge from our engagement with it.[1]

A psychoanalytic ethics is especially pertinent to the study of pornographic aesthetics because, as de Kesel puts it, it is founded on a 'notion of enjoyment (*jouissance*)' (2009, 9) that 'rethink[s] ethics beginning with the moral indifference of the polymorphous-per-verse drive' (2009, 48). In this, de Kesel further notes, a psychoanalytic ethics of the clinic is an '"ethics of the singular": an ethics that is centred not on general, universally valid rules, but on a singular enjoyment that, by definition, withdraws from all forms of gen-erality or universality' (2009, 9). This is in opposition to traditional ethics, what Lacan describes as 'the cleaning up of desire', through a 'modesty', and 'temperateness' (1997, 314) required by the social group where, often, pre-established 'ethical premises' 'fill out in advance the drive's open, polymorphously perverse nature with one's own wishes and fantasies' (de Kesel 2009, 48). Themi points out that a psychoanalytic ethics is thus based on 'the real – as opposed to an imaginary ethics, caught in the ima-ginary' of 'Western moralism' (2015, 312). A psychoanalytic ethics can nevertheless shed light on the role of the individual within a broader social project by means of the work of sublimation – 'satisfaction of the drive, without repression' (Lacan 1998, 165). Indeed, for Freud, what distinguishes civilization is 'the capacity for sublimation': that is, the ability to 'displace' the sexual instinctual 'aim without materially diminishing its intensity' and to 'exchange' it for 'another one, which is no longer sexual but which is psychically related to the first aim' ([1908] 2001, 187). Lacan takes up this notion of sublimation where it underpins the function (and form) of aesthetics in cultural production, as I detail later, and is central to my suggestion that the pornographic film may be read as an aesthetic document of the libido. To establish how, I want to begin by reconsider-ing how 'aesthetics' is mobilized in both art and screen discourses to nominate a 'quality' screen/visual text from the point of view of a psychoanalytic ethics. I then introduce Roland Barthes' ([1980] 2000) work on the 'punctum' to consider how the viewer of por-nography may be 'pricked' by what I want to articulate as the intractability of the porno-graphic aesthetic to its libidinal referent. To isolate one (or several) examples from the plethora of pornographic films in existence risks reducing the concept of pornography's aesthetic to a genre, or 'type', immediately contradicted by another (more particular to the reader). Moreover, as John Champagne (1997, 76) has argued, such choices inevita-bly need to be anchored in 'the social and historical conditions in which certain kinds of texts circulate', if not 'the everyday uses to which subjects put such texts', which it is not possible to do here. Instead, I invite the reader to consider how their own experience of pornography might bear witness to what I outline here.

A question of aesthetics

The aesthetic properties of the pornographic film have been subject to a growing field of philosophical analysis evaluating its ability to become 'good' art (for example, Dennis 2009; Maes and Levinson 2015). Often, as Maes and Levinson (2015, 3) point out, 'aesthetic experience' is defined in Kantian terms, as that which aims at and results in a response from a spectator who judges and enjoys the work 'apart from any interest' (Kant [1790] 2008, 36–37); that is, art inspires contemplation, whereas 'pornography aims for a particular response, sexual arousal, that is anathema to artistic contemplation or aesthetic experience' (Maes and Levinson 2015, 3). Screen studies similarly categorize pornography according to its aim/use as an affective 'body genre' (Williams 1991; Church 2017), but further subjects it to a commercial/art distinction: between an audio-visual text that has high production values – a visually appealing *mise en scène*, slickly edited, tastefully lit, and framed with a high-quality camera – and a text that has all this but does something with the audio-visual form that asks the viewer to contemplate its meaning. Bourdieu's definition of commercial cinema's 'popular aesthetic' might stand in for commercial pornography that 'subordinate[s]' visual 'form to function' ([1984] 2010, 24) where 'formal experiments and specifically artistic effects' are employed 'only to the extent that they can be forgotten and do not get in the way of the substance of the work' ([1984] 2010, 25). Such aesthetics have been in use since porn's home-video revolution to a greater or lesser extent. Indeed, many producers now deploy a visual style that is glossy, polished, and adept at using montage and ellipses to create what Heath describes as the 'artifice of continuity and coherence' in narrative cinema's 'performance of time' (1981, 114).

Yet where digitization and the storing and retrieval function of the internet has opened up access to a vast back-catalogue of pornographic film, I suggest we are better able to appreciate the specific aesthetic modalities of pornography that distinguish it from other forms of screen entertainment. It may be tempting, here, to isolate the 'high-end' visually sophisticated films – including those with rich or complex narratives – from productions that have little or no scenario, less professional cameras (visual style and editing), amateur performers, low budgets, or rough or gonzo footage. But the aesthetic modes of all are, as Maes and Levinson (2015, 7) suggest, shaped by '[m]arket forces' (see also Church 2017), and I want to argue here that these visual and narrative differences do not significantly alter the ethical aesthetic of pornographic films. In fact, most critiques of pornography's aesthetic remain tied to a distorted valuation in the category of aesthetics that psychoanalysis can shed light on. As Terry Eagleton points out:

> Aesthetics was born as a discourse of the body. In its original formulation by the German philosopher Alexander Baumgarten, the term refers not in the first place to art, but, as the Greek *aisthesis* would suggest, to the whole region of human perception and sensation, in contrast to the more rarefied domain of conceptual thought. (1990, 13)

Where aesthetics is recognized as a theory of affect located in the body is the point at which psychoanalysis has ventured to evaluate specific artistic or cultural products for their ability to inspire a contemplation of ethics. Indeed, as de Kesel argues, it is precisely '[t]he ethical function that Lacan attributes to the aesthetic' that 'reveals the contours of his conceptualisation of psychoanalysis' (2009, 9). This relocates the discussion of aesthetics away from formal mastery (visual style) to a question of the diegesis informing the affective experience of the work, as it is in tragedy.[2] Both Freud and Lacan follow Nietzsche here in recognizing the 'sensual' interest with which all art is in some way invested. Nietzsche is sceptical of attempts to understand an aesthetic object as 'pleasure without interest', mocking Kant's naiveté in suggesting that 'one can *even* view undraped female statues "without interest"' (Nietzsche [1887] 1989, 104; original emphasis), and argues, instead, that in an aesthetic state, 'sensuality is not overcome', but rather 'transfigured' where it 'no longer enters consciousness as sexual excitement' ([1887] 1989, 111). In this 'transfiguration', Nietzsche prefaces a central issue in a psychoanalytic ethics where it meets aesthetics: sublimation. Where sublimation, as Lacan (1997, 95) quotes Freud, '[i]s a process that concerns object libido', it is, I aim to show, central to our ethical estimation of moving image pornography.

An ethics of psychoanalysis: *das Ding* and sublimation

Where an ethics of psychoanalysis speaks to the question of a pornographic aesthetic is in its articulation of the principal relation a subject has to the discovery at the heart of the Freudian revolution: to the truth of one's desire vis-à-vis the Freudian 'thing', *das Ding* (the Thing), the primary repressed 'archaic' libidinal 'nucleus' of the subject's cathected partial drives (see Lacan 1997, 93; Themi 2014, 15–18). Where *das Ding* comes to name the unconscious 'polymorphous-perverse libidinal base' of the subject-as-'pleasure animal', de Kesel notes, it is felt as an 'intimately distant thing' that is the origin of our desire (2009, 83–87). And, as de Kesel further observes (2009, 53), '[t]he aim of analysis lies entirely and exclusively in a confrontation with desire and the only ethical question that counts here is whether the analysand has "acted in conformity with the desire that is in [him]"' such that they can choose to act in accordance with this knowledge. The question of desire relevant to the pornographic film (if not all film) is the intervention of the signifier into the subject's experience and the subsequent formation of the Freudian thing – *das Ding* – as it relates to Lacan's *objet petit a*, the partial drives, erogenous zones, and cathected part-objects. Lacan points to a subject's emergence in the signifying chain of symbolic meaning – the 'I' that speaks and is represented as a coherent identity for an Other – at a threshold of experience that leaves something behind, *das Ding*, a 'beyond-of-the-signified' (1997, 54) tied to the 'primordial law' of the incest taboo associated with 'the maternal thing, the mother, insofar as she occupies the place of that thing, of *das Ding*' (1997, 67). That is, 'the first apprehension of reality by the subject' (Lacan 1997, 51) is a consequence of 'the signifying structure impos[ing] itself between perception and consciousness'. Subsequently, where the imposition of the signifier orients *das Ding* as something 'foreign' to the subject – 'the first outside' – it also sets up a 'search for satisfaction' in something that can signify *das Ding* or at least act as a 'point of reference' for 'the world of desires' (1997, 52). In this moment, the 'division in the experience of reality' (1997, 52), the subject finds itself within the operations of the pleasure and reality principles that mediate and regulate distance to *das Ding*. Lacan notes that '[d]as Ding is to be identified with an impulse "to find again" which "characterize[s]" *das Ding* "as a lost object"' (1997, 58). Yet there is a transition in Lacan's work that sees *objet petit a* as representative of the lost object where, Dylan Evans notes, it becomes 'any object which sets desire in motion, especially the partial objects which define the drives', further noting that 'the drives do not seek to attain the *objet petit a,* but rather circle around it' (1996, 125).

Here, Lacan shows where the signifier intervenes in the libidinal life of the subject, and through this, I argue, we can begin to see pornography as a document of libido, where a fascination with the partial drives and part-objects circling out from *objet a* become representative of the libido's substitutive pleasures. Following Freud, Lacan distinguishes the drive as a 'terrain of energy', a 'constant force' seeking satisfaction but, importantly, as it is not a purely biological function, its satisfactions can be found through displacement – through sublimation: a 'satisfaction of the drive, without repression' (Lacan 1998, 165) – essential to the topic of aesthetics. We see this sublimation more obviously in the articulation of the partial drives where, for example, in the oral drive 'it is not food that satisfies' but, rather, 'the pleasure of the mouth' (1998, 167) in its relation to the 'series' of satisfactions that circle out from the original source of oral pleasure, the breast. Lacan describes the partial drives in terms of montage, 'as having neither head nor tail – in the sense in which one speaks of montage in a surrealist collage' (1998, 169), and being 'that montage by which sexuality participates in the psychical life' (1998, 176). For where the signifier intervenes into the subject's libidinal life, a synchronic 'scaffolding of signifiers' provides a 'metonymic' substitution (1998, 176) and 'series of satisfactions that are tied to the relation to the object' in the subject's search for it (Lacan 1997, 58). A non-pornographic example of the substitution between the libido and the signifier cited by Lacan is the classical comedy of Aristophanes in *The Clouds*, 'where the id gets the upper hand, [and] pulls on the boots of language for its own use', and in doing so, shows us '[w]hat enters at the start in the dialectic of language – namely, sexual needs most especially, all hidden needs in general – is what you see produced right before your eyes' (2017, 122).

It is here that pornography's aesthetic modality may be distinguished from other forms of screen culture – specifically, narrative cinema and television – where the former strips back the layers of sublimation and substitution circling out from *das Ding* to engage the viewer openly with those earliest, originary substitutions – the part-objects and aims – while the latter works on a plane of substitution that keeps the original libidinal truth masked and displaced. That is, pornography offers a more direct (less sublimated) satisfaction to the subject – in Nietzsche's terms, there is no 'transfiguration' into non-sexual aims – by animating (to varying degrees) a montage of part-objects representing the aims of the partial drives circling out from *objet a*, what Lacan demarcates as 'the effective presence, as such, of desire' or 'what now remains to indicate desire' (1998, 153). This it does regardless of its success as a screen object vis-à-vis plot or visual style. Pornographic GIFs are particularly illustrative of the discordant nature of this aesthetic, especially where it departs from our expectations of culturally specific symbolic structures, ideals, and taboos that bar access (relatively) to our libidinal truth – that is, those symbolic modalities which narrative film and television work to reproduce. The porn GIF stages what much feature film pornography does in extended form: the polymorphous perversity of the partial drives – oral, anal, genital, invocatory, and especially scopic – and their search for substitutive pleasures in a medium or aesthetic modality that does not (necessarily) fill out these drives beforehand with ideals via elaborate plots or scenarios.

No doubt some narrative film and television works in close proximity to this pornographic aesthetic, showing us, seemingly contrarily, where the signifier/s of symbolic culture are still invested within the pornographic aesthetic. Equally, too, much narrative-rich pornography attempts to add more substitutive layers of signification around the animation of the part-objects and drives, especially those genres aimed towards couples and women, which leads to an important distinction apropos the pornographic aesthetic: where the partial drives are already invested in the signifier via 'metonymic' substitution (Lacan 1998, 176), then no pornography can arouse without a signifier. That is, the pornographic aesthetic is not necessarily a pure, direct – unmediated – animation of the drives or, indeed, consistent in this effect. To the extent that all pornography – whether 'high-end', amateur, gonzo, or otherwise – animates the libidinal truth of the Freudian revolution, it does so through a signifying structure. To articulate how, I turn to Roland Barthes' concept of the 'punctum' (Barthes [1980] 2000), where it correlates to both a 'third meaning' in film (Barthes 1977) and the Lacanian Real, before approaching how a pornographic aesthetic may be considered ethical.

The pornographic aesthetic and the punctum

I want to suggest that Barthes 'punctum' – that detail in the image that 'attracts or distresses me' ([1980] 2000, 40) – can be applied to the pornographic aesthetic already outlined to show where its animation (and documentation) of the drives, part-objects, and aims is, at once, tied to a Real referent that marks this aesthetic out from narrative film and television, and yet, simultaneously, arouses by virtue of the effect of the signifier.

Insofar as the pornographic aesthetic may be distinguished by its capturing of real genitals and explicit acts, it may be likened to Barthes' thesis that the photogram 'is never distinguished from its referent (from what it represents) or at least it is not *immediately* or *generally* distinguished from its referent' ([1980] 2000, 5; original emphases); rather, 'they are glued together' ([1980] 2000, 6) such that the image 'has something tautological about it: a pipe, here, is always and intractably a pipe' ([1980] 2000, 5). That is, no matter how many layers of symbolic meaning are woven into/over the pornographic image, the image also (always) signifies the Real genitals and bodily objects: this is its intractable aesthetic. Nevertheless, where 'the signifying structure imposes itself' between the subject and the Real thing (Lacan 1997, 51) the pornographic referent is metonymically cathected to a signifying structure: breasts, buttocks, phalli, and so on, are the referent for part-objects; sexual play with lips, mouths, vaginas, and anus are also already erotogenic orifices and connote the oral, anal, and genital drives. Not to mention the scopic and invocatory drives that are realized in the play of signifiers. Here signification may work through a particular texture, pitch, or timbre of a sound or word (dirty talk or otherwise), a gesture (bodily movement, the affect of a performer), the physical attributes of a performer's body/genitals, a particular 'look' (costume and styling), some element of *mise en scène* (including urine, semen, saliva), camera-work or editing, the particularity of scenario or establishment of a taboo (incest, etc.), or the absence thereof, or that infinitesimal minutia of meaning established in the conflation of one or more of these signifiers coming together. All of these wrap the image-referent – genitals and sexual acts – in a particular signifying system.

Where the pornographic referent is metonymically cathected to the partial drives and aims 'circling out' from that Thing in the Real, however, something is signified that cannot be fully known in symbolic terms. Barthes alludes to this Real when he puts it that the photogram:

always leads the corpus I need back to the body I see; it is the absolute Particular, the sovereign Contingency, matte and somehow stupid, the This (this photograph, and not Photography), in short, what Lacan calls the *Tuché*, the Occasion, the Encounter, the Real, and its indefatigable expression. ([1980] 2000, 4)

Despite the intractability of the referent, however, it is the signifier that Barthes is interested in, theorizing that his fascination with photography is animated when a particular (often incongruent) signifier 'pricks' or 'pierces' ([1980] 2000, 26) his otherwise 'general interest' in the image. He calls this 'prick' the 'punctum' ([1980] 2000, 27) – that element that disturbs, 'breaks', or 'punctuates' the 'average affect' of reading the image as a cultural, political, or socio-historical artefact – and terms the latter the 'studium' ([1980] 2000, 26), an engagement with the image via 'demi-volition' that is produced through one's 'education' into the myths of culture ([1980] 2000, 27–28). Yet Barthes marks out the erotic from the pornographic image, suggesting the latter is 'naïve', without 'intention' or 'calculation', and is 'constituted by the presentation of one thing: sex: no secondary untimely object ever manages to half conceal, delay, or distract' ([1980] 2000, 41). The erotic image, on the other hand, 'has been disturbed, fissured', and thus transformed ([1980] 2000, 41), where, for instance, the 'close-ups of genitalia [shift] from the pornographic to the erotic by photographing the fabric of underwear at very close range: the photograph is no longer unary, since I am interested in the texture of the material' ([1980] 2000, 42). Here Barthes' disinterest or displacement from genital to material suggests that the genital in itself cannot be erotic,[3] but, I argue, the genitals and real part-objects signify because, as I have already outlined, they refer to real part-objects/ drives that are nonetheless already cathected to the signifier for the speaking being.

Therefore, where Barthes suggests that pornography's document of genitals and sexual acts is 'without intention' (and thus do not signify), I suggest, instead, that the intractable referent is cathected to that 'series' of satisfactions which circles out from the original source of pleasure, where it may 'pierce' the viewer. Indeed, Barthes' description of the punctum perfectly describes porn's intractable signifying aesthetic: where 'the image launche[s] desire beyond what it permits us to see' ([1980] 2000, 59). Insofar as they are moving images, however, we might question how our perception of what is signified therein is engaged. Barthes suggests that the punctum is often only realized 'after the fact, when the photograph is no longer in front of me and I think back on it' ([1980] 2000, 53) such that, he argues, film does not allow for the punctum because 'in front of the screen, I am not free to shut my eyes; otherwise, opening them again, I would not discover the same image' ([1980] 2000, 55). Here, Eagleton's (1990, 13) reminder that aesthetics is 'a discourse of the body' that engages with 'human perception and sensation', over 'conceptual thought', becomes useful in thinking about the ethical way in which pornography's intractable aesthetic may 'pierce' the viewer. Although, for Barthes, 'there is no punctum in the pornographic image; at most it amuses me (and even then, boredom quickly follows)' ([1980] 2000, 59), I suggest we can conceive of the punctum in pornography in relation to the physical 'discourse of the body' that is 'pierced' by arousal and, consequently, can inspire the 'reflection' of the punctum – why did that arouse me? – especially where the arousal contradicts one's conscious investment in symbolic identifications and ideals. For as Barthes puts it, 'once there is a punctum, a blind field is created' ([1980] 2000, 57) where 'a secondary action of knowledge or reflection' is required to make sense of it ([1980] 2000, 5).

Where we can see how the punctum works in the pornographic aesthetic is, I suggest, through Barthes' notion of 'third meaning' in film, which correlates to Lacan's notion of the Real. In film, Barthes identifies a first 'informational' 'message' (denotation) which informs the second-level meaning of intended symbolic connotations (connotation) (1977, 52); a 'third meaning', however, refers to something 'obtuse' that escapes symbolic meaning (Barthes 1977, 52) – a 'supplement that my intellection cannot succeed in absorbing, at once persistent and fleeting, smooth and elusive' (1977, 54), something 'that cause[es] my reading to slip' (1977, 55). This follows Lacan's (1997, 121) formulation of the Real as a 'gap or hole' in the symbolic realm (of language, meaning, culture) that the Thing represents, what, in the punctum, Barthes ([1980] 2000, 57) calls a 'blind field'. Lacan puts it that 'to a certain extent, a work of art always involves encircling the Thing' (1997, 141). Indeed, while art 'imitates the objects they represent [...] their end is certainly not to represent them' but, rather, to 'make something different out of that object': specifically, to 'establish a certain relationship to the Thing' and 'to encircle and to render [it] both present and absent' (1997, 141). Insofar as the pornographic aesthetic intractably represents those Real part-objects, drives, and erotogenic orifices that metonymically 'stand in' for the Thing, their particular presence may be said to simultaneously 'encircle' a gap in the symbolic that nevertheless signifies a 'third meaning' for the viewer. It is here that the particularity of the viewer is important, for the punctum does not necessarily correlate to the intended (first and second) meanings; as Barthes puts it, 'the detail that interests me is not [...] intentional', but rather 'it occurs in the field of the photographed thing like a supplement that is at once inevitable and delightful' ([1980] 2000, 47). That is, the porn that 'pricks' may not be the porn one thought one was looking for, and what one finds erotic in it may not be obvious to another. Barthes' conception that this meaning is 'obtuse' – in the punctum what 'animates me' ([1980] 2000, 20) – may, I suggest, 'pierce' the viewer in the form of a traumatic encounter, felt as anxiety, what Lacan calls a 'signal of the Real' (2014, 157) – a 'cut' or 'furrow' (2014, 76) that may elude immediate understanding. Whether this encounter is 'chance' – Lacan's *tuché* – or unconsciously aimed at through repetition (see Lacan 1998, 53–64) is where a question of ethics may be introduced to this aesthetic.

The ethics of the pornographic aesthetic

Where pornography's intractable aesthetic can be of ethical import is where it can teach the subject something about the truth of their desire and *objet a* beyond socio-symbolic values of 'good' representations, or politically 'bad' pornography. No doubt this assumes an ideal viewer, if not ideal pornography, but, as Todd McGowan has argued, in the focus on 'contextual factors' of production and reception, 'we lose the possibility of being able to see the way in which an aesthetic object like a film might not fit within the context where it appears' (2007, ix) – as Barthes' punctum also indicates. Indeed, this article follows McGowan's (2007, x) in theorizing a spectator that pornography 'demands', rather than an empirical one.

The ethics of the analytic clinic regards the tenor of substitution that has been adopted by the subject and the extent to which they have allowed their desire to be inhibited by external censorship – the common morality of the social group that requires a certain amount of what Themi calls 'instinctual abatement' (2014, 27) – for cohesion. It is here that sublimation – in the form of substitution – becomes an ethical issue for the individual but also, de Kesel notes (2009, 9), for 'the wider culture'. Themi follows de Kesel in observing three realms of culture into which Lacan argues we might sublimate our drives – 'art, religion, and science' – but further notes these all hold just as much potential for a repressive treatment of the drives when there is a 'repressing' of 'some portion of the truth' (Themi 2014, 27). As Freud foresaw in 1908, for example, capitalist orders function by siphoning substitutive pleasures towards objects found in cultural industries that can deceptively distort the origins and aims of the drives (Freud [1908] 2001, 182–183).

The philosophy of art might typically be introduced here to distinguish valued forms of sublimation from commercial industries but, although pornography is largely a commercial product, it can be distinguished from other entertainment forms by its intractable Real referent and less indirect substitutions. In aesthetic criticism applied to art/screen objects, a distinction is placed on the establishment of a suitable distance from the 'thing' (*qua* Kant) – through the play of substitutive signifiers circling out from it – such that a space for contemplation and 'objective' regard of its content and beauty effect is created. For Barthes, this is the *studium* engagement of a 'sympathetically interested' 'docile cultural subject' towards 'what the photograph has to say', which is ultimately tied to cultural value: images that signify 'respectability, family life, conformity' ([1980] 2000, 43). Where these substitutions take on a baroque-signifying chain of re-substitutions, then, they can fetishistically, if not, as Themi (2014, 27) notes of religion, neurotically, play with the subject matter in a hysterical 'encircling' and 'obsessional' 'displacement' of the Thing. Here, the beauty-effect of the signifying chain may distort the drives, and thus make neurosis beautiful, evident in art-cinema such as Lars von Trier's *Antichrist* (2009) and *Nymphomaniac* (2013), or, invoking the weight of social morality, Steve McQueen's *Shame* (2012). Equally, body-genres esteemed for achieving affective thrills through a formal mastery of the visual and thematic field show society's repressed sexual content as distorted and horrific (see Creed 1993; Wood [1986] 2003), evident in films such as de Palma's *Carrie* (1976).

The pornographic aesthetic is ethical insofar as its documentation of the polymorphous perversity of partial objects and drives is not immediately displaced; however, this is not to say that its signification is without distortion. Although a spectator, like Lacan's articulation of de Sade's libertine thesis, 'is invited to pursue to the limit the demands of his lust, and to realize them' beyond any sentimental morality (1997, 79), it is the particular signifying structure that frames these parts, acts, and aims of a libidinal impulse that becomes important. Is the libidinal drive/act framed within a context of innocence, curiosity, violence, or trauma? What taboo is invoked so it can be transgressed? In this way, pornography may distort the libido in the same neurotic, perverse, or violent manner as other moving image cultural production; however, I suggest that the intractability of the image to its referent (the real genitals, part-objects, and drives) disturbs whatever socio-cultural or ideological signifying system is in play, and this may 'pierce' our 'average' engagement with the film.

What arises, then, is the question at the heart of a psychoanalytic ethics regarding the subject's relation to *das Ding* and their management of desire: is the subject's super-ego injunction on enjoyment stronger than their commitment to the truth of their desire? What defence might be mounted to manage the lack of distance in pornography's push towards the real polymorphous perversity of the drives? The punctum of pornography may effectively invoke that element of classical tragedy felt by the spectator – guilt – where, Freud estimates, even if one can reject or negate the material of their unconscious, one is 'nevertheless bound to be aware of this responsibility as a source of guilt whose basis is unknown' ([1917] 2001, 331). It is here that psychoanalysis plays its ethical role in untangling the subject's conscious reactions to unconscious thoughts and impulses. The preoccupations of the clinic, de Kesel observes, 'is a guilt with respect to desire *itself* (2009, 53 original emphasis), and the only 'cure' that can be imagined is one where the subject resolves the conflicting demands upon desire – the moral super-ego (the law) – and thus answers the question 'Have I acted in accordance with my desire?' because, 'from an individual point of view, the only thing of which one can be guilty is of having given ground relative to one's desire' (Lacan 1997, 319, quoted in de Kesel 2009, 53). In an analogy with pornography, the spectator may react with repudiation, disgust, or repulsion because the signifiers of beauty providing that 'necessary distance' – the studium – are absent or reduced. For Barthes, for example, pornography 'represents the sexual organs' as 'a motionless object (a fetish), flattered like an idol that does not leave its niche' ([1980] 2000, 57–59). But this assumes a still-image that one may turn away from in defence ('it bores me', 'I'm not interested'): in the intractability of the pornographic aesthetic there is less time to negate the truth – those unconscious desires felt in the body's arousal, especially where that image is moving (i.e. repeats and insists) as opposed to Barthes' photogram, where one may reject its distressing punctum and admire it only through the studium (see [1980] 2000, 36). That is, where Barthes argues that the moving-image leaves no space for reflection, I argue that the insistence of the moving-image leaves little space for negating the libido: if I shut my eyes, the intractable Real is still there when I open them – perhaps even more so than before (likewise if I choose another pornographic film). Although one may focus on the signifying elements of the image – the scenario, the performers' styling, the editing, and so on – it is difficult to ignore the punctum of arousal. Indeed, as Barthes notes, 'the *punctum* shows no preference for morality or good taste: the *punctum* can be ill-bred' ([1980] 2000, 43; original emphases), because 'if the studium is ultimately always coded, the punctum is not', such that, in the punctum, 'I dismiss all knowledge, all culture, I refuse to inherit anything from another eye than my own' ([1980] 2000, 51). Here we encounter the particularity of the subject's libidinal truth, including the particularity of jouissance achieved in the negation of super-ego moral injunctions, where one's unique mode of enjoyment may be intensified because it is achieved beyond the pleasure principle.

On the other hand, the punctum of arousal may inspire a stronger defence as a result, particularly if one has 'fill[ed] out in advance the drive's open, polymorphously perverse nature with' their 'own wishes and fantasies' (de Kesel 2009, 48), and thus perceive the documented libido as originating from a deliberately – ideologically or pathologically – amoral place. The feminist interpretation of pornography as a symptom of patriarchy's misogyny, for example, presumes that the libidinal acts documented in pornography originate from an intent to demoralize or humiliate women, whose libido has been 'filled out in advance' with innocence. Undoubtedly, however, pornography also stages neurotic, obsessional, and distorted expressions of libido, as I consider in the Conclusion.

Conclusion: distortions to pornography's ethical aesthetic

Lacan holds that psychoanalytic practice can claim 'the status of an ethics' precisely because it aims at exposing the ethics at work within the individual – one's own censorship – as opposed to those of the community. In this, pornography can afford a confrontation within those particular inhibitions that limit the realizing of libidinal enjoyment, but can also encourage us to brave our internal censorship in order to access the particularity of our desire where, as Lacan notes, the 'liberating truth' of analysis is '[n]ot a universal truth, of course, but a particular truth' that 'appears to everyone in its intimate specificity' (1997, 24).

A psychoanalytic ethics also informs the production of pornography's on-screen aesthetic. Many involved in the porn industry may routinely go beyond their own limits (and particular libidinal truth) in pursuit of economic or career gain; here, a difference between action and desire may be discerned in each performer's rationale for working in the industry, what Lacan describes as 'return[ing] to the meaning of action … whether it be healthy, sick, normal or morbid' by way of 'the desire that inhabits it' (1997, 312–313). Where desire for money disguises other, unconscious motivations for entering the industry, the lack of (ethical) libidinal knowledge is felt in the on-screen aesthetic: in unconscious gestures, reactions, or the creation of a particular persona. Over time, these unrealized motivations can either become inhibited by an external criticism too great for the performer to bear, or they confront their own ethical limitations that the pursuit of money has obscured, as the subjects of Bauer and Gradus' documentary *Hot Girls Wanted* (2015) illustrate.

Where pornography remains tied to the service of goods and aims at increasingly displaced forms of libidinal transgression to cash-in on page-views, we can arguably see, at the level of aesthetics, the animation of the death-drive. Lacan opens seminar seven by posing a question about the 'attraction to transgression' the analysand brings with them to the clinic, somewhere between the fantasy of the murder of the father and of a deeper 'more obscure and original transgression' of the death drive (1997, 2). The pornographic industry certainly requires a modest confrontation with the latter, in that a performer's health is always potentially at risk, if not because of the ruinous expenditure involved in pursuing desire. But this documentation of a death-drive stripped of 'objective' beauty asks us to consider the psychoanalytic distinction between 'normal' pleasure and pleasure that goes beyond – that is, jouissance – in our engagement with pornography's intractable aesthetic of the Real where, de Kesel notes, from a psychoanalytic point of view 'enjoyment can no longer be situated inside the limits of desire and the pleasure principle, but is to be regarded as an exponent of the *death drive*' (2009, 125; original emphasis). Towards the end of his ethics seminar, Lacan notes that an 'ethics of psychoanalysis has nothing to do with speculation about prescriptions for, or the regulation of, what I have called the service of goods' and is, rather, an ethics 'that is expressed in what we call the tragic sense of life' (1997, 313). Where pornography is tied up in the service of goods, it does, nevertheless, contradict capitalist imperatives to sublimate the drives in displaced forms of production and consumption. This is arguably the significance of pornography's ethical aesthetic: its recognition of desire, the taboos that inhibit it, and confrontation with libidinally honest satisfactions so often obscured by the service of goods can, if realized, subvert those attempts to displace our desire towards objects and ideals antithetical to our best interests.

Notes

1. Williams claims some psychoanalytic insight in her analysis, but it is psychoanalysis at the service of feminism which, as I have argued (Horbury 2017), tends to focus only on those

aspects of Freud that serve the pre-established wishes and (unconscious) fantasies of feminist discourses.
2. I would note that in narrative cinema, visual mastery is often used to create affect – as in the horror genre.
3. A disingenuous reading on Barthes part, where, as Michael Halley (1995, 289) has observed, his 'aversion' to the eroticized violence of *Story of the Eye* (Bataille [1928] 2012) is 'a pure clerk's reaction'.

Disclosure statement

No potential conflict of interest was reported by the author.

References

Barthes, Roland. 1977. *Image, Music, Text*, translated by Steven Heath. London: Fontana Press.
Barthes, Roland. [1980] 2000. *Camera Lucida: Reflections of Photography*, translated by Richard Howard. London: Vintage Books.
Bataille, George. [1928] 2012. *Story of the Eye*. London: Penguin Classics.
Bauer, Jill and Ronna Gradus, dir. 2015. *Hot Girls Wanted*. USA.
Bourdieu, Pierre. [1984] 2010. *Distinction: A Social Critique of the Judgment of Taste*. London and New York: Routledge.
Champagne, John. 1997. '"Stop Reading Films!": Film Studies, Close Analysis, and Gay Pornography.' *Cinema Journal* 36 (4): 76–97.
Church, David. 2017. 'Introduction.' *Porn Studies* 4 (3): 257–262.
Creed, Barbara. 1993. *The Monstrous Feminine: Film, Feminism, Psychoanalysis*. London: Routledge.
de Kesel, Marc. 2009. *Eros and Ethics: Reading Jacques Lacan's Seminar VII*, translated by Sigi Jöttkandt. Albany: State University of New York.
Dennis, Kelly. 2009. *Art/Porn: A History of Seeing and Touching*. Oxford and New York: Berg.
de Palma, Brian, dir. 1976. *Carrie*. USA.
Eagleton, Terry. 1990. *The Ideology of the Aesthetic*. Maldon: Blackwell Publishing.
Evans, Dylan. 1996. *An Introductory Dictionary of Lacanian Psychoanalysis*. London and New York: Routledge.
Freud, Sigmund. [1908] 2001. '"Civilised" Sexual Morality and Modern Nervous Illness.' In *The Standard Edition of The Complete Psychological Works of Sigmund Freud Volume IX (1906-1908)*, edited by James Strachey, Anna Freud, Alix Strachey and Alan Tyson, 181–204. London: Vintage Books, The Hogarth Press and the Institute of Psycho-analysis.
Freud, Sigmund. [1917] 2001. 'The Development of the Libido.' In *The Standard Edition of the Complete Psychological Works of Sigmund Freud, Volume XVI*, translated by James Strachey, Anna Freud, Alix Strachey and Alan Tyson, 320–338. London: The Hogarth Press and the Institute of Psychoanalysis.
Heath, Stephen. 1981. *Questions of Cinema*. Bloomington: Indiana University Press.
Halley, Michael. 1995. ' … And a Truth for a Truth: Barthes on Bataille.' In *On Bataille: Critical Essays*, edited by Leslie Anne Boldt-Irons, 285–294. Albany: State University of New York.
Horbury, Alison. 2017. '"What Does Feminism Want?".' *Continental Thought & Theory: A Journal of Intellectual Freedom* 1 (3): 567–592.
Kant, Immanuel. [1790] 2008. *Critique of Judgement*, translated by James Creed Meredith. Oxford: Oxford University Press.
Lacan, Jacques. 1997. *The Seminar of Jacques Lacan, Book VII: The Ethics of Psychoanalysis 1959–1960*, translated by Dennis Porter, edited by Jacques-Alain Miller. New York: W. W. Norton & Company.
Lacan, Jacques. 1998. *The Seminar of Jacques Lacan: Book XI The Four Fundamental Concepts of Psychoanalysis*, translated by Alan Sheridan, edited by Jacques-Alain Miller. New York: W. W. Norton & Company.

Lacan, Jacques. 2014. *The Seminar of Jacques Lacan, Book X: Anxiety*, translated by A. R. Price, edited by Jacques-Alain Miller. Cambridge: Polity.

Lacan, Jacques. 2017. *The Seminar of Jacques Lacan: Book V, Formations of the Unconscious*, translated by Russell Grigg, edited by Jacques-Alain Miller. Cambridge: Polity.

Maes, Hans, and Levinson Levinson, eds. 2015. *Art & Pornography: Philosophical Essays*. Oxford: Oxford University Press.

McGowan, Todd. 2007. *The Real Gaze: Film Theory After Lacan*. Albany: SUNY.

McQueen, Steve, dir. 2012. *Shame*. UK.

Nietzsche, Friedrich. [1887] 1989. 'On the Genealogy of Morals.' In *On the Genealogy of Morals and Ecce Homo*, edited by Walter Kaufmann, 15–163. New York: Random House.

Themi, Tim. 2014. *Lacan's Ethics and Nietzsche's Critique of Platonism*. Albany: SUNY.

Themi, Tim. 2015. 'Bataille and the Erotics of the Real.' *Parrhesia* 24: 312–335.

von Trier, Lars, dir. 2009. *Antichrist*. Denmark.

von Trier, Lars, dir. 2013. *Nymphomaniac Volume I and II*. Denmark.

Williams, Linda. 1991. 'Film Bodies: Gender, Genre, and Excess.' *Film Quarterly* 44 (4): 2–13.

Williams, Linda. 1999. *Hard Core: Power, Pleasure, and the 'Frenzy of the Visible'*. Berkeley: University of California Press.

Wood, Robin. [1986] 2003. 'The American Nightmare: Horror in the 70s.' In *Hollywood From Vietnam to Reagan ... And Beyond*, 63–84. New York: Columbia University Press.

The social/political potential of illusions: enthusiasm and feminist porn

Maggie Ann Labinski

ABSTRACT
What are the social/political possibilities of 'feminist porn?' How might feminists broach these films within the context of their wider communities? Given the uncertainty that surrounds the future of this genre, many feminists have embraced a posture of 'ambivalence' about feminist porn. In what follows, I argue against the necessity of such an approach. More specifically, I suggest that Sigmund Freud offers a compelling example of what it might look like to lead with 'enthusiasm' when faced with the unknown. I conclude by exploring how Freud's insights might be used to expand the impact of feminist porn within the social/political sphere.

Historical origins

The set of films that tend to be classified as 'feminist porn' is diverse. Still, within the United States, the bulk of this media shares similar origins. In the 1980s, feminist scholars and activists were fully entangled in debates about the consequences of 'mainstream pornography' (Dworkin 1981; Dworkin and MacKinnon 1988; Cornell 2000; Spector 2006; Taormino et al. 2013; Bronstein 2015).[1] The vast majority agreed that the traditional industry was perpetuating a culture of sexism, racism, and classism. However, they disagreed about how those who identified with the feminist movement should respond: what course of action do these films demand?

Some maintained that the only appropriate solution was engaged resistance (MacKinnon 1987; Russell 1988; Ramos 2000).[2] As Andrea Dworkin and Catherine MacKinnon suggest, pornography not only appears to depend upon the commodification of human sexuality; it also supports the notion that this commodification is desirable. It implies that to dominate another, to render them an object, is sexy. More specifically, pornography would seem to especially eroticize the domination of women:

> Pornography is a systematic act against women on every level of its social existence. It takes rape culture to require and permit it. It takes acts against women to make it; selling it is a series of acts (transactions) that provide the incentive to make it and mass-produce the abuse; consuming it is an act against women and spawns more acts that make many more women's actual lives dangerous, meaningless, and unequal. (Dworkin and MacKinnon 1988, 62)

Given that the acceptance of such violence would run contrary to the basic principles of feminism, individuals like Dworkin and MacKinnon advocated on behalf of legislation that would prohibit the production and distribution of porn.[3]

Others embraced a policy of creative retrieval (Tisdale 1994; McElroy 1995; Bright 2011; Dodson 2011; Dodson 2013).[4] As Louise Lush/Ms. Naughty explains, the issues plaguing the mainstream industry then and now are hardly limited to pornography alone. The pervasiveness of phenomena like sexism and racism, the extent of such patterns of domination, suggests that these issues are due to broader systems of power and privilege. So understood, one need not throw the proverbial baby out with the bathwater. Instead, feminists might encourage one another to make porn that precisely serves to bring these systems into relief:

> I didn't buy into the prevailing Dworkinesque wisdom that all porn was evil ... I knew porn wasn't perfect but that didn't mean I had to dismiss it completely. Surely, I reasoned, it would be better to change it, to make it more positive and include a woman's perspective in the process ... To me, making porn was a positive solution to a difficult question. (Lush 2013, 71–72)

Feminist porn, thereby, arrived on the scene as an (albeit unconventional) answer to an otherwise suspect industry. Directors like Candida Royalle and Nina Hartley set out to develop a body of work that served a liberatory agenda – that challenged a tradition of social/political marginalization and prompted critique. The origins of feminist activism are, in other words, origins of feminist activism.

Present-day ambivalence

Initially, the introduction of this unique form of activism did not reunite feminist communities in the United States. If anything, it fuelled the debates. What had started as an external point of mutual concern now existed as an internal source of deep divide. Much of the controversy centred on determining the actual social/political potential of feminist porn: is there sufficient distance between these films and the violence that first worried Dworkin and MacKinnon? Are some institutions simply too broken to bring about positive change in the world? Many insisted that feminist porn was a vivid illustration of 'false consciousness', a failure to fight an ongoing history of sexual exploitation. Others argued that a feminist-driven rejection of this genre could only result in a new era of totalitarianism, one where even feminists deny people the right to make informed choices about their bodies.[5]

As the (so-called) 'sex wars' raged, an increasing number of feminists began to seek a different approach – a middle way. In particular, several concluded that any evaluation of these films must acknowledge the inherent uncertainty of their social/political future. As Mireille Miller-Young (2013) explains, while feminist porn may eventually effect sweeping change, the verdict is still out. Like any example of long-term activism, the results of these films are, as yet, unknown. More pressingly, insofar as it continues to operate within a 'mainstream' culture, feminist porn remains susceptible to the very systems it hopes to critique:

> Feminist pornography is a for-profit enterprise that relies upon sex workers to manufacture subversive fantasies and build its consumer base ... Though feminism seeks to dismantle structural and discursive exploitation and oppression of women and marginalized populations, our feminist praxis is not external to or untouched by hegemonic systems of domination. (Miller-Young 2013, 107)

Perhaps feminist porn will, at some point, provide viewers with the means to alter their sexual landscapes. However, it is also possible that these films will fall short – will fail to adequately untangle themselves from the problematic narratives that compelled feminists to act in the first place. Because of this lack of clarity, it would seem that feminists are all but forced to conclude that this genre demands a posture which stands between – that avoids either optimism or despair.

As Jane Ward argues, allegiance to this middle way can be seen across feminist circles today. More specifically, feminists would appear to be all but expected to respond to feminist porn with a spirit of 'ambivalence':

> Given that I am a feminist dyke and a professor of women's studies, I recognize that it is a bit of a cliché to say that I am ambivalent about porn. Academics are arguably ambivalent about everything, and most feminists are keenly aware of the gendered and racialized forms of violence and exploitation that undergird much of the adult film industry, even as they oppose censorship, support sex workers' rights, and enjoy the porn they enjoy. (Ward 2013, 130)[6]

The ubiquity of this ambivalence, the pervasiveness of this 'cliché', has only been reinforced by recent changes in the production and distribution of pornography writ large – for example, the rise of amateur porn. As Susanna Paasonen (2010) suggests, one of the advantages of amateur porn is its ability to blur the lines between otherwise distinct genres. This flexibility has enabled feminist pornographers to expand their work in unanticipated and exciting directions. Nevertheless, such ambiguity also calls into question the possibility of assessment. How can one pinpoint the political success or failure of a film whose very being complicates the labels we may wish to track? From what, or whose, 'feminist' standard would such evaluation rightly occur?

The risks of ambivalence

This feminist ambivalence towards porn has had obvious practical advantages. Most notably, it has tamed the 'wars'. When I now disclose the content of my teaching and research to my feminist colleagues, the majority seem to find the subject entirely passé. Ambivalence about feminist porn has become so ingrained that the conversation barely seems worth having. Although I do appreciate aspects of this newfound lack of fireworks, I would also argue that there are risks inherent to the space between. As Constance Penley (2013, 181) argues, these risks are especially evident when the subject of feminist porn is broached in the public sphere. Within the United States, the complexity that ambivalence is intended to capture is often lost in translation. Popular culture continues to hear what it wants, and evidence suggests that what it wants is confirmation that feminists hate sex. In the public arena, discussions about these films remain strongly anti-feminist and anti-porn. Clarissa Smith and Feona Attwood explain:

> [I]n most public debates, arguments that do not begin from a suspicion of pornography are relatively invisible, and the discussion there can only operate within certain limits because the terrain has been so clearly demarcated by a framework of concern … Thus, while anti-porn feminism has been extensively critiqued … it has retained significant purchase in both academic and more populist spheres as a perspective that can only ever be circumnavigated. (2013, 47)

Positions like ambivalence may be complex in theory. Unfortunately, due to the biases that define many political climates in the West, they are rarely received as such in practice. By extension, while the middle way may suit the conceptual realities of feminist porn, it is unclear whether it carries the prescriptive weight needed to foster substantial change in 'mainstream' communities. Ambivalence would seem, in other words, to be a luxury for the already converted. It would not appear to function as a convincing platform from which to transform a broader culture.

Given that such transformation is essential to any example of feminist activism, my goal in what follows is to explore an alternative to ambivalence. Can one locate a nuanced response to feminist porn that recognizes the un-nuanced assumptions of popular opinion? Is it possible to acknowledge the uncertainty of these films and still avoid playing into the hand of sex-negativity? More specifically, I would like to argue for the benefits of embracing a particular kind of 'enthusiasm' – that is, the enthusiasm modelled by Sigmund Freud in *The Future of an Illusion* ([1927] 1961, 65). While Freud's tendencies towards sexism and essentialism have been well documented, several feminists have insisted that these shortcomings need not suggest that his corpus is entirely beyond use (Mitchell 1974; Chodorow 1978; Irigaray 1985; Dinnerstein [1976] 1999). There are moments where Freud's insights can be used to support the work of feminists. However, these moments often unfold in unexpected places. To this end, I will begin by briefly sketching the nature of Freud's enthusiasm. Special attention will be paid to the way Freud justifies his optimism by grounding it in a distinct critical process. With this in mind, I will analyze three moments where the feminist industry would also appear open to such evaluation. I will argue that, insofar as feminists embrace Freud's critical method, they may also adopt his enthusiastic spirit. I will conclude by outlining some of the implications of turning to Freud in this regard: how might a posture of enthusiasm expand the impact of these films within the social/political sphere?

Enthusiasm

In *The Future of an Illusion*, Freud makes his case against religion. He argues that the ideas and principles which structure this entity are not the results of rigorous analysis, but rather stem from 'the oldest, strongest, and most urgent wishes of mankind':

> [T]hey are illusions … [T]he benevolent rule of a divine Providence allays our fear of the dangers of life; the establishment of a moral world-order ensures the fulfillment of the demands of justice, which have so often remained unfulfilled in human civilization; and the prolongation of earthly existence in a future life provides the local and temporal framework in which these wish-fulfillments shall take place. ([1927] 1961, 38)

As illusions, religious doctrines soothe human beings into a state of complacency (Freud [1927] 1961, 39). Freud contends that such a condition not only thwarts the full development of the individual. It also threatens the progress of civilization; it prevents us from accepting the realities that would otherwise allow us to flourish with and alongside each other ([1927] 1961, 63). Because of this, Freud ([1927] 1961, 68–69) urges readers to abandon the illusions of religion and take solace in the 'primacy of the intellect' – that is, the promise of science.

As Freud fleshes out the features of this scientific enterprise, his own sentiments about his project become clear. Freud ([1927] 1961, 65) admits that he is wholly 'enthusiastic' about the capabilities of science. He is all but unwavering in his belief that, one day, human beings will use such tools to overcome the mental and social impasse set about by religion ([1927] 1961, 67). The unrelenting character of Freud's optimism is so evident that it prompts his hypothetical interlocutor to accuse him of falling victim to his own illusions – that is, wishes about the future of reason:

> We seem now to have exchanged roles: you emerge as an enthusiast who allows himself to be carried away by illusions, and I stand for the claims of reason, the rights of skepticism. What you have been expounding seems to me to be built upon errors which, following your example, I may call illusions, because they betray clearly enough the influence of your wishes. (Freud [1927] 1961, 65)

Freud, of course, has no way of knowing whether or not a society guided by reason will succeed. Perhaps up and coming 'generations' will find their lives rehabilitated by the powers of science. However, it is also possible that even the most rationally driven of human beings will cling to the religious notions of the past. More pressingly, Freud cannot be sure that he has completely unravelled himself from the temptation of such illusions. After all, Freud shares the same 'mainstream' world as his interlocutor, one largely influenced by the lure of 'wishes', the ideas of religion. It is entirely likely that, despite his best efforts, traces of these inclinations continue to influence him.

Doubtlessly aware of this haziness, Freud concedes in part to his opponent. He acknowledges that it is altogether conceivable that his desires 'are of an illusory nature' ([1927] 1961, 67). At the same time, Freud also refuses to assert that these ambiguities force him to abandon his enthusiasm and adopt a spirit of ambivalence about his work. Instead, he uses his interlocutor's suspicions as an opportunity to reaffirm the depths of his optimism. Freud distinguishes between his own potential illusions and those of religion. He suggests that while all illusions share a similar beginning – that is, arise from wishes – they are not necessarily held in kind. More specifically, Freud ([1927] 1961, 65–71) argues that, unlike the naïve hopes that define the religious, his enthusiasm is tied to an important critical process; his ideas are submitted to a precise form of evaluation. This process serves as a system of checks and balances, ensuring that Freud's optimism does not get the best of him. As a result, while it is unclear how 'the claims of reason' will ultimately unfold, Freud finds no evidence that compels him to accept the middle way.

The distinction Freud draws yields immediate rewards. By grounding his enthusiasm in a critical framework, Freud locates the wiggle room he needs to authentically 'chase' the vision he longs for. Freud, in effect, alters the terms of his interlocutor's allegation. He posits that, although the future is unknown, the work he desires to accomplish, the path of scientific conversion, does not depend upon the assurances of tomorrow. What matters is that he is willing to hold his efforts accountable to ongoing appraisal 'today'. As such, Freud is able to grant the theoretical ambiguity of his position and still bypass the practical pitfalls of postures like ambivalence. Freud's critical method allows him to defend 'the primacy of the intellect' from a standpoint that grapples with the popular assumptions of his community – assumptions that would, arguably, interpret any hesitation as an excuse to uphold the ideological tradition of religion (Freud [1927] 1961, 68).

Such 'wiggle room' would seem to be potentially valuable when it comes to restructuring current conversations about feminist porn. Freud's approach confirms that it is possible to acknowledge the uncertainty that characterizes the future of these films without succumbing to the trappings of the space between. His project suggests that so long as feminists are willing to adopt his critical tactics, they might also welcome his enthusiasm. The question, thereby, becomes: is there any indication that the ideas which propel feminist porn are amenable to Freud's method? Do those who participate in this activism promote such critical efforts, or are the hopes of feminist porn rooted in the same 'complacency' that classifies religion (Freud [1927] 1961, 39)?

Openness to correction

To answer this question, one must dig a bit deeper into the particulars of Freud's critical process. One of the first characteristics that Freud outlines concerns whether or not an idea is open to correction. Freud argues that his system of checks and balances requires that an individual be receptive to the possibility that their ideas might change. This receptivity serves to distinguish potential illusions from something far more dangerous – that is, delusions:

> But I hold fast to one distinction. Apart from the fact that no penalty is imposed for not sharing them, my illusions are not, like religious ones, incapable of correction. They have not the character of a delusion. If experience should show – not to me, but to others after me, who think as I do – that we have been mistaken, we will give up our expectations. (Freud [1927] 1961, 67)

Freud explains that some illusions are held so stubbornly that no amount of conflicting evidence has the power to alter them. Even the wisdom of experience holds little sway. This intractability implies that these ideas are delusional – that is, absent of any tie to reality (Freud [1927] 1961, 39). To assume that such empirical arguments are utterly irrelevant suggests that one's ideas are fundamentally unhinged. While this assumption may define many of the ideas inherent to the religious, Freud ([1927] 1961, 68–69) argues that his own commitment to science remains open. Freud is willing to re-evaluate his work based upon the conclusions of future 'generations'. So understood, Freud's critical process impels him to avoid equivocating between optimism and obstinacy.

Feminist porn has a well-regarded history of cultivating a similar kind of openness. Perhaps the most obvious example of this is the fact that the definition – the idea – of feminist porn has, itself, remained in a state of flux (Penley et al. 2013, 9–10). Such fluidity of meaning is largely due to the persistent reflection that has personified the feminist industry from the beginning. As Lynn Comella (2013, 82) argues, unlike its mainstream counterpart, feminist porn has held itself accountable to the social/political 'feedback' of consumers, activists, academics, and sex industry workers alike. Insights about the oppressive systems that feminist pornographers hope to challenge continue to develop. Theories about what counts as a properly 'feminist' perspective continue to evolve. Because it is receptive to such information, the very notion of feminist porn necessarily stands as a work in progress.

For example, one might consider the transformation that has occurred around the idea that feminist porn should be 'women friendly'. Many industry trailblazers argued that, in order to support the political goals of feminism, these films should prioritize the kind of sex that 'women might enjoy' (Ward 2013, 134–135). Initially, this led directors to replace the 'hardcore' scenes common in mainstream pornography with on-screen romance and 'vanilla'-flavoured couples-play (Williams 1989). Drawing from her own time behind the camera, Candida Royalle explains:

So I began to think about making porn movies that were aimed at women, and which couples could share together. I felt that adult entertainment could be very valid and life-enriching, but it wasn't being done with that in mind ... So I began Femme with three aims in mind. I wanted to show that it was possible to produce explicit porn that had integrity, I wanted to show that porn could be nonsexist, and I wanted to show that porn could be life-enriching. (1993, 23)

'Women friendly' porn was, in other words, understood as synonymous with 'women friendly' activism. By catering to women viewers, these films sought to confront the misogynistic practices of the traditional industry and distribute media that would allow individuals to reclaim the 'valid and life-enriching' power of sex.

However, later advocates argued that the notion of 'women friendly' porn inevitably reinforces certain stereotypes about those who identify as 'women' and the 'essence' of women's pleasure. To infer that women prefer sex that occurs within the context of romantic relationships only exacerbates the myth that women are uninterested in sex per se – that is, that sex without emotion holds little 'feminine' value. So, too, the pursuit of 'women friendly' porn would appear to perpetuate the general collapse of gender and sexuality. As Jane Ward argues, despite numerous 'experiences' to the contrary, these films imply that the best way to think about sex is to think through gender:

[These] approaches to sexuality privilege women's genuine desires and experiences, but it does so without much critical reflection on who we think women are, and how they come to desire what they do ... [B]iological maleness and femaleness is hardly the most interesting or erotic way to organize or represent sexuality. (2013, 135)

What is striking about this criticism is not that aspects of feminist porn were shown to be anything but 'valid and life enriching'. What is striking is the openness that the majority of those in the industry demonstrated in response. Pioneers like Royalle not only listened to such feedback; they heard it and responded in kind. They acknowledged that their own ideas about feminist porn were in conflict with the sexual realities of their communities. As a result, the face of feminist porn evolved. Some expanded the range of sexual content captured in their films, aiming to disassociate this genre from unnecessary sentimentality (Royalle 2013). Others sought to carve a space for sex that resisted the conventions of gender normativity – that is, that refused to limit the subject of sex/sexuality to the confines of a binary gender system (Lee 2015). This openness has only continued today. The idea of feminist porn remains elusive and in motion. By holding their ideas lightly, feminist pornographers have cultivated a space for the diverse and shifting needs of those around them. They have prioritized the wisdom of their communities and, thereby, insisted that if feminist porn desires to change the world it must be willing to undergo change itself.

Logos

The advantages of such openness are enticing. Still, questions remain: by what criteria is one to determine whether their ideas are falling short? How might an individual decide whether their potential illusions are in need of immediate correction? Freud shares his own guidelines regarding this second aspect of his critical method in the passages that follow. More specifically, he argues that his ideas operate under the guidance of a particular kind of 'god':

> Our god, *Logos*, will fulfill whichever of these wishes nature allows, but he will do it very gradually, only in the unforeseeable future, and for a new generation of men ... [I]n the long run nothing can withstand reason and experience, and the contradiction which religion offers to both is all too palpable. (Freud [1927] 1961, 69)

Freud suggests that the rule of *Logos* is two-fold. First, as mentioned earlier, Freud's ideas will be judged based upon their compatibility with the insights of human experience. At the same time, however, they will also be held accountable to the basic principles of reason. As such, Freud proposes that his ideas are submitted to a holistic god that expects both empirical and rational acumen. Unfortunately, due to the complexity of this one–two punch, Freud's critical process is burdened by certain temporal restrictions. The efforts of *Logos* – the completion of this multifaceted operation – will take time.

Feminist porn has long since begun to serve under the direction of a similarly balanced, if not slow-moving, god. For example, this both/and is evident in the ways the feminist industry has sought to assess its ideas about the politics of producing sex. On the one hand, feminist pornographers have demonstrated a clear commitment to processing such concerns from the standpoint of human experience. More pointedly, as Tristan Taormino (2013) argues, part of what has set feminist porn apart is its willingness to honour the experiences of the under-represented. Feminist porn is a business, and, traditionally, businesses have favoured the experiences of their stakeholders – the 'bottom line'. In contrast, feminist porn has striven to include the perspectives of those on set. As a result, this industry has its own tradition – that is, one of producing sexual 'goods' that are irreducible to economic gains alone. Most notably, many directors have placed a special emphasis on the idea of just working conditions. Taorimino explains:

> Feminist porn ... must be a fair and ethical process and a positive working environment for everyone. Performers set their own pay rates and know up front what I am hiring them to do; there is absolute, explicit consent and no coercion of any kind. (2013, 260)

In this way, feminist porn has not only submitted itself to the conclusions of the empirical realm; it has also prompted additional dialogue about whose realms are deemed valuable. The feminist industry has, in other words, contrived a 'fair and ethical' *Logos* – one which demands that the production of sex grapples with the experience of workers' rights.

At the same time, feminist porn has also proven itself accountable to the stipulations of reason. While feminist porn is surely invested in the production of sexual goods, it is equally dedicated to the production of sexual ideas. As Miller-Young (2013, 2014) suggests, many of the ideas that have been implicitly and explicitly articulated by mainstream pornography are simply unsound. Most obviously, the majority of these films have a history of reinforcing social/political stereotypes – that is, falsehoods that uphold some sexual lives to the detriment of others. For instance, this has been especially clear in the stereotypes that surround the representation of Black sexuality:

> Within this hierarchy black bodies are some of the most degraded, and their degradation mobilizes the very fetishism driving their representations ... [B]lack-cast pornography tends to be organized around a view of black sexual deviance and pathology – often a low-budget affair presenting pimps and players trolling the 'hood' for hoes and hookers. (Miller-Young 2013, 107)

In response, feminist porn has worked to produce counter-representations – that is, sound ideas. These ideas have only multiplied as an increasingly diverse group of directors have stepped behind the camera. As Miller-Young (2013, 106) concludes, to 'author' one's own narrative about sex is to reclaim the truth that sits at the intersection of identity and eroticism.[7] Such truths challenge others to recognize and unpack those contradictory ideas that are irreconcilable with the principles of reason. So understood, feminist porn exemplifies what it means to develop sexual concepts that seek to end the allure of widespread error within the political world.[8]

Today, feminist allegiance to this bi-partisan god has led to an increased emphasis on the importance of genuine collaboration between the 'Ivory Tower' and the film set. As Kari Kesler (2002, 232) argues, much of the discourse about sex work in general has assumed the centrality of the 'academic-as-knower'. Such an interpretive lens has tended to present sex work and sex workers as objects to master – 'things' desperately in need of the evaluative criteria only a scholar can provide. By underscoring the empirical and rational frameworks present within their industry, feminist pornographers have flipped the discourse. They have highlighted the ways in which their films are already privy to a *Logos* of their own. The presence of this *Logos* suggests that feminist porn is more than capable of standing as the foundation of its own activism. Despite the priority often given to the hermeneutic credentials of academia, feminist porn is no less suited to serve 'as a valid basis for feminist theory and social transformation' (Kesler 2002, 240).

Education in reality

Once again, the benefits of embracing this aspect of Freud's critical process are clear. Yet, here too, questions arise: how might one know whether they are following Freud's god correctly? What can an individual expect to occur if they commit their ideas to experience and reason? To this end, Freud outlines a third and final component of his critical method. In particular, he argues that the primary consequence of such a journey is education:

> [I]nfantilism is destined to be surmounted. Men cannot remain children forever; they must in the end go out into 'hostile life.' We may call this 'education to reality.' Need I confess to you that the sole purpose of my book is to point out the necessity for this forward step. (Freud [1927] 1961, 63)

Freud argues that this unique example of education will be uncomfortable, will require a 'forward step' towards the 'hostilities' of life. However, the value of abandoning 'infantilism' cannot be underestimated. Freud suggests that an 'education to reality' will 'increase our power' ([1927] 1961, 70). This increase enables human beings to better order and 'arrange' their lives. In this way, Freud would appear to come full circle. Such a result stands in stark contrast to his earlier assessment of the effects of religious ideas – that is, the tendency of these illusions to diminish the individual and halt the development of civilization ([1927] 1961, 63). In contrast, Freud concludes that his critical process allows his own potential illusions to strengthen the self and its community.

Feminist porn has dared to advance a similarly 'real' education. More specifically, many have worked to create porn that encourages those on and off set to contend with the potentially 'hostile' realities of sex. This has been especially evident in the development of feminist Queer and Lesbian porn (Hollibaugh 1996; Ryberg 2013). As Greta Christina

(1992) argues, popular culture in the West is only too eager to police the boundaries of sexual activity – to restrict sex to the experiences of those who identify as cisgender and heterosexual. Such policing has had violent repercussions for those individuals whose longings do not reflect these labels. It has cultivated a sexually dangerous world where certain acts are needlessly deemed 'unnatural' or 'inhuman'. By developing media that call such expectations into question, feminist porn has exposed the risks of this policing. Ingrid Ryberg explains:

> Such a negotiation of social relations is also central in the queer, feminist, and lesbian porn film culture ... [T]he performers share their hard-won experiences of sexual pleasure as well as the pain and difficulties in living in a sexist, homophobic, and racist world. Their conversations and their sexual performances work through the norms, conventions, and taboos shaping and pressing on their lives, bodies, and desires. (2013, 151)

To name those forces that condition a culture's ideas about sex is to reclaim the 'power' of the individual. It is to take a 'forward step' towards an education in the diverse sexual realities that are otherwise lost behind aggressive practices of control.

These 'forward steps' continue to be achieved across a variety of formal and informal venues today. For example, within the United States, a growing number of faculty have elected to bring feminist porn into the space of higher education (Tarrant 2015). Classes devoted to porn in general, and feminist porn in particular, have become a regular occurrence on university campuses. As Constance Penley (2013) argues, the pedagogical benefits of these films are pointed. Because of the social/political positionalities reflected in this genre, to expose college students to feminist porn is to expose them to 'reality'. More specifically, unlike other mediums, the social, political, and economic 'hostilities' that compel the production of these films are often easier to pinpoint. As such, they are easier to learn. By extension, Penley maintains that feminist porn is at its educational best when it inspires students to bring such multi-faceted learning to the members of their communities:

> [I]t keeps teaching. My students tell me that the minute they leave class, they must report to their roommates, friends, parents, folks back home in Australia, what went on in class that day. They constantly have to explain the class, why it's important to study pornography, why it's crucial to have informed opinions ... It's the class that keeps on teaching. (2013, 198)

By engaging in these classes, students may well experience an increase in their individual 'power'. However, the hope is that this power will embolden them to become future educators – that is, sexual leaders who are eager to usher in the 'generational' changes that their feminist elders may not yet envision.

To be clear, none of this is to suggest that participating in such education is easy. While certain media outlets may imply otherwise, in the West the Academy remains a largely conservative institution – often dependent upon the ideological prerogatives of a small set of trustees and donors. As Penley concludes, this conservativism often takes the form of 'infantilism':

> The local anti-porn activists, for example, accused me of exposing children to pornography in my classroom, to the anger and dismay of my students who vocally spoke out against their characterization as children. (2013, 181)

For some, it is not enough to 'arrange' their existence so as to 'remain children forever'. Many anti-porn activists have attempted to ensure that others avoid 'stepping forward' too. Given this, the presence of feminist porn on university campuses is simultaneously common and precarious – an uphill battle designed to confront the status quo. Within this context, the status quo emerges as the assumption that sex is unworthy of academic consideration and best left to the dimly lit and dirty. By attempting to dismantle such an assumption, the sheer existence of these courses contributes to the broader social/political goals of these films. It suggests that an 'education in reality' can be but another name for feminist activism.

Why Freud?

Must the uncertainty that surrounds the future of feminist porn foster ambivalence in the present? Are feminists destined to be caught in a space between optimism and despair? I have argued that a provocative alternative can be found in the example of Freud. By attaching his own would-be illusions to a unique critical process, Freud locates a way to preserve enthusiasm. More specifically, by opening his ideas to correction, following the guide of *Logos*, and engaging in a crucial form of 'education', Freud distinguishes his desires from the unruly sentiments of religion. As such, he offers an (arguably demanding) method for all those who wish to remain hopeful until the verdicts of the future unfold. It is a method that would appear to be more than conducive with the industry of feminist porn. From its earliest beginnings, feminist porn has encouraged a similarly critical approach. If Freud is right, this approach may be used to defend feminist optimism and, thereby, restructure contemporary conversations about such sexual activism.

To be fair, one might argue that this interpretive conclusion is misplaced – that is, a faulty extension of Freud's analysis of religion to the topic of sex and sexuality. However, although it is true that Freud is focused on the religious in *The Future of an Illusion*, he is also clear that human illusions are not limited to religion alone. If anything, Freud ([1927] 1961, 43) invites readers to explore the full range of their ideas, including those that influence their 'erotic' lives. As James DiCenso (2007) argues, this suggests that Freud's goal within his text is more comprehensive than the debunking of religion per se. Freud does not examine the religious for its sake alone. Instead, he writes to 'further a more ethically-oriented human co-existence' (DiCenso 2007, 163). While Freud would doubtlessly be pleased to learn that he had inspired some to abandon their religious illusions, the parameters of his project are all-encompassing. Accordingly, although the subject of porn may fall beyond the purview of religion, it does not fall beyond the set of experiences that Freud would have us assess.

By extension, Freud's dedication to the full range of these experiences confirms the benefits of using him to inform modern-day discussions about feminist porn. Most notably, Freud offers feminists an opportunity to extend the impact of this activism. First, and as hinted earlier, Freud models a compelling way for feminists to wrestle with the mainstream biases of their communities. Unfortunately, for many in the United States, positions like ambivalence inevitably feed into anti-feminist and anti-sex rhetoric (Penley 2013; Smith and Attwood 2013). Hermeneutic messiness is often swallowed by prejudicial outrage. This drastically reduces the social/political success of these films. It increases the severity of the roadblocks with which activists are forced to contend. To allow feminists to lead with enthusiasm is to package such work in a way that avoids reinforcing the very cultural assumptions feminist porn hopes to overturn.

Secondly, Freud also presents feminists with the means to rally their base. The problem with ambivalence is that it rarely powers a movement; it rarely inspires individuals to go out and effect systemic change. While the 'sex wars' were a regrettable time in feminist history, they did prompt a high level of political passion. This passion drove feminists to organize. Such organization is no less crucial today than it was in the 1980s. As Taormino (2013) argues, much of the violence that first concerned Dworkin and MacKinnon has persisted in the mainstream industry. This violence continues to have lasting consequences, shaping everything from technology (Butterworth 1996; Patterson 2004; Kinnick 2007) to fashion (Bishop 2007; Harvey and Robinson 2007). Assuming that these cases demand a response, it is unclear whether feminists can afford to be ambivalent about porn – can afford to embody any posture that might diminish their own willingness to take action.

Finally, Freud urges feminists to remember the complexity inherent in any form of sexual activism. We live and move in a sexually imperfect world. Given this, it is altogether likely that our attempts at sexual revolution – attempts like feminist porn – will be imperfect as well. Freud reminds us that our willingness to act need not be contingent upon the infallibility of our desires. However, he also reminds us that to engage in such activism – to have enthusiasm about feminist porn – will be risky. Those who elect to lead with optimism are surely susceptible to the finger-wags of the next 'generation'. Still, this risk is the condition of the possibility of sexual change. In order for sex to exceed the limits of our societal imaginations, we need individuals who are willing to put their own imaginations to the test. As Candida Royalle (2013, 69) argues, because of this, enthusiasm will require courage – that is, the 'courage to explore what is uniquely [ours] about sex', the courage to share those insights with others. So understood, the social/political possibilities of feminist porn need not be contingent upon the laws of certainty. They need only be contingent upon our willingness to allow each other to hope.

Notes

1. To be clear, like feminist porn, the set of media that tends to be labelled as 'mainstream pornography' is diverse. Still, the vast majority of feminist scholarship continues to use both phrases. Herein, I will follow their lead.
2. The history of pornography has, of course, included more than film alone. However, in what follows, I will focus on this medium in particular.
3. See the Anti-pornography Civil Rights Ordinances.
4. Many, here, have followed the insights of self-identified 'pro-sex' or 'sex-positive' feminists (Califia 1981; Rubin 1984).
5. Echoes of this can be heard across the field of feminist philosophies of sex (Jackson and Scott 1996; Johnson 2002).
6. One can also see this in the claim that 'ambivalence' is 'at the core of sex worker feminisms' (Kesler 2002, 233).
7. See also Parrenaz Shimizu (2007) and Cruz (2016a, 2016b).
8. This includes those ideas that have not always been popular amongst feminists themselves (Kipnis 1992).

Disclosure statement

No potential conflict of interest was reported by the author.

References

Anti-Pornography Civil Rights Ordinance. The City Council of the City of Minneapolis. Accessed December 1, 2018. http://www.nostatusquo.com/ACLU/dworkin/other/ordinance/newday/AppA.htm.

Anti-Pornography Civil Rights Ordinance. Indianapolis and Marion County. Accessed December 1, 2018. http://www.nostatusquo.com/ACLU/dworkin/other/ordinance/newday/AppB1.htm.

Bishop, Mardia J. 2007. 'The Making of a Pre-Pubescent Porn Star.' In *Pop Porn*, edited by Ann C. Hall, and Mardia J. Bishop, 45–56. Westport and London: Praeger.

Bright, Susie. 2011. *Susie Bright's Erotic Screen*. Santa Cruz: Bright Stuff.

Bronstein, Carolyn. 2015. 'Clashing at Barnard's Gates.' In *New Views on Pornography*, edited by Lynn Comella, and Shira Tarrant, 57–76. Santa Barbara: Praeger.

Butterworth, Dianne. 1996. 'Wanking in Cyberspace.' In *Feminism and Sexuality*, edited by Stevi Jackson, and Sue Scott, 314–320. New York: Columbia University Press.

Califia, Pat. 1981. 'Feminism and Sadomasochism.' *Heresies* 12 Sex Issue 3 (4): 30–34.

Chodorow, Nancy. 1978. *The Reproduction of Mothering*. Berkeley and Los Angeles: University of California Press.

Christina, Greta. 1992. 'Are We Having Sex Now or What.' In *The Erotic Impulse*, edited by David Steinberg, 24–29. New York: Tarcher.

Comella, Lynn. 2013. 'From Text to Context.' In *The Feminist Porn Book*, edited by Tristan Taormino, Celine Parrenas Shimizu, Constance Penley, and Mireille Miller-Young, 79–93. New York: The Feminist Press.

Cornell, Drucilla, ed. 2000. *Feminism and Pornography*. Oxford: Oxford University Press.

Cruz, Ariane. 2016a. *The Color of Kink*. New York: New York University Press.

Cruz, Ariane. 2016b. 'Sisters Are Doin' It For Themselves: Black Women and the New Pornography.' In *The Philosophy of Pornography*, edited by Lindsay Coleman, and Jacob Held, 225–248. Lanham: Rowman and Littlefield.

DiCenso, James. 2007. 'Kant, Freud, and the Ethical Critique of Religion.' *International Journal for Philosophy of Religion* 61 (3): 161–179.

Dinnerstein, Dorothy. [1976] 1999. *The Mermaid and the Minotaur*. New York: Other Press.

Dodson, Betty. 2011. *My Romantic Love Wars*. Bad Media LLC.

Dodson, Betty. 2013. 'Porn Wars.' In *The Feminist Porn Book*, edited by Tristan Taormino, Celine Parrenas Shimizu, Constance Penley, and Mireille Miller-Young, 23–31. New York: The Feminist Press.

Dworkin, Andrea. 1981. *Pornography: Men Possessing Women*. New York: Putnam.

Dworkin, Andrea, and Catherine MacKinnon. 1988. *Pornography and Civil Rights*. Minneapolis: Organizing Against Pornography.

Freud, Sigmund. [1927] 1961. *The Future of an Illusion*. Translated and edited by James Strachey. New York and London: W.W. Norton and Company.

Harvey, Hannah B., and Karen Robinson. 2007. 'Hot Bodies on Campus.' In *Pop Porn*, edited by Ann C. Hall, and Mardia J. Bishop, 57–74. Westport and London: Praeger.

Hollibaugh, Amber. 1996. 'Seducing Women Into 'A Lifestyle of Vaginal Fisting'.' In *Policing Public Sex: Queer Politics and the Future of AIDS Activism*, 321–336. Boston: South Bend Press.

Irigaray, Luce. 1985. *Speculum of the Other Woman*. Translated by Gillian C. Gill. New York: Cornell University Press.

Jackson, Stevi, and Sue Scott, eds. 1996. *Feminism and Sexuality*. New York: Columbia University Press.

Johnson, Merri Lisa. 2002. *Jane Sexes it Up: True Confessions of Feminist Desire*. New York: Thunder's Mouth Press.

Kesler, Kari. 2002. 'The Plain Clothes Whore.' In *Jane Sexes it Up: True Confessions of Feminist Desire*, edited by Merri Lisa Johnson, 231–240. New York: Thunder's Mouth Press.

Kinnick, Katherine. 2007. 'Pushing the Envelope.' In *Pop Porn*, edited by Ann C. Hall, and Mardia J. Bishop, 7–26. Westport and London: Praeger.

Kipnis, Laura. 1992. '(Male) Desire and (Female) Disgust: Reading Hustler.' In *Cultural Studies*, edited by Lawrence Grossberg, Cary Nelson, and Paula A. Treichler, 373–391. New York: Routledge.

Lee, Jiz, ed. 2015. *Coming Out Like a Porn Star*. Berkeley: ThreeL Media.

Lush, Louise. 2013. 'My Decadent Decade.' In *The Feminist Porn Book*, edited by Tristan Taormino, Celine Parrenas Shimizu, Constance Penley, and Mireille Miller-Young, 70–78. New York: The Feminist Press.

MacKinnon, Catherine. 1987. *Feminism Unmodified: Discourses on Life and Law*. Cambridge: Harvard University Press.

McElroy, Wendy. 1995. *XXX: A Woman's Right to Pornography*. New York: St. Martin's Press.

Miller-Young, Mireille. 2013. 'Interventions.' In *The Feminist Porn Book*, edited by Tristan Taormino, Celine Parrenas Shimizu, Constance Penley, and Mireille Miller-Young, 105–120. New York: The Feminist Press.

Miller-Young, Mireille. 2014. *A Taste for Brown Sugar*. Durham: Duke University Press.

Mitchell, Juliet. 1974. *Psychoanalysis and Feminism*. New York: Vintage Books.

Paasonen, Susanna. 2010. 'Labors of Love: Netporn, Web 2.0 and the Meanings of Amateurism.' *new Media and Society* 12 (8): 297–312.

Parrenaz Shimizu, Celine. 2007. *The Hypersexuality of Race*. Durham: Duke University Press.

Patterson, Zabet. 2004. 'Going On-Line.' In *Porn Studies*, edited by Linda Williams, 104–123. Durham: Duke University Press.

Penley, Constance. 2013. 'A Feminist Teaching Pornography.' In *The Feminist Porn Book*, edited by Tristan Taormino, Celine Parrenas Shimizu, Constance Penley, and Mireille Miller-Young, 179–199. New York: The Feminist Press.

Penley, Constance, Celine Parrenas Shimizu, Mireille Miller-Young, and Tristan Taormino. 2013. 'Introduction.' In *The Feminist Porn Book*, edited by Tristan Taormino, Celine Parrenas Shimizu, Constance Penley, and Mireille Miller-Young, 9–20. New York: The Feminist Press.

Ramos, Norma. 2000. 'Pornography is a Social Justice Issue.' In *Feminism and Pornography*, edited by Drucilla Cornell, 45–47. Oxford: Oxford University Press.

Royalle, Candida. 1993. 'Porn in the USA.' *Social Text* 37: 23–32.

Royalle, Candida. 2013. 'What's a Nice Girl Like You … .' In *The Feminist Porn Book*, edited by Tristan Taormino, Celine Parrenas Shimizu, Constance Penley, and Mireille Miller-Young, 58–69. New York: The Feminist Press.

Rubin, Gayle. 1984. 'Thinking Sex.' In *Pleasure and Danger*, edited by Carole S. Vance, 267–319. Boston and London: Routledge and Kegan Paul.

Russell, Diana E. H. 1988. 'Pornography and Rape: A Causal Model.' *Political Psychology* 9 (1): 41–73.

Ryberg, Ingrid. 2013. "Every Time we Fuck, we win:' The Public Sphere of Queer, Feminist, and Lesbian Porn as a (Safe) Space for Sexual Empowerment.' In *The Feminist Porn Book*, edited by Tristan Taormino, Celine Parrenas Shimizu, Constance Penley, and Mireille Miller-Young, 140–154. New York: The Feminist Press.

Smith, Clarissa, and Feona Attwood. 2013. 'Emotional Truths and Thrilling Slide Shows.' In *The Feminist Porn Book*, edited by Tristan Taormino, Celine Parrenas Shimizu, Constance Penley, and Mireille Miller-Young, 41–57. New York: The Feminist Press.

Spector, Jessica, ed. 2006. *Prostitution and Pornography*. Stanford: Stanford University Press.

Taormino, Tristan. 2013. 'Calling the Shots.' In *The Feminist Porn Book*, edited by Tristan Taormino, Celine Parrenas Shimizu, Constance Penley, and Mireille Miller-Young, 255–264. New York: The Feminist Press.

Taormino, Tristan, Celine Parrenas Shimizu, Constance Penley, and Mireille Miller-Young, eds. 2013. *The Feminist Porn Book*. New York: The Feminist Press.

Tarrant, Shira. 2015. 'Pornography and Pedagogy.' In *New Views on Pornography*, edited by Lynn Comella, and Shira Tarrant, 417–430. Santa Barbara: Praeger.

Tisdale, Sallie. 1994. *Talk Dirty to Me: An Intimate Philosophy of Sex*. New York, London, Toronto, Sydney, and Auckland: Anchor Books.

Ward, Jane. 2013. 'Queer Feminist Pigs.' In *The Feminist Porn Book*, edited by Tristan Taormino, Celine Parrenas Shimizu, Constance Penley, and Mireille Miller-Young, 130–139. New York: The Feminist Press.

Williams, Linda. 1989. *Hard Core: Power, Pleasure, and the 'Frenzy of the Visible.'*. Berkeley: University of California Press.

More than vanilla sex: reading gay post-pornography with affect theory and psychoanalysis

Peter Rehberg

ABSTRACT
New regimes of representation in the realcore of Porn 2.0 seem to operate beyond psychoanalytic accounts of subjectivity and desire. 'Fantasy' and 'identification' do not quite capture the forms of attachment emerging out of these new post-pornographic cultures. Their temporalities and binding forces appear to be too ephemeral in order to produce the psychoanalytic subject through pornographic interpellation. But does that mean we are now living within a post-psychoanalytic pornographic universe? Is our sexuality currently shaped by forces that make any account of the dynamics detected by psychoanalysis obsolete? The first part of this article will look at the Dutch transnational fanzine *Butt* as an example of gay post-pornography within the past 15 years that operates affectively as well as sexually. In the second part of the article, I discuss the intersection of affect and sex as presented in *Butt* through the juxtaposition of Eve Sedgwick's affect theory and Sigmund Freud's theory of the drives. In so doing, I specify the ways it is possible – and not – to distinguish between drives and affects. This dialogue between competing theories helps us to grasp *Butt's* culture of affective sexualities.

Pornography and affect

Affect theory suggests that in our contemporary post-disciplinary society of control and its media culture the binding forces of the symbolic are less stable than Lacanian psychoanalysis would lead us to believe. A discussion of affect, therefore, would allow us to address newly shaped experiences, and differently constructed subjectivities and entanglements, beyond a linguistically informed psychoanalytic account of the social and the subject. It would mean working with a different understanding of the semiotic – including not only signs, but aesthetic forms as well – beyond regimes of representation and thus offers us new access to a different reality. What is the place of sexuality within this affective, mediated configuration?[1]

Beyond a dialectics of repression and liberation, and after the emergence of queer theory as a new field of study in the early 1990s, sexuality no longer benefitted from the same critical attention it received in previous decades (Hardt and Negri 2000) – a tendency that has also reached parts of queer theory itself (Sedgwick 2003). While attempts at downplaying and trivializing the role of sexuality in analyses of contemporary culture should be understood and criticized as an effect of political and economic forces (Tim Dean 2015), it is also true that our globalized digital present offers and necessitates new ways of thinking about sexuality. In this sense we must acknowledge, or even welcome, the 'trivialization of sexuality'. This is not to say that the discussion of sexuality has become superfluous, but rather that the debate about sexuality as 'trivial' should be considered important.

These renegotiations of the significance of sexuality, its representation, and its functionality, or dysfunctionality, within an affective mediated environment have been the concern of some of the most important, recent works in the field of porn studies (Hillis 2009; Paasonen 2011). On a theoretical level, these shifts have led us to question the legacy of psychoanalysis as the most nuanced and powerful paradigm when talking about sexuality in the twentieth century (rivalled only, to an extent, by Foucault), and its status for analyzing contemporary porn culture. My engagement with affect theory here is aimed against gestures which would substitute sexuality with affect as a central conceptual paradigm. The current inevitability of addressing affect when talking about the body and the ways in which it is mediated, as an object of cultural analysis, offers instead an occasion to rethink sexuality through affect.

This strategy seems adequate given the culture of post-pornography in the 2000s. Within a new digital media environment, a DIY-porn culture emerged that continually worked at dismantling the forces of a heteronormative pornographic paradigm (Jacobs 2007; Stüttgen 2010). Not only did it produce alternative representational codes, it also directed critical attention to forces beyond representation, and thus to new potential for research within porn studies (Paasonen 2011). Along with new forms of self-presentation and connection online, it also helped develop a new culture of porn film festivals and of alternative publications such as fanzines (Bronson and Aarons 2008, 2014).

Here I take the Dutch gay fanzine *Butt* as an example of post-porn. Published in print between 2001and 2011, *Butt* has inspired the production of new queer fanzines for more than 15 years around the world. Inspired by online pornography and remediating its aesthetics by bringing the characteristics of images circulating online – such as amateurism and scenes of domesticity – back into print, contemporary gay visual culture, as in *Butt,* displays a new style of sexuality. It presents a post-dramatic mood, which can no longer be grasped by the 'traumatic' accounts of ego shattering, or sexual difference, and their entailing mythologies that psychoanalysis has to offer. Given the relaxed sexual everydayness of these images, the psychoanalytical lexicon seems at first glance to have little to offer in making sense of them (Figure 1). Thus, contemporary sexual and pornographic cultures raise questions about an 'end of psychoanalysis' – as they have been announced many times since the turn of the century.

With its documentary-style photographs of imperfect, naked young men, often in private rooms, not hiding everything that would not straightforwardly lead to sexual satisfaction, one way to describe this scenario would be to say that *Butt* is about affects. What I mean by this is that *Butt* displays a variety of pleasures and interests in activities and objects that are connected to, but not always centred around, the sexual. Taking such a preliminary characterization of the pictures in *Butt* as a point of departure, the question is: how, then, would affect theory provide new vocabulary for talking about sensations and attachments which pervade this new media landscape (Figure 2)? How would

Figure 1. Jason Whipple, picture by Miguel Villalobos.
Note: reproduced from Jop Van Bennekom and Gert Jonkers, eds. (2006) *Butt* 18 (Winter): 14.

affect theory help us grasp the low-key, mediated sexual lifestyle presented in *Butt*? While the extraordinariness of sex is questioned in these pictures, sex does not seem to be repressed or sacrificed. It is not vanilla either. Sex in *Butt* might be tender, yet dirty. *Butt* does more than substitute the sexual with the affective, the fanzine asks a difficult question: how do sex, sexuality, and affect intersect?

This article has two parts. In the first, I briefly describe *Butt*'s aesthetics and its culture between intimacy and kink. As an example of contemporary post-porn, it presents material that provokes questions about the place left for psychoanalysis in understanding contemporary pornographic culture. In the second part, I take up this question theoretically by juxtaposing some characteristics of Eve Sedgwick's version of affect theory and of Freud's theory of the drives. While Sedgwick's writings have been foundational to the field of affect studies since the mid-1990s, turning to Freud when thinking about the relationship between affect and sexuality might not necessarily be our first intuition. As Leo Bersani reminds us, thinking about forms of attachment beyond sexuality is already a part of Freud's project: 'the first major theoretical attempt to desexualize pleasure was not Foucault's *History of Sexuality* but about seventy years earlier, Freud's *Three Essays on the Theory of Sexuality*' (1995, 98).

Strategically, I suggest a double movement: to use affect theory in order to critique and extend Freudian notions of sexuality – or the standardized forms in which they circulate – while at the same time avoiding its tendency to silence sexuality. This allows a reimagining of the relationship between affect and drive. This way, I hope to develop a notion of an affective sexuality that helps us grasp the reinvention of sex, sexuality, and desire in *Butt*'s post-pornographic aesthetics.

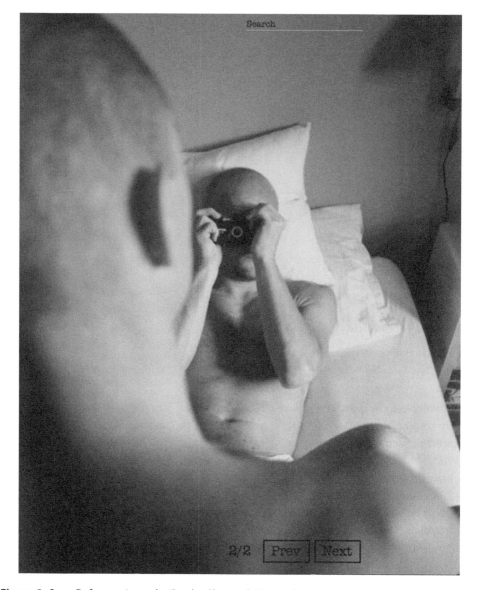

Figure 2. Bavo Defurne, picture by Sander Plug and Werner Damen.
Note: reproduced from Jop Van Bennekom Jop and Gert Jonkers eds. (2001) *Butt* 2 (Autumn): 12–15.

Butt magazine

The proliferation of pornographic online imagery has had a double effect. While the 'pornification' of society popularized pornographic norms (Paasonen, Nikunen, and Saarenmaa 2007), it has also led to a post-pornographic counter-culture. As in earlier versions of feminist appropriations of porn, queer post-porn can challenge the hierarchical and normative structures of the pornotopic field and its formal stagnations. This concerns both questions of gender and desire. *Butt*, a transnational project founded by the Dutch journalists Gert Jonkers and Jop van Bennekom accompanied by German Wolfgang Tillmans as their signature photographer, rearticulates images of same-sex masculinity and maleness, and queers the notion of desire, itself ambiguously moving between affective and sexual attachments.

Butt partakes in the contemporary popular culture of de-sublimation without establishing sex as the master-signifier of its pictures or narratives. As opposed to the rigid functionality of sexual desire in mainstream porn, both gay and straight, the post-porn in the gay male fanzine *Butt* introduces an affective diffusion of sexual interest. The fanzine displays sexual and affective attachments on the 'superficial' level of liking things, as in pop art starting with Warhol (Flatley 1996; Muñoz 2009a), and has received more critical attention recently in the context of web culture (Ngai 2012). *Butt* addresses all kinds of 'hobbies' – for example, playing an instrument or gardening – both visually and textually on the same level as sexual preferences (Figures 3 and 4).

This strategy of decentring that applies to sexual interests also manifests itself when *Butt* presents its interviews with the young male models. The superficiality of the documentary-style stories that accompany the pictures – informed by a tradition of new journalism and its ethics and aesthetics of publishing conversations that appear as if they were not edited – does not turn the interviews of the *Butt* boys into biographical accounts or psycho-pathological case studies. More than narratively stabilizing the visual representation of the post-pornographic celebrity on the pages of *Butt*, these interviews open up the contingency of attachments that cannot necessarily be explained as symptoms of a psychoanalytic subject; stars and ordinary people appear side by side (Figure 4).

Example headlines include 'Fashion Homo From Germany Grew Up Naked And Makes Clothes In Paris' (Van Bennekom and Jonkers 2006, 285) or 'French Horticulturist Makes up to 1500 Euros per Night' (Van Bennekom and Jonkers 2007, 25). What would be the best way to make sense of these headlines? Bruce LaBruce paraphrases them as follows: 'what started out as a more fashion fag-based magazine has branched-out to include all sorts of sordid sissies: a macho cow farmer who loves udders and deals with fireworks on the side, a random boring fag' (2006, 11).

While sexual interests usually represent a point of departure for portrayals of gay men in *Butt*, the fanzine contextualizes sex and sexuality within the ordinariness of everyday life. Aesthetically, this mundane world is connected to the realcore aspects of amateur porn presented in online chatrooms. This contextualization sacrifices the extraordinary status of sexuality as a realm of fantasy, ritualistically separated from everyday life. There is no longer a categorical distinction between sexual desire and other needs or wishes.

The portrayals and stories in *Butt* do not aim to document a social reality.[2] Rather, they look at everydayness both erotically and aesthetically. That is to say, these portrayals register unforeseen connections and the pleasure that can be gained from them. Following Lauren Berlant (2011), I understand affective attachments here in distinction to emotions as neither expressions of an individual subject or a historical structure of feeling, but in the first place as a production of relations between people and things. With this logic of and–and conjunctions, the question arises whether we should think of the *Butt* boys as Deleuzian desiring-machines – assemblages that connect to the world through the production of attachments without a hidden script or an original narrative that directs its trajectory.

One of the problems with such a reading, however, is that it cannot explain the humour in *Butt*'s aesthetic and journalistic strategies; for instance, 'Tom the Carpenter is Good with Wood and Likes Men Who Work with Their Hands' (Van Bennekom and Jonkers 2011). In their juxtaposition of mundane things, *Butt*'s headlines (as well as, occasionally, its images)

Figure 3. Andy Butler, picture by Andreas Larsson.
Note: reproduced from Jop Van Bennekom and Gert Jonkers, eds. (2008) *Butt* 23 (Summer): 29.

provoke laughter (Figure 5). If we follow Freud, the laughter of the joke depends on the mobility of the meaning. One of the examples in Freud's (2003) book on jokes, which was originally published in 1905 (the same year as the *Three Essays* which will be at the

Figure 4. Xavier Simonneau, picture by Regis Trigano.
Note: reproduced from Jop Van Bennekom and Gert Jonkers, eds. (2007) Butt 21 (Late Autumn–Early Winter): 24.

centre of the second part of this text), is the dirty joke ('*die Zote*'). In this heterosexist context, the sexual joke gains its meaning through the exposure of the female as 'lacking' the phallus. As a phallic tale, the dirty joke enjoys the hierarchy of power from a position of control. A style of joke that projects the loss of meaning onto the other, and that Freud also names 'Roman' in distinction to the 'Jewish', self-inflicted, joke. Applied to the headlines in *Butt*, I argue that the way they construct humour positions sex on a different plane than affects and attachments to non-sexual objects or activities. The jokes point to a hierarchical difference between sex and whatever else they mention or depict. People's habits are pursued here only almost with the same interest as their sexual behaviours. The authority of the sexual is not so much ignored or left behind, but continually exposed to the contingency of its surroundings – the details and objects of one's life. What *Butt* achieves with its narrative and aesthetic strategies is less an overcoming than a repeated return to the sexual. The value of the sexual is established – the *Butt* boys will always be sure to prove how kinky they are – only so it can later be betrayed; for example, 'Thomas Engel Hart Is A Non-Vegetarian American Menswear Fashion Designer Living In Paris Who Loves To Be Beaten Up Every Now And Then And Is Married To A Lesbian' (Van Bennekom and Jonkers 2006, 347) (Figure 6).

One way to describe the structure of the stories in *Butt*, as presented by its headlines, then, would be to read it as a form of pornographic castration humour. But, if castration humour celebrates the destruction of the phallic power of the sexual, in *Butt* humour is not performed as feminist revenge – as in some forms of White Trash Porn (Penley 2004), and to whose aesthetic *Butt* also owes quite a bit – but rather as self-inflicted

Figure 5. Tom the Carpenter, picture by Black Little.
Note: reproduced from *Buttmagazine.com*, 12 August 2011. Accessed September 17 2018. http://www.buttmagazine.com/magazine/interviews/tom-the-carpenter-is-good-with-wood-and-likes-men-who-work-with-their-hands/.

from a gay male subject position. The inevitability of the jokes in *Butt* indicates, paradoxically, I would argue, that sexual pleasure and affective attachments do not (yet?) operate on the same level. *Butt*'s editor Jop van Bennekom says 'we always try to make a connection between sexuality and for instance doing dishes and psychotherapy' (Needham 2006, 42). But in the world of *Butt* we are still a step away from the possibility that we could look at, say, diet and sexuality, or doing the dishes and sexuality for that matter, in the same way – a utopian de-dramatization of the sexual suggested both by Halperin and Bersani, following Foucault (Bersani 1995, 56).

Still, the authoritative legacy of a psychoanalytically legible sexuality is constantly undone in the context of affective attachments, which both texts and pictures present with, for example, the headlines of the interviews or the playfulness of the images. While the power of the regime of sex and sexuality must still be dealt with by means of a joke, the presentation of the gay male self opens to an affective world beyond identification and fantasy.

It is this movement from the sexual to the affective – a movement that also continually returns to the sexual – presented in *Butt*'s pictures, headlines, and stories that I take as the occasion to turn to a question about the relationship between the respective theories of affects and drives in the works of Sedgwick and Freud. How can they help us in reading the queerness in desire in *Butt*? Or, conversely, how can *Butt* help us to position psychoanalysis and affect theory vis-à-vis pornography?

Figure 6. Thomas Engel Hart, picture by Katja Rahlwes.
Note: reproduced from Jop Van Bennekom and Gert Jonkers, eds. (2006) *Butt Book: The Best Of the First 5 Years Of Butt – Adventures In 21st century Gay Subculture*, 347 (Cologne: Taschen, 347).

Affect and drive

> I've continued to find this disconnect between drive and affect extraordinarily helpful, and wish a lot more people were willing to engage with it. (Barber and Clark 2002, 261)

The dissociation of affect from drive is a foundational moment in affect theory. Especially within the context of queer theory – for which both Freud and Lacan have been decisive – affect theory following Sedgwick presents itself as, in part, a critique of psychoanalysis. Sedgwick writes:

> I find it helpful to have [...] a[n] angle of vision [...] that is more programmatically resistant to some of the assumptions that have shaped psychoanalysis in (what I think of as) its Oedipal mode: the defining centrality of dualistic gender difference; the primacy of genital morphology and desire; the determinative nature of childhood experience and the linear topology toward a sharply distinct state of maturity. (2011, 289)

Such a critique of psychoanalysis was of course already foundational to its feminist and queer re-reading. For the relationship between psychoanalysis and affect theory, however, two points in particular seem to be of importance: the dominance of drive theory in understanding sexuality, and the symbolic structuring of the libido through Oedipal law.

Sedgwick's earlier work, which has been constitutive for the field of queer studies, followed the paradigm of desire, sexuality, and knowledge identified by Foucault – a conceptual framework which enabled her rigorous analysis of the entanglement of sexuality and power in western modernity. In the second half of the 1990s, Sedgwick became more critical of her earlier style of analysis (which she would call now 'paranoid'), particularly with respect to the relationship between affects and drives. About a psychoanalytically informed project of queer studies, she says:

> This consensus view does not exclude emotions, but it views emotion primarily as a vehicle of manifestation of an underlying libidinal drive [...] Reducing affect to drive in this way permits a diagrammatic sharpness of thought that may, however, be too impoverishing in qualitative terms. (Sedgwick 2003, 18)

What is at stake in Sedgwick's self-criticism, inspired by Melanie Klein and Silvan Tomkins, is the autonomy of affect in relation to the libido. Affects are understood as a system with its own logic, which structurally and operationally must be differentiated from the system of the drives. Thus, affects should display a certain amount of freedom from the forms of organization identified by psychoanalysis, as Jonathan Flatley summarizes:

> For Tomkins, one of the key differences separating the affects from the drives was their degree of freedom in object and duration; [...] Affects are not necessarily attached to any one object, indeed can attach to any object, and are free to modify each other and to change one's experience of the drives as well. (2008, 13)

Sedgwick makes a similar point when she writes:

> Affects have far greater freedom than drives with respect to, for example, time (anger can evaporate in seconds but can also motivate a decades-long career of revenge) and aim (my pleasure in hearing a piece of music can make me want to hear it repeatedly, listen to other music, or study to become a composer myself). Especially, however, affects have greater freedom with respect to object, for unlike the drives, 'any affect may have any object.' This is the basic source of complexity of human motivation and behavior. (2003, 19)

From the perspective of psychoanalysis, the turn towards affect is justified at least inasmuch as Freud has no comprehensive theory thereof to offer; the relationship between affects and drives within psychoanalysis remains unclear. How do drives and affects belong together – or not?

What is characteristic of affects in Tomkins' view, however, and what is supposed to explain a categorical difference between drives and affects – for instance, the fact that affects are independent of their objects – can already be found as a description of the libido in Freud's *Three Essays On the Theory of Sexuality* from 1905. As the Freudian text unfolds, it turns out that the libido cannot be modelled after the one-dimensionality and directionality of hunger. Freud writes:

> We are thus warned to loosen the bond that exists in our thoughts between instinct [German *Trieb*, better translated as drive] and object. It seems probable that the sexual instinct is in the first instance independent of its object; nor is its origin likely to be due to its object's attractions. ([1962] 2000, 14)

Sedgwick herself points out that Freudian libido theory shows a certain proximity to affect: '[...] sexuality is clearly the least constrained (most affect-like) of the drives' (2003, 18). Or, as Tomkins also said about sexuality, '[it is] the drive in which the affective component plays the largest role' (as quoted in Sedgwick 2003, 20). So, if the indeterminacy towards the object promised by affect theory is already a part of Freud's argument about the libido, how would it be both possible and necessary to insist on a difference between affect and libido as Sedgwick and Tomkins do?

Without a doubt, the position of the drive in Freud is ambivalent to the extent that its non-systematic potential is domesticated through normative narratives of sexual maturation; as, for instance, Guy Hocquenghem remarked early on: 'Freud discovers the libido to be the basis of affective life and immediately enchains it in the Oedipal privatization of the family' (1993, 59). On the one hand, Freud's drive theory offers the potential for its own deconstruction, and on the other it remains bound to a normative regime of power and knowledge, as Sedgwick (along with Bersani and Beckman[3]) points out: but to the (limited) degree that sexuality is a drive, it shares the immediate instrumentality and the defining orientation towards a specified aim different from itself that finally distinguishes the drives from the affects (Sedgwick 2003, 19).

Therefore, the relationship between psychoanalysis and affect theory hinges on which Freud we pick. For Sedgwick, Freud's perspective offers an openness to sexuality, which does not materialize within the context of drive theory. Even if sexuality proves to be a more open negotiation of libidinal attachment, from the perspective of affect theory, this potential of sexuality is eventually consumed by its interpretation as drive and its insisting instrumentality. Through drive theory, sexuality becomes identifiable within a network of intentions and objects. Despite creative detours, the libido eventually turns out to be spatially restricted, with regards to the object, and temporally restricted, with regards to seeking satisfaction. In this way, sexuality as drive gains meaning in distinction to a potentially affective sexuality. Within the dialogue of psychoanalysis and affect theory, then, 'affect' would be the name for a deconstructive and deterritorializing potential for sexuality, as long as it would not be recognizable and bound as drive. It is only as drive that sexuality receives a history. With affects, this is not the case. Berlant, for instance, writes that 'in affect theory laws, norms and events are not seen as determining anything' (2009, 263).

Affectivity would be a form of sexuality that is both beyond the attachment to unconscious fantasies and without the libidinal restriction to aim and function. From a psychoanalytic perspective, affect would be the name for a radically decentred sexuality. To talk about affects would mean to insist on the fact that sexuality does not have to become a drive – that it would not only name a preliminary stage within the development of libidinal life – but that it can remain, in fact, affectively effective.

In Sedgwick's perspective the repertoire of affects, consequently, would be broader than that of the drives. She writes:

> Affects can be, and are, attached to things, people, ideas, sensations, relations, activities, ambitions, institutions, and any number of other things, including other affects. Thus, one can be excited by anger, disgusted by shame, or surprised by joy. (Sedgwick 2003, 19)

Eventually, affects can relate to anything, including themselves. This leads to a self-generating system of, according to Sedgwick, 'autotelic' affects (2003, 19). In this account, affects would be self-generating, without following a historical scheme, and without repetitions. Affects, so to speak, have no memory and produce no history or knowledge – unless they turn into emotions.

However, given the ambivalence of the drive in Freud, such distinction between drive and affect must remain unstable. With the complications and variations of the drive – wholeheartedly confessed by Freud – it remains problematic to maintain a distinction between drive and affects regarding their spatial or temporal structure. Freud's concept of sexuality can also be thought of as affectivity (Flatley 2008, 53). From the perspective of affect theory, this would mean that affects cannot always be distinguished from sexuality. If Freud's libido – in its ambivalence between undirected movement and symbolic manifestation – can initially be thought of as affect, we could also say that Deleuze and Guattari's 'desire', understood as affective movement of intensities, is still sexuality (this is a perspective on sexuality – a sexuality beyond sexuality, we might say – which was particularly important to Guy Hocquenghem). Elizabeth Grosz writes in her reading of Deleuze that 'desire does not create permanent multiplicities; it experiments, producing ever new alignments, linkages, and connections, making things' (1994, 168).

If we start off with a structural similarity between libido and affects, and if this affective potential of a psychoanalytically understood sexuality is eventually restricted again by the drive theory, then we might ask on what basis does this restriction occur? What is the force in Freud that leads to an authority which limits an affective sexuality and transforms it into an identifiable drive with a specific narrative, aim, and temporality? Here, I think, we do indeed have a difference between psychoanalysis and affect theory, and consequently a categorical distinction between drives and affects. Contrasted with the drives and their relative independence, affects, with their greater potential of freedom, do not lead back to a history of origin, which would organize their itinerary (Sedgwick 2003, 146). In the context of psychoanalysis, this origin is posited, as in Freud and Lacan, as either sexual difference and the symbolic structures thus generated, such as castration (Sedgwick 2003, 21), or, as in Bersani, as also a masochistic ego shattering. In psychoanalysis, we have the contextualization of sexuality as drive structure, through which meaning is generated. This is not the case for affects, which do not follow a genealogy and do not develop a teleology.

The dramatic dimension of sexuality within psychoanalysis – which in the context of queer theory manifests itself particularly with those voices summarized under the rubric 'anti-social turn' – goes back, in Bersani as much as in Lacan, to an anthropological understanding of sexuality.[4] Psychoanalysis translates anthropological moments – such as anatomical sexual difference or the premature untimeliness of human birth – into generative mythologies, which eventually organize what we are used to calling a 'sexuality' based on drives. Affect theory does not have this narrative framework based on trauma.

Unlike the system of drives, the system of affects – if we follow this distinction made by Tomkins (Sedgwick 2003, 20) – is not immediately bound to the survival of the subject. The freedom of affects takes place precisely because they do not follow an existential need, as is the case for a psychoanalytic understanding of sexuality as drives.[5] Consequently, psychoanalytic sexuality is always connected to powerful mythologies and the violence inherent in them.

The question is, then, what does it mean to think of affects – including affective sexualities – as without origin, beyond anthropological conditions and their translations into generative mythologies? To my knowledge, Sedgwick is not interested in answering this question, but precisely moving away from the generative power that narratives of origin bring about. Bersani comments more generally on this scepticism about narratives of origin within queer theory: 'like Eve Sedgwick, most [...] [queer theorists] feel that accounts of origin of sexual preference and identity in individuals run counter to politically gay-affirmative work' (2010, 40). José Muñoz (2009b) points out that within the field of affect theory Sedgwick's critique of psychoanalysis must be distinguished from Massumi's, which takes Deleuze as its point of departure. To my mind, this is a moment where it seems productive to turn from Sedgwick to Deleuze. As we know, Deleuze offers us an ontology of an immanent desire which radically devalues psychoanalytic mythologies and their conception of desire as lack.

Here, a recognizable drive does not stabilize an unorganized sexuality or affectivity because it does not have to respond to a traumatic origin. Rather, Deleuze insists on the primacy and persistence of the pre-Oedipal as an affective-sexual universe in relation to which every solidification of sexed or gendered positions – as a mythological translation of an original trauma – is secondary. As Massumi writes, 'Deleuze and Guattari do not deny the reality of sexual difference. They simply argue that it does not lie at the foundation of subjectivity' (1992, 86). By starting from plenitude and movement, from the very start human animals live within an affective environment as assemblages. Thus, Deleuze provides the philosophical foundations for an affect theory prior to castration that does not know of any categorical distinction between affects and sex.

I want to end this article by coming back to the question regarding how a juxtaposition of affect in Sedgwick and drive in Freud, which shows both their affinities and differences, helps us to understand the post-pornographic sexual culture in *Butt*. To call the sexuality in *Butt* 'affective' would suggest the fanzine presents a sexuality without origin, a sexuality without trauma; a sexuality of occasional attachments and superficial forms of pleasure, an alternative sexual sensorium in the context of post-pornography. As documentation of a gay subculture and a remediation of real porn aesthetics, *Butt* points to a reinvention of sexuality through affects 20 years after the beginning of the AIDS crisis, at the beginning of the twenty-first century. In my mind, *Butt*'s project consists of a diffusion of the sexual – to which its images and interviews give evidence. In *Butt*, pornography becomes the stage for a movement towards a point where the affective and the sexual become indistinguishable. Without going too much into detail concerning the historical specificity of *Butt*'s aesthetics, I claim that this strategy is not only a form of remediating online aesthetics, such as amateur porn and realcore. Within the history of gay sexuality, it also offers a form of reconciliation and solace. *Butt*'s affective-sexual programme demonstrates that gay sex culture has survived AIDS.

However, this tender world on the pink pages of *Butt* also has its limits. The 'monarchy of sex' (Foucault) is not yet quite dead. An anthropologically authorized sexuality generated through trauma, as it is decisive for the discourse of psychoanalysis in distinction to affect theory, has not yet been overcome in Porn 2.0 and its remediations. The 'rule of sex', however, is not extended here through the imperative of being serious as in a conventional frame of pornographic representations. Paradoxically, it is the laughter, provoked by its headlines, interviews, or the images themselves, which reminds us that leaving the obscene sovereignty of sexuality behind – a sexuality about which psychoanalysis has had so much to say – is still a work in progress. For porn studies, this means that psychoanalysis loses its status as porn's master narrative. However, we have not quite left psychoanalysis behind with the twentieth century, as so many have claimed. Psychoanalysis keeps returning to us like laughter from a dirty joke.

Notes

1. This question was raised prominently 10 years ago by Marie-Luise Angerer ([2007] 2014), and it also constitutes the point of departure for Halley and Parker's (2011) *After Sex? On Writing Since Queer Theory*.

2. HIV and other unambiguously identifiable social and political issues such as gay marriage are mostly banned from the magazine (see LaBruce 2006).
3. Bersani continually emphasizes this double function of psychoanalysis. In distinction to representatives of affect theory, however, he is interested in developing alternatives out of a reading of psychoanalysis itself: 'Psychoanalysis has justifiably been considered an enemy of anti-identitarian politics, but it also proposes a concept of the sexual that might be a powerful weapon in the struggle against the disciplinarian constraints of identity' (Bersani 1995, 101). Frida Beckman writes on this point:

> [...] Freud's important configuration of desire as libido decodes previous conceptions of desire as related to object or aims, and frees it up as an abstract force. At the same time, however, he recodes desire by delimiting it to the family, thereby obscuring the wide open spaces glimpsed for a moment. (2013, 147)

4. As Bersani remarks: 'The origin of the excitement inherent in this erasure may, as I speculated in *The Freudian Body*, be in the biologically dysfunctional process of maturation in human beings' (1995, 100).
5. This existential understanding of sex and sexuality is of course widespread, also beyond psychoanalysis. Zygmunt Bauman (1998, 25), for example, assumes a tragic dimension of the sexual in distinction to the affective.

Disclosure statement

No potential conflict of interest was reported by the author.

References

Angerer, Marie-Luise. [2007] 2014. *Desire after Affect*, translated by Nicholas Grindell. Lanham: Rowman & Littlefield International.

Barber, Stephen M., and David L. Clark, eds. 2002. *Regarding Sedgwick: Essays on Queer Culture and Critical Theory*. New York: Routledge.

Bauman, Zygmunt. 1998. 'On Postmodern Uses of Sex.' *Theory, Culture & Society* 15 (3–4): 19–33.

Beckman, Frida. 2013. *Between Desire and Pleasure: A Deleuzian Theory of Sexuality*. Edinburgh: Edinburgh University Press.

Berlant, Lauren. 2009. '. 'Neither Monstrous Nor Pastoral, But Scary and Sweet: Some Thoughts On Sex and Emotional Performance in *Intimacies* and *What Do Gay Men Want?*' *Women and Performance: A Journal of Feminist Theory* 19 (2): 261–273.

Berlant, Lauren. 2011. *Cruel Optimism*. Durham and London: Duke University Press.

Bersani, Leo. 1995. *Homos*. Cambridge and London: Harvard University Press.

Bersani, Leo. 2010. *Is the Rectum a Grave? And Other Essays*. Chicago: University of Chicago Press.

Bronson, A. A., and Philip Aarons, eds. 2008. *Queer Zines*. New York: Printed Matter.

Bronson, A. A., and Philip Aarons, eds. 2014. *Queer Zines 2*. New York: Printed Matter.

Dean, Tim. 2015. 'No Sex Please, We're American.' *American Literary History* 27 (3): 614–624.

Flatley, Jonathan. 1996. 'Warhol Gives Good Face: Publicity and the Politics of Prosopopeia.' In *Pop Out: Queer Warhol*, edited by Jennifer Doyle, Jonathan Flatley and José Esteban Munoz, 101–133. Durham and London: Duke University Press.

Flatley, Jonathan. 2008. *Affective Mapping: Melancholia and the Politics of Modernism*. Cambridge and London: Harvard University Press.

Freud, Sigmund. [1962] 2000. *Three Essays on the Theory of Sexuality*, translated and revised by James Strachey. New York: Basic Books.

Freud, Sigmund. 2003. *The Joke and Its Relation to the Unconscious*, translated by Joyce Crick, Introduction by John Carey. New York: Penguin Classics.

Grosz, Elizabeth. 1994. *Volatile Bodies: Toward a Corporeal Feminism*. Bloomington and Indianapolis: Indiana University Press.

Halley, Janet, and Andrew Parker, eds. 2011. *After Sex? On Writing Since Queer Theory*. Durham and London: Duke University Press.

Hardt, Michael, and Antonio Negri. 2000. *Empire*. Cambridge and London: Harvard University Press.

Hillis, Ken. 2009. *Online A Lot Of the Time: Ritual, Fetish, Sign*. Durham and London: Duke University Press.

Hocquenghem, Guy. 1993. *Homosexual Desire*, translated by Daniella Dangoor. London and Durham: Duke University Press.

Jacobs, Katrien. 2007. *Netporn: DIY Webculture and Sexual Politics*. Lanham: Rowman & Littlefield.

LaBruce, Bruce. 2006. 'Fats and Femmes Please: An Introduction to Butt Magazine.' In *Butt Book: The Best Of the First 5 Years of Butt – Adventures In 21st Century Gay Subculture*, edited by Jop van Bennekom and Gert Jonkers, 9–13. Cologne: Taschen.

Massumi, Brian. 1992. *A User's Guide to Capitalism and Schizophrenia*. Cambridge and London: MIT Press.

Muñoz, José Esteban. 2009a. *Cruising Utopia: The Then and There of Queer Futurity*. New York and London: New York University Press.

Muñoz, José Esteban. 2009b. 'From Surface to Depth: Between Psychoanalysis and Affect.' *Women & Performance: A Journal of Feminist Theory* 19 (2): 123–129.

Needham, Alex. 2006. '1/2 Of Butt: Jop van Bennekom.' In *Butt Book: The Best Of the First 5 Years of Butt – Adventures In 21st Century Gay Subculture*, edited by Jop van Bennekom and Gert Jonkers, 36–42. Cologne: Taschen.

Ngai, Sianne. 2012. *Our Aesthetic Categories: Zany, Cute, Interesting*. Cambridge and London: Harvard University Press.

Paasonen, Susanna. 2011. *Carnal Resonance: Affect and Online Pornography*. Cambridge and London: MIT Press.

Paasonen, Susanna, Kaarina Nikunen, and Laura Saarenmaa. 2007. *Pornofication: Sex and Sexuality in Media Culture*. Oxford: Berg.

Penley, Constance. 2004. 'Crackers and Whackers: The White Trashing of Porn.' In *Porn Studies*, edited by Linda Williams, 309–331. Durham and London: Duke University Press.

Sedgwick, Eve Kosofsky. 2003. *Touching Feeling: Affect, Pedagogy, Performativity*. Durham and London: Duke University Press.

Sedgwick, Eve Kosofsky. 2011. 'Melanie Klein and the Difference Affect Makes.' In *After Sex? On Writing Since Queer Theory*, edited by Janet Halley and Andrew Parker, 283–301. Durham and London: Duke University Press.

Stüttgen, Tim, ed. 2010. *Post/Porn/Politics*. Berlin: BBooks.

van Bennekom, Jop, and Gert Jonkers, eds. 2006. *Butt Book: The Best of the First 5 Years of Butt – Adventures In 21st Century Gay Subculture*. Cologne: Taschen.

van Bennekom, Jop, and Gert Jonkers, eds. 2007. *Butt 21* (Late Autumn – Early Winter).

van Bennekom, Jop, and Gert Jonkers, eds. 2011. 'Tom the Capenter is Good with Wood and Likes Men Who Work with Their Hands.' *Buttmagazine.com*. August 12. Accessed September 17 2018. http://www.buttmagazine.com/magazine/interviews/tom-the-carpenter-is-good-with-wood-and-likes-men-who-work-with-their-hands/#.

Index

Page numbers in **bold** refer to tables and those in *italic* refer to figures.

accurate–specific–detailed–contingent level 17
adult film workers 67
affect theory 111–14
'Alex Mason's Birthday Gang Bang' 80–1
amateur pornography 26
Antichrist (2009) 92
Atlantic, the Independent, and Vice (newspaper)
   27–8
Audiovisual Media Services Regulation 2014 59
autonomous sensory meridian response (ASMR)
   whispering 8
Azoulay, Ariella 23

Baker, Nicholson 8
barebacking 75–8
'Bareback Sex and Queer Theory across Three
   National Contexts' 73
Barthes, Roland 72; archons 42; authenticity
   effect 36–8; 'blind field' expression 41; digital
   archives 42; porny proliferation 42–3
Bauman, Zygmunt 30
BDSM communities 50–1, 59
'Behind the Scenes' 26
Being and Nothingness (1992) 24
Berger, John 1
Berlant, Lauren 51, 115
Bersani, Leo 72
Bhabha, Homi K. 51–2
black-cast pornography 104
Black Mirror (2016) 29
body–practice–pleasure–pressure level 17
Brokestraightboys.com 38, *38*
Brooker, Charlie 29
Brooks, Cleanth 15
Butler, Andy 52, *116*
Butler, Judith 46, 47
Butt, Dutch gay fanzine 112–13, 112–19

Camera Lucida see Barthes, Roland
Canadian settler multiculturalism 50
Carrie (1976) 92
Champagne, John 85
chemsex 75–8

Cheng, Anne Anlin 46
Christina, Greta 105–6
Cole, Liam 71, 76
Comay, Rebecca 6
Comey, James 28–9
Cooper, Dennis 65, 66
Copjec, Joan 65
Creet, Julia 60
CumControl101's videos (2018) 40–1

Damen, Werner *114*
Daubney, Martin 28
Davis, Oliver 73
Deakin, John 14
Dean, Tim 59, 72, 74
Defurne, Bavo *114*
'Described Video': available sartorial objects 10;
   defined 8; multiple competing valuations 12;
   narrator's vocality 13, *14*; 'purely descriptive
   (objective)' encounter 9–12; 'Schoolgirls
   Squirting' 11; twofold experimentation 9
describing voice 17
descriptive porn videos 15
*Diagnostic and Statistical Manual of Mental
   Disorders* 21
DiCenso, James 107
Dombek, Kristen 21
Dworkin, Andrea 97

Edelman, Lee 59
'Eligible for melancholic incorporation' 51
enthusiasm 100–2
'epidemic of narcissism' 20, 21
Essaisur l'origine des langues 8

fade–dissolve–close-up system 15–16
false hole 66
Fanon, Frantz 50
feminist ambivalence 99–100
feminist pornography 98
Ferguson, Frances 14–15
Fighting Chance (1990) 49, 53
Fink, Bruce 72

Foucauldian artefact of 'knowledge-pleasure' 85
Foucault, Michel 51
Four Fundamental Concepts of Psycho-Analysis 25
Freud, Sigmund 45, 100, 102–3, 116
Frisk 65–6
Fung, Richard 46, 49, 53, 54
The Future of an Illusion (1927) 100

Gallagher, Ryan 28
Garcia, Christien 72
Gay Pornography: Representations of Sexuality and Masculinity (2017) 73
Georgis, Dina 54
Gone Wild Audio 8
Gordon, Bette 60, 61
Greenwald, Glenn 28
Greteman, A. J. 73
Grim, Ryan 28

Habib, Conner 67–8
Halperin, David 51
Hard Cuts I (2014) 77
Hard Cuts II (2015) 77
Hartley, Nina 98
Hart, Thomas Engel *119*
Hawkes, Brent 48
hermeneutic messiness 107
heteronormative and homonormative conception 76
Hocquenghem, Guy 77
'Homemade' 26
Homosexual Desire 77
Huffington Post article 28

Žižek, Slavoj 24, 26, 47–8, 52–3
infantilism 105
'instinctual abatement' 91–2
interpretability of pornography 17

Jacobellis v. Ohio (1964) 8
jouissance 75–8; and language 72
Joyce, James 64

kairos, neutral moment 37
Kaite, Berkeley 65
'Kant with Sade' 59
Klossowski, Pierre 9
Kusruti, Kani 2, 3, 5

Lacan, Jacques 25, 52, 59, 61, 71, 75, 84
Laplanche, Jean 17
Larsson, Andreas *116*
Lee, Jiz 67
Levinson, Levinson 86
'Limited Intimacy: Barebacking and the Imaginary' (2013), 72
Little, Black *118*
'Live Sex Cam' 26
local anti-porn activists 106

'Looking For My Penis' 54
Louise Lush/Ms. Naughty 98
Lyon, David 30

MacKinnon, Catherine 97
Maes, Hans 86
'male gaze' 60, *62*
Marcuse, Herbert 50
Maslin, Janet 60
Mason, Alex 80
masturbators 67
mathesis singularis 36
mattering and muttering 74–5
McCaskell, Tim 49, 51
McGowan, Todd 91
McLeod, Sandy 63
McQueen, Steve 59, 92
media manufacturers 28
melancholia 45–6
Memories of a Machine (2016) 1, 2, *4*
Men Loving Themselves (1980) 54
Mercer, John 73
metalanguage of pornography 17, 18
Michaels, Anne 2
Miller-Young, Mireille 59, 98, 104
Morel, Geneviève 68
Morin, Jack 54
Mormonboyz.com *39*, 39–40
Morris, Paul 76
Mulvey, Laura 1, 60

'The Name of Your First Pet and the Street You Grew Up On' 67
Nancy, Jean-Luc 41
narciphobia 21
the National Crime Agency 28
The News Minute 5
'The New Surveillance Normal' (2014) 22
The New York Times 29
Niedzviecki, Hal 21
Nietzsche, Friedrich 87
Nymphomaniac (2013) 92

Oedipus complex 46
online pornography providers 23
orgasm 4
Orientations: Lesbian and Gay Asians (1986) 49, 50
Overload (2013) 77

Paasonen, Susanna 98
Padindala, Shailaja 1, *2*, 4–5
pale of bourgeois respectability 73
'paradox of phallocentrism' 61
'paranoid' reading 49
Patton, Cindy 23
Peeping Toms 21, 22, 24, 29
Pei-Hsien, Lim: 'The/beginning of my love affair/ with others/and myself' 53–4; inaugural loss 47;

Lake Ontario 48–9; racism, xenophobia, homophobia 49; sexual fantasy 52; sexual pedagogy 53
Penley, Constance 106
Perlroth, Nicole 29
personal webcam materials 29
phallocentrism 76
Phillips, Adam 72
The Pleasure of the Text (1975) 72
Plug, Sander *114*
Pontalis, Jean-Bertrand 17
The Pornhub Network 26, 27
Pornographos 14
pornography 57, 61, 67, 97
The *Pornography Industry* 27
Porn Studies issue 5
post-racial/pan-racial universalism 47
Price, David H. 22
psychoanalysis 67
psychoanalytic ethics: aesthetic properties 86–7; das Ding and sublimation 87–9; individual, role of 85; 'modesty' and 'temperateness' 85; 'notion of enjoyment (jouissance)' 85; pornographic aesthetic and punctum 89–91
pussy–cock–cum system 15–16

'quirky questions' series 2

racial melancholia 46
Rahlwes, Katja *119*
'ransomware' 28
rathimoorcha (orgasm) 4, 6
RawFuckClub.com 71, 79–80
remote administration tools 28
Re:Orientations (2016) 49
Rooney, Ellen 15
Royalle, Candida 98, 108
rule of *Logos* 104
Ryberg, Ingrid 106

Sartre, Jean-Paul 22, 24–5
Schor, Naomi 17
Sedgwick, Eve 49, 113, 119–23
'self-imposed impotence' 66
Seminar XX Encore: On Feminine Sexuality, The Limits of Love and Knowledge 1972–73 71
Seminar XXIII 57
Sexualities 73
'sex wars' 98, 108
Shame (2011 & 2012) 59, 92

'Shut Up and Dance' 29
signalling jouissance 68
Simonneau, Xavier *117*
Slammed (2012) 77
Snowden, Edward 20
social approbation 21
social power 51
Spivak, Gayatri 49
spluttering 75, 78–9
Stoller, Robert 23
'The Subversion of the Subject and the Dialectic of Desire in the Freudian Unconscious' 75
Sutherland, Harry 48

Taormino, Tristan 108
Tarrant, Shira 27
technocultural paranoia 27–32
technocultural voyeurism and pornographic gaze 23–5
Tom the Carpenter *118*
Track Two: Enough is Enough (1982) 48
transcribing voice 17
transitional phenomena 50
Trigano, Regis *117*
'trivialization of sexuality' 112

Unlimited Intimacy: Reflections on the Subculture of Barebacking (2009) 72
'unrealistic'/'parasitic dependency' 59

Variety (1983) 60–4
'Variety: The Pleasure in Looking' 61
Végsö, Roland K. 68
'Visual Pleasure and Narrative Cinema' 1
volunteer audiodescribers 9
von Trier, Lars 92

Ward, Jane 98
'Webcam' 26
Weiss, Margot 50–1
The Well-Wrought Urn (1947) 15
'Western moralism' 85
Whipple, Jason *113*
Wiegman, Robyn 49
'wiggle room' 101
Williams, Linda 68, 85
Winnicott, Donald 50

Zuckerberg, Mark 29